The Rights
of
Children

to Annie

The Rights of Children

edited by

BOB FRANKLIN

Basil Blackwell

© Basil Blackwell Ltd 1986

First published 1986

Basil Blackwell Ltd
108 Cowley Road, Oxford OX4 1JF, UK

Basil Blackwell Inc.
432 Park Avenue South, Suite 1503
New York, NY 10016, USA

British Library Cataloguing in Publication Data

The Rights of children.
  1. Children's rights—Great Britain
  I. Franklin, Bob
  323.3'52'0941   HQ789

  ISBN 0-631-14711-X
  ISBN 0-631-14712-8 Pbk

Library of Congress Cataloging in Publication Data

Main entry under title:

The Rights of children.

  Includes index.
  1. Children's rights—Great Britain. I. Franklin,
Bob, 1949–   .
HQ789.R533 1986   305.2'3   85-30675
ISBN 0-631-14711-X
ISBN 0-631-14712-8 (pbk.)

Typeset by Alan Sutton Publishing Limited, Gloucester
Printed in Great Britain by Billings Ltd, Worcester

Contents

Acknowledgements

My contribution to this book was written while I was teaching in Newcastle upon Tyne and I wish to record my thanks to the polytechnic for the research and clerical facilities which made the work possible. Particular thanks are owed to Austin McArthy, Glenda Francis and to Mike Jones of Sunderland Polytechnic. The editorial staff at Blackwell's have surprised and delighted me with their efficiency in producing the book and I am grateful for their helpful comments which enhanced the manuscript at earlier stages.

Two special thanks are necessary even at the risk of embarrassing the people concerned. The first is to my good friend and ex-colleague Tony Jeffs who initially kindled my interest in the problems facing young people. His own contribution to this field of study is well known and justly prized. The second is to my closest friend, Annie Franklin, who in conversations too numerous to recount has criticized, discussed and helped to formulate so many of the ideas which are here attributed to me. Her contribution to this book cannot easily be overstressed and it is therefore dedicated to her.

Bob Franklin

Foreword

Patricia Hewitt

It is astonishing and disturbing how little attention has been paid to the rights of children in this country. There are, of course, the regular outbreaks of public fury and concern about the deaths of children, the repeated 'This must never happen again' editorials and press campaigns. They are not to be sneered at. Indeed they provide a real opportunity to direct attention towards a more searching examination of the legal, social, political and economic status of children and young people. But, as the press itself acknowledges, these campaigns have happened before. There has also been – less often and more muted – public concern about the rights of parents who have found themselves bewildered and frustrated by the absence of clear, quick legal procedures to challenge a decision to take or keep a child in care. But there has been very little consistent and comprehensive consideration of the problems and issues which underlie these visible and vociferous concerns. Nan Berger's pioneering work,[1] the study by the Cobden Trust and Mind[2] of children in care, the work of the Children's Rights Centre and the writing of Norman Tutt[3] stand out in the last two decades.

This volume, which covers a wide range of issues and which fully reviews previous studies, is therefore particularly welcome. I fear, however, that it may receive the same kind of treatment that the National Council for Civil Liberties (NCCL) received when it launched its early Children's Rights Campaign 15 years ago. Publication of a Children's Rights Charter and the organization of a conference on the subject provoked a national outcry at this apparent excess of 1960s permissiveness. All the caricatures were there; babies abandoning their prams for collectives; two-years olds with the vote; terrifying toddlers negotiating with their cowed parents. More sinister was the trial and conviction of Viv Berger (whose mother, Grace Berger, was chair of NCCL at a crucial point in the children's rights campaign) and his colleagues for their part in the 'Schoolkids'' issue of *Oz*. The NCCL campaign deserved better. And so does this book. It is a serious effort to summarize current thinking – from different perspectives – on children's rights and children's welfare, to explore the extent to which our laws and legal procedures protect or harm children and to make proposals for reform.

This publication is, of course, particularly timely. The deaths of Jasmine Beckford and other children at the hands of parents (whether natural parents, step- or foster parents), the serious injury of many more, and reports that child abuse is not only far more widespread than previously suspected but is on the increase, have rekindled public debate about the rights and role of parents, social workers and others in authority over children. The debate has at least reminded the nation that children are too important to be left to their parents. Children are *not* – or should not be – their parents' 'property', and the 'rights' of parents cannot be unrestricted. The logic – which runs wholly counter to the prevailing anti-statist mood – is that the state must have a role to play in the care and protection of children.

The outcome of the present debate is likely to be legislation which tries to ensure that any decision about whether or not a child lives with his or her natural parents, or with a step-parent, or with foster parents, or in a local authority home must be made 'in the best interests' of the child. The 'welfare of the child' is to be paramount. Yet, Gerry Lavery and Robert Adams point out in their essays in this volume, that will not solve all our problems. A 'welfare' approach, where the court determines the issue in the children's best interests, may lead to children placed in institutions where their own rights are ignored. It may leave parents ill-placed to argue their side of the story. It will encourage action to remove the child from danger rather than action to tackle the social and economic realities of poverty, bad housing and poor parenting which desperately need attention. And it may leave the older child who has a clear view of what she or he wants without the legal right to ensure that those views are respected.

The present debate raises these important general questions about the society in which children are brought up. As the NSPCC has made clear, child abuse is directly related to unemployment, to family debt and to marital problems. Family debt and marital problems are, of course, likely to increase as unemployment increases. The 'party of the family' which forms the current government believes, of course, that families should, by and large, be left to manage by themselves. Alongside the 'right to buy' has come a rapid increase in mortgage debt, in evictions, in the numbers of homeless families and those living in inadequate housing. The prime minister who wants 'our children to grow tall' has been responsible for a reduction in the availability of free school meals, a deterioration in educational standards and resources, a cut in the real value of child benefit, gross inadequacies in child care provision and a scandalous increase in the number of children living in poverty. As Mrs Thatcher herself boasted, some children will grow taller than others.

Politicians who believe that individual freedom is enhanced by 'rolling back the State' will be fixed with horror at the sexual abuse, injuries and deaths inflicted on children and forced to realize that the needs of many children will remain unmet and the rights of children unrespected unless the state plays its part. That part must involve effective legislation and social work provision to deal with physical and emotional abuse. But it must also involve financial provisions – the most important of which is the provision of an adequate level of child benefit – to assist in redistributing income from adults without children to adults with children, and from adults at the time of their lives when they are without children to that time when children are dependent on them. It must entail the provision of care at an early age for the children of parents who want (as the vast majority do) to share their responsibility for part of the time, and the best possible education and health facilities for *all* children: those in the most derelict inner city areas as well as those in more affluent suburbs; children from the ethnic minority communities as well as white children. And it must also provide for a redistribution of employment time so that *all* parents – fathers as well as mothers – are encouraged and enabled to play a full part in bringing up children. Just to approach these goals will require major changes in the use of national resources and in our view of what 'full employment' means in a modern community. It will also require far more thorough consideration of the rights, as well as the needs, of children.

This publication is particularly helpful in stimulating that consideration. The very fact that we are dealing with an age span which stretches from infancy to somewhere between sixteen and twenty-one and an age span which encompasses the individual's most concentrated and rapid period of emotional, intellectual and physical growth makes it exceptionally hard to make proposals for 'rights' which are applicable to everybody. It is also exceptionally easy to dismiss the notion of 'rights' for children as obvious nonsense, or to caricature, for instance, a discussion of children's political rights with the notion of votes for two-year-olds (something that, as Bob Franklin himself points out, no-one is actually proposing). Such caricatures can, of course, be countered with the obvious anomalies of today's laws: Oxford's brightest maths student this century, for instance, is several years away from the right to vote.

But the issue is too serious to caricature. It is not so very long since the notion of rights for women, or rights for slaves, was also dismissed as obvious nonsense. Adults have not proved themselves such good judges of children's interests, or such effective protectors of their well-being, to allow us to go on believing that only those who have outgrown childhood should be permitted to decide upon its requirements. That is why, although I fear that some adult readers of this book may fall into the trap of ridicule, I expect that some of the most intelligent and fruitful responses will come from children and young people themselves.

Notes

1 Nan Berger, *The Rights of Children and Young Persons* (Cobden Trust, 1967).
2 L. Taylor, R. Lacey and D. Bracken, *In Whose Best Interests* (Cobden Trust, 1980).
3 For example, see Norman Tutt, 'Observation and assessment', in *Providing Civil Justice for children*, eds H. Geach and E. Szwed (Edward Arnold, 1983).

1

Introduction

Bob Franklin

During the 1960s and 1970s the movements for black liberation and women's liberation heightened social awareness of the existence of racism and sexism and the deleterious effects of such prejudicial views on blacks, women and society as a whole. The irrationality and immorality of systematic and institutionalized discrimination against individuals on the basis of their gender or race has, to some degree, been established. However, the equivalent discrimination against people on the basis of their age has proven more resilient to change. Children continue to be the chief victims, but old people also suffer from this ageism. What distinguishes ageism from sexism and racism is that, while there is some degree of consensus that women and blacks have suffered and been discriminated against, in the case of children such a consensus is absent. As Martin Hoyles observed, 'indignation is often expressed that women or blacks are treated like children, but not so often that children are treated the way they are.'[1] Hoyles is right to compare the position of women and blacks with that of children, not because their logic is necessarily similar, but because their history is so.[2]

Children because of their age are denied rights which as adults we consider to be basic human rights. They have their freedom and autonomy limited in a number of ways which range from the relatively unimportant to the highly significant: from being denied the right to choose which films to see, or at what time to go to bed, or which clothes to wear, to being denied the right to vote. Children form a large, long-suffering and oppressed grouping in society, 'a silent and unrepresented minority',[3] undeserving of civil rights. They share the forgotten and excluded status of other minority groups in history which Martin Luther King, Jr, has called 'nobodyness'.[4]

The disadvantages which are consequent upon being a child can be stated briefly. First, children are denied any political rights. They are disfranchised, unable to lobby and cannot participate in the political affairs of their society. Second, children are economically disadvantaged. They enjoy little, if any, independent financial power, they cannot own property, they are legally excluded from the labour market and have no access to, or control over, any substantial cash reserves. Third, the legal status of children is essentially passive, and they are considered the property of their parents. They are an expensive investment costing on average £32,000 to support to the age of eighteen and demanding an investment of time which has been calculated to be around fifty hours a week.[5] Fourth, children are obliged to attend educational institutions for a minimum of eleven years, during which time they will be subject to the arbitrary authority of teachers, may receive physical and non-physical punishments and will be the subject of a confidential file to which they will have no access.[6] Finally, at home the child is under the constant supervision of parents who can legitimately inflict a range of punishments to discipline and control behaviour.

Children reflect the wider society of which they form a part and therefore they are a heterogeneous group. Some are rich, others poor, yet others black, white, male, female; there is an almost endless diversity. However, all children will, without regard to this diversity, suffer these political, economic, legal, educational and domestic restrictions as a consequence of that which they hold in common: their status as children. Again, like adult society, children from certain groups will suffer more than others, and race, gender, class[7] and physical or mental handicaps are obvious factors which will reinforce the injustices deriving from age. Children of the poor are less likely to survive the first year of life,[8] to receive higher education, to enjoy a healthy diet and occupy good housing; conversely they are more likely to enter residential care and contract and die from certain diseases.[9] Physically and mentally handicapped children must confront particular difficulties to secure their rights, and it is regretted that it has not proved possible to include a more substantial discussion of their special concerns. Some children will therefore be subject to additional hardship, poverty, physical, mental or sexual abuse at home, school or in a range of other social welfare or penal institutions.

As adults we are reluctant to acknowledge the severity which this picture of childhood presents. Our perception of childhood is somehow clouded by a more socially acceptable, if idealized, view of adult and child relationships. This is because children suffer the same processes which Simone de Beauvoir observed in operation against the elderly. In reality, society's treatment of both groups is harsh and uncaring and yet its attitude towards them is paternalistic and protective. To save itself from this potential schizophrenia, society dehumanizes the young and old alike, denying them the status of people. In de Beauvoir's words:

> As far as old people are concerned, this society is not only guilty but downright criminal . . . old people are condemned to poverty . . . wretchedness and despair. . . . To reconcile this barbarous treatment with the humanist morality they profess to follow, the ruling class adopts the convenient plan of refusing to consider them as real people; if their voices were heard, the hearers would be forced to acknowledge they were human voices.[10]

In the same way, young people are refused a voice, and their legitimate protest is muted and denied by the hypocrisy of adult attitudes which to borrow de Beauvoir's phrase are 'distorted by the myths and clichés of Bourgeois culture.'[11]

One such myth suggests that the adult treatment of children is based upon respect and a concern to protect the best interests of the child. According to this idealized perception, children are elevated to a central position in the fulfilled adult life. Children provide the motivation and purpose, as well as much of the meaning, to many areas of adult life; to be childless is to court pity. Within the context of family life it is children who are believed to 'make a marriage'. As parents we want to do 'the best' for our children and to that end we work, save and deny ourselves so that our children have 'the best possible start in life' or at least 'a better start than we had ourselves'. This idealized adult concern for children has informed and found institutional expression in much post-war social legislation, in areas such as education and social welfare, aimed at promoting the best interests of the child. However, legislation, such as the Children and Young Persons Act: (1969), can create practices which generate still further arbitrary and unjust treatment of children which denies their rights, and enhances adult intervention in their lives and purposes.[12] This idealized view of adult–child relationships means that when cases of child abuse are spotlighted in the media, as for example the case of Maria Colwell or Jasmine Beckford, public opinion is not only morally outraged but incredulous. We believe that such cases must be aberrant, exceptional or quite rare; in reality they are not. As one director of a social services department expressed it, 'we cannot ignore that children are still abused, neglected, deprived and put at risk by parents to the extent that if it happened to dogs we would ban people for life . . . somehow we are apparently not ready for such declarations.'[13]

It is important to acknowledge that, no matter how dreadful the circumstances of particular cases, they cannot be understood at the level of individual pathology as the actions of especially violent or callous persons. Child abuse is related to poverty and inequality and, as Parton reminds us, by 'concentrating on dangerous individuals' we risk ignoring 'dangerous conditions'.[14]

A second myth about childhood is perhaps even more influential in informing our attitude towards children: the myth of childhood as a 'golden age'.[15] According to this myth, childhood is a special period of our lives when, because of our innocence and weakness, we are protected from the harshness and adversity of adult life. The child is spared the responsibilities and anxieties of economic life, the world of work and the many worries which are to be inherited upon maturity. Childhood is a period of unconstrained freedom, a time for play, education and learning. We are encouraged to 'enjoy ourselves while we are young', since, 'these are the best days of our life'. It is remarkable that this myth of childhood as a period of freedom, pleasure and discovery can survive when each adult has necessarily lived through this period and experienced at first hand the injustices and frustrations which occur in childhood. The resilience of the myth is even more remarkable in the light of some data about childhood.

It is known that one in three schoolchildren have a part-time job, other than babysitting, and that 80 per cent of these jobs are illegal by virtue of long hours, unsocial hours, or because the children are below the legal working age of thirteen. Moreover, one-sixth of the children are in heavy manual jobs such as work on construction sites or furniture removals and are being exploited by employers as cheap labour.[16] Paradoxically, young people over school-leaving age face enormous difficulties in finding work. In June 1985, 106,800 school-leavers were unemployed, and unemployment totals for those aged eighteen and under were 172,804.[17] An additional 370,220 young people are removed from these unemployment statistics by their presence on a Youth Training Scheme, but, on completion, they are unlikely to find permanent work.[18]

Children rather than the elderly now bear the burden of poverty in Britain. 879,000 children live in families on supplementary benefit, 660,000 live in single-parent families on supplementary benefit, and the number of children living below the poverty line doubled between 1979 and 1981.[19] According to DHSS figures, the number of children living at what it acknowledges to be low-income levels (140 per cent of supplementary benefit levels) exceeds three and a half million, or one in three.[20]

During the 1950s, 62,000 children were in care, and this figure increased by 1 per cent per annum during the 1960s and 1970s.[21] In 1981 over 44,500 children were received into care in England and Wales[22] and by March 1982 the number of children in care was 7.8 per 1000 population.[23] Life in care is not easy. The National Association of Young People in Care (NAYPIC) claim that no matter how 'badly treated young people may have been in the past there is no assurance ... that they won't be treated in a similar way whilst in care.'[24] The disciplinary regime is harsh and the invasion of privacy total. Confidential files are kept on all children in care, and young people are denied participation in the major decisions which affect their lives, such as the review.[25]

Research literature is now beginning to discover that child sexual abuse is a serious problem. Home Office data for 1980 recorded 312 cases of incest and 3109 cases of unlawful intercourse.[26] In 1979 there were 8967 conceptions among girls under the age of sixteen.[27] The reluctance to acknowledge the existence of this abuse means that such figures substantially understate levels of incidence. A review of research by the National Children's Bureau suggests that between a quarter and a third of all children and adolescents have had at least one sexual experience with an adult.[28]

Data for the physical abuse of children is equally notoriously unreliable, and difficulties are exacerbated by a lack of clarity concerning what constitutes abuse; definitions range from physical violence, through emotional neglect, to sexual exploitation.[29] The existence of a range of agencies dealing with child abuse, from social services departments to voluntary organizations such as the NSPCC, creates further difficulties in producing reliable data. However, in 1979 there were at least 50,000 young people listed on child abuse registers,[30] and the NSPCC reported 15,000 new cases of child abuse in 1982.[31] Jobling suggests that between 2400 and 4600 children are seriously injured each year. Around 450 children are physically incapacitated for life, while estimates of child fatalities range from 100 to 750. Exact numbers have become a 'controversial guessing game'.[32] However, violence against children is certainly more widespread than these data suggest, since some forms of physical abuse – like corporal punishment – are readily accepted as part of a system of discipline in educational and welfare institutions. The Society of Teachers Opposed to Physical Punishment (STOPP) has estimated that in schools in England and Wales a child is beaten once every nineteen seconds of the teaching day, culminating in a quarter of a million beatings per annum. In Scotland, where official figures of

such incidents are not recorded, estimates suggest corporal
punishment is inflicted on two and a half million occasions per
annum, or once every two seconds.[33] Young people in care may be
subject to corporal punishment or the use of behaviour-controlling
drugs – 'the liquid cosh'.[34]

At the international level the deprivations of children are even
greater, with more awful consequences. It is a particular irony
that during the International Year of the Child 15 million children
died from starvation, with 10.3 million of those deaths occurring
in the first eleven months of the child's life. In the same year, 400
million children under six did not have access to health services
and 100 million children suffered from malnutrition.[35] There is no
more fundamental right than the right to sufficient food and shelter
to sustain life, but it is being denied on a scale that is devastating.

In the light of these data, the myth of childhood as a 'golden age'
looks less credible. The facts are stated here as starkly as possible in
order to shake us out of our cultural complacency about the
conditions in which children are obliged to live. Children lack basic
human rights and are subject to treatment which, if inflicted upon any
other grouping in society, would be considered a moral outrage and
would undoubtedly become the source of substantial political
activity. Moreover, the size of the problem is vast. In Britain alone
11.7 million children constitute nearly one-fifth of the total
population.

The different essays contained in this book attempt to dispel some
of the myths concerning childhood. By focusing attention on a
particular aspect of children's concerns, whether at school, in care,
in the juvenile justice system, or their political or sexual rights,
each chapter tries to clarify the problems and needs of children, the
difficulties they confront, and the ways in which attitudes and
institutional procedures serve to limit their rights. Each chapter
is prescriptive as well as descriptive and advocates reform which will
enforce the existing rights which children possess, extend their rights
to protection and acknowledge their dignity. We need to reassess
both attitudes and policies towards children in many fields including education, child care, juvenile justice, work and sexual relations.

However, the issue of children's rights is complex; problems
relating to the definition of terms are particularly acute. Two fairly
lengthy digressions are needed at the outset for purposes of
clarification. The first will consider the changing nature of childhood,
the second some of the complexities of the term 'rights.'

What is a child?

The attempt to answer the question 'What is a child?' involves extraordinary complexities. Simple definitions prove elusive. A little probing dispels certainty and prompts further questions. Would the response to the question be the same today as it was in Victorian England? Did Dickens's Artful Dodger experience childhood in the same way as Casper in Barry Hines's novel *A Kestrel for a Knave*? Do Western accounts of childhood require reconsideration when confronted with the realities of life in the Third World, where economic necessity creates an expectation that children should work from an early age? Given the variety of the experience of childhood, we should be doubtful about the prospect of alighting upon some simple formula which will capture this diversity.

It is important to make five points about childhood at the outset. First, childhood is not a single universal experience of any fixed duration. It is rather a historically shifting, cultural construction. Anthropological studies, such as Turnbull's account of the Mbuti pygmy community, illustrate the cultural diversity and relativity of the phenomenon of childhood. Judged by contemporary Western conceptions of childhood, Mbuti children would be considered precocious in many respects. Their sexual activities and their participation in the economic life of their society would perhaps offend Western mores. For the Mbuti, of course, there is nothing exceptional in all this.[36] The work of historians further reveals that the dividing line between childhood and adulthood has been drawn arbitrarily and has varied widely across the different historical periods.[37] Since the dividing line has proved to be a wavering line, it seems probable that the existing conception of childhood may yet prove ephemeral.

Second, the existing division between the two age-states is not only arbitrary but also incoherent. In Britain sexual, criminal and electoral activities have different qualifying ages at one and the same time, so that people may be deemed too young for some activities, yet old enough for others. On this basis it is possible to become an adult not all at once but in stages, being deemed capable of electoral activity at eighteen, sexual activity at sixteen and criminal activity at ten. Further, the boundaries are drawn at different ages for different genders.

Third, children are defined in a negative way as 'non-adults'. Childhood spans a wide age range from early infancy to eighteen years and within this broad span is an enormously varied range of needs, abilities and potentials. Therefore what is appropriate and suitable for one group of young people may not be so for another. Yet this diversity is clouded by the assumption that all young people are 'children' and alike in the sense that they are incapable of adult activities. A four-year-old person and a sixteen-year-old person, though more disparate in their capacities, capabilities and requirements than eighteen-year-olds and twenty-one-year-olds, are equally considered to be children because they are 'not adult'. This can lead to trivial jibes and ill-thought-out arguments about children's rights – 'What, two-year-olds driving, voting, having sex?'[38]

Fourth, the term 'child' has a connection less with chronology than with power. The term has tended to specify a power relationship rather than to denote any particular age and was originally used to describe those of low status.[39] There is therefore no requirement to be young in order to be called a child. This is important, since it illustrates the fact that the question 'What is a child?' is answered by those in authority – those who have power in society. The powerful can impose their conceptions of childhood on socially subordinate adults. In this way slaves in the southern states of America appeared to display many of the characteristics of subservience and dependence that inform the current conception of childhood. They were accordingly called 'boy' or simply by their first name, their master or mistress retained the right to punish them, and the slave was often considered 'a natural companion for children, sharing some of their simple pleasures and fears'.[40]

Fifth, childhood is a fairly recent invention, and most historians would endorse Plumb's judgement that 'the very idea of childhood is a European invention of the last 400 years'.[41] Before then, 'as soon as the child could live without the constant solicitude of his mother, his nanny, or his cradle rocker, he belonged to an adult society.'[42] Holt observes that this isolation of childhood as a special phase in life is part of a more general tendency of modern societies to become concerned with age divisions. Instead of life being considered an uninterrupted continuum of development from birth to death, increasingly it is fragmented into a number of phases, with a crisis accompanying the transition from one phase to another. Childhood is thus an artificial period which 'has divided that curve of life, that wholeness, into two parts, one called childhood, the other adulthood or maturity.'[43]

By 1600 childhood was beginning to develop, and 'the age between seven and adolescence was rapidly becoming a world of its own'.[44] Prior to the Renaissance children were typically depicted in contemporary art as small adults, and this reflected their role in society. The suggestion that the emergence of childhood as a special period in life developed in the early seventeenth century is underlined by changes in European vocabulary which occurred at the same time.[45] Children were so little differentiated from adults that there was no special vocabulary to describe them, and the words *boy, garçon, Knabe* were used indiscriminately before the seventeenth century to mean a male in a dependent position. Moreover, a vocabulary and language especially for addressing children – 'childrenese' – became fashionable in the seventeenth century.[46]

The concept of childhood which emerged with the advent of the seventeenth century and informs the contemporary account stressed the innocence and weakness of the child. Children, by virtue of their 'sweetness, simplicity and drollery', became a source of amusement and relaxation for the adult.[47] Childhood came to be associated with very negative qualities such as weakness, irrationality, helplessness and dependence. Holt believes that childhood is best understood by the metaphor of a walled garden in which children 'being small and weak are protected from the harshness of the outside world until they become strong and clever enough to cope with it'.[48] The metaphor is apt, since English language uses the word 'nursery' as a place where both plants and children are nurtured.

This perception of childhood as a period of innocence and weakness which bestowed upon adults 'the duty . . . to safeguard the former and strengthen the latter'[49] emerged in the seventeenth century, and many changes in children's lives can be dated to that period. The sum effect of these changes was to separate children from contact with the adult world of which they were previously a part.[50] Ariès notes how prior to that date children were represented in contemporary art as small men or women, but after that date 'paintings of children became commonplace'.[51] At around the same time children ceased to be dressed similarly to adults and, whereas previously differences in dress signalled status rather than age, clothing was now designed specifically for children.[52] Games which children were to play apart from adults,[53] children's toys[54] and books written and published for children, all date from this period.[55]

The most significant changes in young people's lives which occurred with the development of childhood involved the curtailment of their sexual relations, their removal from the world of work and their increased involvement in education and schooling.

In this chapter entitled 'From Immodesty to Innocence', Ariès shows how the current moral necessity for 'adults to avoid any reference . . . to sexual matters in the presence of children . . . was entirely foreign to the society of old.'[56] Ariès's quotations from Heroard's *Journal sur l'enfance et la jeunesse de Louis XIII*, which is a detailed account of the Dauphin's early life, testify to the degree to which children were exposed to, and participated in, the sexual practices of adult life. While much of the behaviour which the *Journal* discusses might shock a modern-day reader, in 1600 when it was written these sexual experiences for children were considered perfectly natural'.[57] Biographical evidence must be treated with caution because it may deal with untypical individuals and, in the Dauphin's case it was important that as the last male heir, he should produce children. It must also be remembered, however, that when life expectancy is only thirty,[58] marriage for girls at thirteen becomes 'very common'.[59]

The other major change removed young people from a working life and placed them in educational institutions. Children at the age of seven or eight were often sent to another home to serve an apprenticeship which usually involved domestic service. In return parents would receive other children into their home brought in for work and training. Apprentices were workers who became somewhat similar to 'extra sons or extra daughters';[60] in return for their labour children were clothed, fed and educated. Child labour within the family was hard, and poor children could begin as early as three,[61] but it was with the development of the factory system that the worst excesses and exploitations took place.[62]

As children ceased to work they began to study, and between 1600 and 1800 there were substantial changes in education. Education as an activity in the Renaissance period was indifferent to age and was considered to be an activity which should span the entire life, and therefore people of all ages learned together.[63] Over a short period education had become an activity confined to childhood. The extension of the period of study, its concentration in childhood and the introduction of corporal punishment led to rioting at Winchester and Eton in the eighteenth century.[64] These educational changes, in tandem with the others mentioned, served to segregate children from the adult world, bestowed upon them a weakness and innocence not previously possessed and made them dependent upon adults and subject to their discipline. However, these changes were not experienced evenly or simultaneously by all children, and gender and class influenced the pace of developments. The first children were middle class and male, since 'childhood did not apply to women'.[65] The emergent bourgeoisie wanted only their sons to be educated in this innovatory fashion, so they could cope with the rapidly developing technological changes in society. Girls learned their future work in the home and therefore did not need the education and training which schools provided. Moreover, the exclusion of girls spanned all social groups, and 'girls of good family were no better educated than girls of the lower classes.'[66]

In much the same way, working-class children worked in the mines, factories and mills, had little need to read and write and therefore were at least initially excluded from childhood. Childhood was, particularly in its early days, class discriminating. However, mass education eventually involved the working class, and the social legislation of the nineteenth and twentieth centuries further controlled their drinking, smoking, gambling and sexual lives with an age of consent. The process of change initiated in 1600 was remarkably slow in reaching some working-class groups, and Plumb observes that

> pictures of working class children of Victorian London or Paris showed them still dressed as adults, usually in their parents' worn out and cut down clothes and we now know that they drank, gambled and rioted sexually and in fact participated in every form of adult life – indeed physically they had no escape from it.[67]

However, while historians concur on the nature of the changes in young people's lives, they disagree about their cause. Ariès's account is rather idealist[68] and explains the changes in childhood as a consequence of the ideas of 'a small minority of lawyers, priests and moralists'[69] who were at the origins of both the concept of childhood and the modern concept of schooling. However, ideas never exist in isolation from the society which nurtures them but are expressions of the needs and interests of particular social groups or movements. Hoyles, Plumb and Firestone identify such a group. The transition from feudalism to capitalism produced a new social class, the Bourgeoisie. It also generated urbanization and industrialization with the inevitable increase in the division of labour. The new society was one in which science and technology were expanding rapidly and was therefore infinitely more complex than its predecessor requiring skilled personnel for commerce and the professions. Schools were established and middle-class males became the first to undergo a long and segregated training for adult life; they became the first children. Males rather than females were selected, since those with newly acquired wealth wished to pass it to successive generations through the male line. In the process of these changes, Plumb observes how

> we forced the growing child into a repressive and artificial world, a prison . . . we can now look back with longing to the

late medieval world when, crude and simple as it was, men, women and children lived their lives together, shared the same morals as well as the same games, the same excesses as well as the same austerities.[70]

The works of Ariès, Plumb, Firestone and others are important to our understanding of the development and changing character of childhood, but we should beware of accepting their findings uncritically, since, as Freeman observes, the evidence offered by history can be selective and 'history is written predominantly by upper class male adults'.[71] What is significant about the historical study of childhood is that, while commonsense beliefs currently view childhood as a fixed and immutable state, the suggestion that it has, and could again, assume a radically different form challenges that commonsense view and indicates the potential for change. Conceptions of childhood and adulthood are continually shifting.

Rights

The phrase 'children's rights' lacks precision and has been described as 'a slogan in search of definition'.[72] The issue of children's rights is certainly complex and raises philosophical, moral and legal as well as social concerns. Part of that complexity derives from the fact that the term 'rights' has been invested with a diversity of meaning as a consequence of the considerable attention it has received and continues to enjoy from political philosophers.[73] But, in part, the complexity reflects the wide variety of rights claimed for children. John Holt argues the case for an extensive list of rights on behalf of children. This includes the right to vote, to work, to own property, to travel, to choose one's guardian, to receive a guaranteed income, to assume legal and financial responsibilities, to control one's learning, to use drugs and to drive.[74] Farson advocates a similar list in *Birthrights*.[75] Pinchbeck and Hewitt seek less ambitious claims which stress the rights of children 'to adequate food, clothing, medical care, to appropriate education and training, protection against exploitation, cruelty and neglect'.[76] NAYPIC's claims are more general but no less basic. Their demands for human dignity include the rights to privacy, autonomy, freedom from labelling and 'the right to be treated with the same respect as any other valid member of the human race'.[77] Now this of course is a very mixed bag, not only in terms of the variety of rights which are being claimed, but the difficulties involved in enforcing them, the resources required to meet them and the social and political consequences upon granting them. Some of this complexity can be resolved by classification, and perhaps the fundamental division to be drawn in a discussion of rights is that which distinguishes legal from moral rights.[78]

A legal right is an entitlement[79] which is 'conceded and enforced by the law of the realm': it is 'the actual law of actual states'.[80] The right to vote, for example, is a legal right conferred by the Representation of the People Act (1969) upon all citizens excluding those disqualified by age, incompetence or other grounds. A moral right, however, finds no such endorsement or recognition in any existing law.[81] I might, for example, claim that everyone who so wishes has the right to vote without regard to age. In making such a claim I cannot refer to legal statute and I am definitely not asserting any statement of fact. What I am doing is appealing to the principle that every human being who is a member of a society has a right to participate in the decision-making procedures which govern it. A legal right therefore describes an existing entitlement; a moral right prescribes a justifiable entitlement. Legal rights are further distinguished from their moral counterparts by the characteristics of enforceability and proof. A legal right must necessarily be enforceable through the judicial machinery of law estate, whereas a moral right cannot always be enforced. To claim that one has the moral right to work is not to say that one is employed. On the contrary, it is precisely unemployed people who are likely to claim this right most keenly. As Cranston notes, 'we are most acutely conscious of a moral right when it is not being conceded.'[82] Moreover, the existence of legal rights can be established by examining laws which have been enacted, by consulting a book, or in discussion with a judge or some other legal authority. A person may claim a moral right to something, but someone else may refute the claim. Each may try to satisfy both claim and counter-claim, but neither can satisfactorily prove the existence of a moral right.

While it is clear that there are substantial differences between legal and moral rights, there are also close relationships between them, although these may vary.

All this can perhaps be best explained by the use of an example. In Britain every young person has the legal right to a full-time education up to their sixteenth year. For those who believe like Pinchbeck and Hewitt,[83] cited above, that children have a moral right to such an education, there is overlap between moral and legal rights. The moral right informs and supports the legal right; this is how things *are* as well as *ought* to be. Alternatively, writers such as Holt and Farson bestow upon young people the moral right to work, to vote, to own property, to control one's own learning, and others, for which there is no corresponding legal right; indeed, in some instances, laws specifically exclude children from the possession of a legal right. In this instance moral rights become a source of criticism of the law and signal a certain direction for change; this is how things *are*, but not how they *ought* to be. Thus, while moral and legal rights are distinct, in practice they are interrelated and can overlap. Advocates of children's rights have stressed the need for the recognition and expansion of both the legal and the moral rights of children, although the emphasis has tended to be on moral rights. However, by claiming that children possess certain moral rights, it is easy to progress to arguments in support of legislative changes which would acknowledge such rights and convert them into statutes.

A recent classification produced four distinct categories of rights under the general heading 'children's rights'.[84] For convenience's sake these categories can be labelled welfare rights, protective rights, adult rights and rights against parents.

Children's rights, understood as welfare rights, find their clearest expression in the United Nations Declaration of the Rights of the Child. Such rights ensure for all children welfare needs of nutrition, medical services, housing and education. In Wald's words, these 'rights against the world' are 'the most important "rights" that could be given to children', since they 'lie at the heart of a child's well being'.[85] However, the achievement of welfare rights does not, in any way, alter the social or legal standing of children, in relation to adults. Moreover, as many children have learned at appalling cost, governments cannot always meet claims to such welfare rights, since 'Courts cannot order that the world be free of poverty'.[86] Claims of this kind are not so much rights as moral, social and political objectives which any humane society would seek to pursue, for adults as well as children; we all desire adequate nutrition, housing, medical and welfare provision. The way to secure these objectives is for society to exercise its political will and choice, enact legislative change, and make the equal provision of these basic goods its highest priority.

The second category, protective rights, is concerned with rights which will protect children from inadequate care, neglect and physical or emotional abuse in the home, or any other form of danger. The range of protections which it is considered necessary to provide for children is considerable and is in some cases contentious. Everyone would probably acknowledge the need for protection to prevent sexual or physical abuse of children, but there would be less unanimity about the need to protect children from the possible hazards of part-time jobs, since some consider that great benefits accrue to children from their involvement in the world of work.[87] Like welfare rights, protective rights do not involve any greater independence for children or alter their subordinate status in relation to adults; indeed, their effect may well be to the contrary. Enhancing children's rights to protection from abuse, at least in the British context, has tended to diminish their autonomy. In cases of child abuse it is adult perceptions of 'the best interests of the child'[88] which have proved influential in decisions concerning the need to invoke the protective mechanisms of the state. Authority and decision-making power over the child's interests in these matters tends to transfer from one set of adults (parents) to another (social workers) rather than being given to children themselves. The attainment of protective rights can therefore entail a substantial degree of paternalism. As Freeman argues, 'I do not think it would occur to the average social worker to ask a child, even an older child, whether he wanted to remain with parents who physically ill treated him.'[89] Protective rights can, and do, restrict autonomy, and there is clearly some measure of tension between these two aspects of children's rights.

The third category of rights, adult rights, suggests that children should have the same rights which are currently enjoyed in monopoly by adults. The claim is based on the judgement that age is an arbitrary and irrational yardstick by which to offer or withhold privilege.[90] Children are currently denied many rights which adults consider essential for living a full, free life. They lack rights to vote, work, marry and drive and are subject to eleven years' compulsory education. Granting these 'adult' rights to young people would massively extend their autonomy and independence in these important areas. The arbitrariness involved in age limits and restrictions is an inevitable consequence of the unevenness of the process of human development and maturation; not all twelve-year-olds are the same. Therefore any law which restricts those under twenty-one from doing X will exclude many twenty-year-olds who have the necessary capacities to do X, while allowing anyone over twenty-one to do X without regard to their capacities and competencies. But to acknowledge the dilemma does not provide a solution. Freeman suggests three options.[91] First, we can accept the inevitability of some age restrictions, even though they may be arbitrary, but try to reduce injustice by ensuring that the specified age is low enough to exclude only the minimal number. Second, we can abolish all age-related restrictions or third – and this is Freeman's preference – we can proceed on a 'case-by-case' basis and thereby identify those twenty-year-olds who may be sufficiently mature to exercise the rights from which the law generally precludes them. The difficulty with this last option is that there is rarely any objective test which allows us to measure any individual's competence to exercise these rights, and the 'case-by-case' approach could lead to discrimination against individuals and to greater arbitrariness. Children are slowly expanding their stock of these 'adult rights' as legislation which imposes age restrictions is reviewed and revised. The reduction from twenty-one to eighteen years as a qualification for franchise in 1969 is an obvious example here.

The final category of children's rights suggest that children should have greater independence from parents before reaching the existing age of majority. These rights against parents would give children autonomy over decision-making across a range of issues, from 'what to eat, the length of a child's hair, what television programmes to watch, to major steps such as leaving home or having an abortion'.[92] As with 'adult rights', the purpose of rights against parents is not to protect children but to extend their personal autonomy. Two limitations of rights against parents should be noted. First, as Wald observes, such rights do not always imply that the power to make decisions simply transfers from parents to children. Children may be required to seek approval for their choices from the courts. In America, some states have given children the right to an abortion without parental consent, while in other states the child must petition the court to order the abortion where there is a dispute with parents.[93] Second, children's autonomy is limited, as is their parents', by the fact that all are part of a family. Communal living requires that we cannot always do what we wish, or win every dispute which emerges as a consequence of conflicting wishes and intentions; a communal and co-operative life makes compromise a necessity for everyone.

The classification of children's rights outlined above is of great interest and has much to recommend it – not least the fact that it imposes order on the chaotic range of claims which have been made by children and on their behalf. However, the divisions are not adequately exclusive, cannot be sustained, and ultimately the four categories collapse into two larger groupings. The rights of children to greater independence from parental decision-making (category 4) is one aspect of the claim that children should have the same rights as adults (category 3). Equally, welfare rights (category 1) are simply a subdivision of protective rights (category 2), and Freeman acknowledges that in the case of welfare rights 'it may be best to conceive of them as protections rather than rights'.[94]

This fourfold classification turns out upon inspection to be an elaborate variant of an older conceptual division between what may be termed the liberationist versus the protectionist orientation towards children's rights. This dichotomy has its roots in the work of Rogers and Wrightsman.[95] The nurturance orientation 'stresses the provision by society of supposedly beneficial objects, environments, services, experiences, etc., for the child'; whereas the self-determination orientation stresses 'those potential rights which would allow children to exercise control over their environments, to make decisions about what they want, to have autonomous control over various facets of their lives'.[96] The distinction drawn here parallels the division Farson makes between those interested in protecting children and those interested in protecting children's rights,[97] and illustrates the two broad schools of thought which have emerged in the discussion of children's rights. One school has stressed that children have special needs which require attention and protection, and it demands particular rights specifically tailored to meet their needs as children.

In opposition to this view, it has been argued that young people should possess the same rights as adults, that the rights of children 'are no greater than the rights of others and no less'.[98] This division between the nurturance and self-determination position on rights, between protecting children and protecting children's rights, is a simple, useful and attractive organizing principle to help order the complex discussion of rights. However, a word of caution is necessary, since like many antitheses the opposition here is more apparent than real. Children are claiming and require an expansion of both kinds of rights, but the pursuit of protective rights should not be seen as antithetical to the achievement of self-determination rights, or vice versa. If the question of age is removed for a moment and the discussion centres on human rather than children's rights, the picture becomes clearer. Adults can, and indeed do, enjoy both self-determination and protectionist rights without any necessary tension between the two, although there are some cases there they may conflict. The law prohibiting women from underground colliery work is an example where a concern with protection inhibits self-determination. Generally, however, an adult at work enjoys the protection from hazardous conditions and exploitative employers provided by health and safety legislation without any sense of loss of autonomy. Similarly if children were given the right to work as Holt, Farson and others have suggested, they like adults, would require protection from poor and dangerous working conditions, but this should be without prejudice to their autonomy and choice in other matters. Protecting children and protecting their rights are therefore not necessarily oppositional but can be complementary objectives; protective legislation must supplement but not supplant the adult rights which liberationists wish to extend to children. It should be added that, in advocating the right to work, Holt is seeking to offer a choice and not impose an obligation. There is a very important difference between having the right to work and being obliged to work.[99]

The different chapters contained in this book express both liberationist and protectionist positions. Bob Franklin's advocacy of the extension of suffrage to children is clearly cast in the liberationist mould, while Emma MacLennan's argument for the need to implement fully the Employment of Children Act (1973) favours a protectionist emphasis. Ruth Adler and Alan Dearling claim that children's rights in the Scottish context can only be understood satisfactorily by recourse to a 'modified protectionism' which they try to elaborate. The questions that arise in the discussion of children's rights are complex, and there is no single answer, no 'slick' formula which can attract consensus and resolve them. The literature on children's rights is characterized by this division between liberationist and protectionist approaches, which is perhaps a consequence of the fact that children's rights are a relatively new area of academic interest and, in their liberationist guise, of political concern. It is therefore appropriate that this collection of essays should embrace and articulate this diversity.

Underlying the different emphases in approaches to rights taken by contributors is a fundamental agreement that children need to expand the rights they currently possess. Schools, courts, welfare and social institutions, and the professions largely concerned with children, must all be reformed if children are to win their rights. This pursuit of rights will require the acknowledgement of children's moral claims, the enactment of claims in legislation, and the implementation, scrutiny and constant re-evaluation of laws. Most important, it will require that adult attitudes towards children change. Without these attitudinal changes, legislative reforms are of only limited value: a first step. The discussions of girls' and black children's rights below reveal that the formal achievements of rights, even where enacted in legislation, does not by itself secure the provision of equal rights for these groups. Children must learn the lessons offered by the movements to secure rights for blacks and women. The existence of legislation to ensure women's rights to work and equal pay does not guarantee a full equality and the eradication of discrimination on the basis of gender. The same experience is true for blacks seeking equal rights. Prejudice is more resilient to change, and legislation can prove itself a blunt tool with which to attack it. It is, however, the starting point, and legislation to improve the rights of children must be promoted by children and adults alike as a matter of urgency.

Notes

1 M. Hoyles, *Changing Childhood* (Writers and Readers, 1979), p. 16.
2 P. Edelman, 'The children's rights movement', in *The Children's Rights Movement: overcoming the oppression of the young*, ed. B. and R. Gross (Anchor, 1977), p. 203.
3 A. Vardin and P. Brody (eds), *Children's Rights: contemporary perspectives* (Teachers College Press, 1979), p. xv.
4 Ibid., p. 9. Awareness of the existence of children as a minority group is reflected in a growing but, as yet, not substantial body of literature advocating an extension of children's rights. The British literature is very recent: M. D. A. Freeman, *The Rights and the Wrongs of Children* (Frances Pinter, 1983); J. Harris, 'The political status of children', in *Contemporary Political philosophy: radical studies*, ed. K. Graham (Cambridge University Press, 1982); C. A. Wringe, *Children's Rights: a philosophical study* (Routledge and Kegan Paul, 1981); M. King (ed.), *Childhood, Welfare and Justice* (Batsford Academic, 1981); P. Adams (ed.), *Children's Rights* (Elek Books, 1971). More specialized studies of aspects of children's rights are offered in A. Morris and H. Giller, *Providing Criminal Justice for Children* (Edward Arnold, 1983), and H. Geach and E. Szwed, *Providing Civil Justice for Children* (Edward Arnold, 1983). For the American literature, see B. and R. Gross (eds), *The Children's Rights Movement*; D. Gottlieb (ed.), *Children's Liberation* (Spectrum Books, 1973); Vardin and Brody (eds), *Children's Rights*; R. Farson, *Birthrights* (Penguin, 1978); J. C. Hogan and M. D. Schwartz (eds), *Child's Rights* (Lexington Books, 1983); J. Holt, *Escape from Childhood* (Penguin, 1975).
5 £14,000 of this figure is loss of the mother's take-home pay at 1980 figures: P. Ashley, *The Money Problems of the Poor* (Heinemann, 1983), p. 10; D. Piachaud, *Round about Fifty Hours a week* (CPAG, 1984).
6 L. Hodges, *Out in the Open: the school records debate* (Writers and Readers, 1981).
7 For a study of the impact of social adversity on the health, family circumstances and educational development of eleven- and sixteen-year-olds, see P. Wedge and J. Essen, *Children in Adversity* (Pan Books, 1982); also R. Holman, *Inequality in Child Care* (CPAG, 1980), especially section 2.
8 UNICEF, *The State of the World's Children, 1985* (Oxford University Press, 1985).

9   S. Fothergill and J. Vincent, *The State of the Nation* (Pluto Press, 1985).
10 S. de Beauvoir, *Old Age* (Penguin, 1985), p. 8.
11 Ibid.
12 A. Morris, H. Giller, H. Geach and E. Szwed, *Justice for Children* (Macmillan, 1980). See also Morris and Giller, *Providing Criminal Justice for Children*, and Geach and Szwed, *Providing Civil Justice for Children*.
13 M. Hawker, 'Children have rights too', *Community Care*, 6 January 1983, p. 16.
14 N. Parton, *Child Abuse* (Macmillan, 1985), p. 152.
15 This is well discussed by Holt, *Escape from Childhood*, p. 22.
16 See Emma MacLennan's discussion of children's rights at work in chapter 6.
17 *Department of Employment Gazette* (July 1985), p. 31.
18 *Regional Trends*, 20 (HMSO, 1985), p. 98.
19 *Youth and Policy*, Monitor section, 2, 2 (Autumn 1983). The number of children living in poverty in 1977 was about 280,000: Hansard, 28 April 1981.
20 H. Sharron, 'The child poverty trap', *The Times Education Supplement*, 10 May 1985.
21 M. Brown and N. Madge, *Despite the Welfare State* (Heinemann Educational, 1982).
22 *Social Trends*, vol. 14 (HMSO, 1984), pp. 114–15.
23 *Regional Trends* (HMSO, 1984), p. 33.
24 NAYPIC, *Evidence to the Select Committee on 'Children in Care'* (NAYPIC, 1983), p. 10.
25 M. Stein and S. Ellis, *Gizza Say? Reviews and young people in care* (NAYPIC, 1983). See also *Locked up in Care* (Children's Legal Centre, 1982). See Gerry Lavery's discussion of children's rights in care in chapter 4.
26 *Criminal Statistics, England and Wales, 1980* (Home Office, 1981).
27 *Social Trends*, vol. 14, p. 14.
28 R. Ives, 'Child sexual abuse and incest', *Highlight*, 50 (July 1982). See chapter 7 on children's sexual rights.
29 R. S. Kempe and C. H. Kempe, *Child Abuse* (Fontana/Open Books, 1982), p. 18. For a useful discussion of the difficulties involved in the definition of child abuse, see M. D. A. Freeman, 'The rights of children in the International Year of the Child', *Current Legal Problems*, 33 (1980), especially pp. 2–12.
30 H. Geach, 'What safety in numbers', *Guardian*, 7 December 1983.
31 J. D. W. Low, 'On child abuse', *Social Work Today*, 14, 42 (1983).
32 M. Jobling, *The Abused Child* (National Children's Bureau, 1977), p. 5.
33 STOPP, *Once Every 19 Seconds* (STOPP, 1982).
34 NAYPIC, *Sharing Care* (NAYPIC, 1983), p. 13.
35 UNICEF, *The State of the World's Children, 1985*, p. 10.

36   C. Turnbull, *The Forest People* (Picador, 1976), pp. 117–18 and 201–4.

37   The most scholarly historical study of childhood is probably P. Ariès, *Centuries of Childhood (Jonathan Cape, 1962). For a critique of Ariès, see L. A. Pollock, Forgotten Children* (Cambridge University Press, 1983). See also Lloyd de Mause, 'The evolution of childhood', in *The History of Childhood* (Souvenir Press, 1976); J. H. Plumb, *In the Light of History* (Penguin, 1972); M. Hoyles, *Changing Childhood*; S. Firestone, 'Down with childhood', in *The Dialectic of Sex* (Bantam Books, 1972), pp. 72–105; J. Walvin, *A Child's World: a social history of English childhood, 1800–1914* (Penguin, 1982); N. Tucker, *What is a Child?* (Open Books, 1977); P. Thane, 'Childhood in history', in *Childhood, Welfare and Justice*, ed. M. King (Batsford Academic, 1981); I. Pinchbeck and M. Hewitt, *Children in English Society*, vols 1 and 2 (Routledge and Kegan Paul, 1973); S. Humphries, *Hooligans or Rebels?* (Blackwell, 1981); H. Hendrick, *Kept from History: aspects of the status of children* (Justice for children, n.d.), parts I and II.

38   B. and R. Gross (eds), *The Children's Rights Movement*, p. 10.

39   Hoyles, *Changing Childhood*, p. 25.

40   Tucker, *What is a Child?*, p. 25.

41   Plumb, *In the Light of History*, p. 153; Ariès, *Centuries of Childhood*, p. 329; P. Laslett, The World We Have Lost (Methuen, 1965), p. 105.

42   Ariès, *Centuries of Childhood*, p. 128.

43   Holt, *Escape from Childhood*, p. 21.

44   Plumb, *In the Light of History*, p. 159.

45   Ibid., p. 153.

46   Firestone, 'Down with childhood', p. 78.

47   Ariès, *Centuries of Childhood*, p. 129.

48   Holt, *Escape from Childhood*, p. 22.

49   Ariès, *Centuries of Childhood*, p. 329.

50   Farson, *Birthrights*, p. 22; Holt, *Escape from Childhood*, p. 32.

51   Ariès, *Centuries of Childhood*, p. 46.

52   Laslett, *The World We Have Lost*, p. 105; Hoyles, *Changing Childhood, pp. 17 and 22; Ariès, Centuries of Childhood*, p. 50; Firestone, 'Down with childhood', p. 78; Pinchbeck and Hewitt, *Children in English Society*, vol. 2, p. 348.

53   Ariès, *Centuries of Childhood*, pp. 62–7; Hoyles, *Changing Childhood*, p. 22; Firestone, 'Down with childhood', p. 78; Tucker, *What is a Child?*, p. 18.

54   Firestone, 'Down with childhood', p. 78; Ariès, *Centuries of Childhood*, p. 70.

55   John Newbury in 1744 was the first person to make the publication of children's books a business: Hoyles, *Changing Childhood*, p. 22; Ariès, *Centuries of Childhood*, p. 119.

56   Ariès, *Centuries of Childhood*, p. 100.

57   Ibid., p. 100.

58   Laslett, *The World We Have Lost*, p. 6.

59 Ariès, *Centuries of Childhood*, p. 103.
60 Laslett, *The World We Have Lost*, p. 3.
61 E. P. Thompson, *The Making of the English Working Class* (Pelican, 1968).
62 C. Hill, *Reformation to Industrial Revolution* (Penguin, 1969), p. 263. See also F. Engels, *The Condition of the Working Class in England*, in *Marx and Engels on Britain* (Lawrence and Wishart, 1954).
63 Hoyles, *Changing Childhood*, p. 20; Ariès, *Centuries of Childhood*, p. 330; Plumb, *In the Light of History*, p. 163.
64 Hoyles, *Changing Childhood*, pp. 24–5.
65 Firestone, 'Down with childhood', p. 81. See also Thane, 'Childhood in history', p. 9, and Hoyles, *Changing Childhood*, p. 3.
66 Ariès, *Centuries of Childhood*, p. 334.
67 Plumb, *In the Light of History*, p. 163.
68 Lloyd de Mause's 'psychogenic' explanation of the changing character of childhood is equally idealist. See his 'The evolution of childhood', p. 3.
69 Ariès, *Centuries of Childhood*, p. 329.
70 Plumb, *In the Light of History*, p. 165. See Hendrick, *Kept from History*, part II, pp. 22–3.
71 Freeman, *The Rights and Wrongs of Children*, p. 12; Tucker, *What is a Child?*, p. 16.
72 H. Rodham, 'Children under the law', *Harvard Educational Review*, 43 (1973), p. 487.
73 R. Flatham, *The Practice of Rights* (Cambridge University Press, 1976), p. 33.
74 Holt, *Escape from Childhood*, pp. 114–205.
75 Farson, 'Birthrights' in B. and R. Gross (eds) *Op Cit* pp. 325–8.
76 Pinchbeck and Hewitt, *Children in English Society*, vol. 2, p. 347.
77 NAYPIC, *Evidence to the Select Committee on 'Children in Care'*, pp. 38–9. For a fairly comprehensive, if unsympathetic, attempt to catalogue the rights claimed for childen see Wringe, *Children's Rights*, pp. 9–16. See also Youth Liberation of Ann Arbor, 'Youth liberation programme', in B. and R. Gross (eds), *The Children's Rights Movement*, pp. 329–33.
78 Rodham, 'Children under the law', p. 488. See M. Cranston *What Are Human Rights?* (Bodley Head, 1973), p. 5; Wringe, *Children's Rights*, ch. 4.
79 For a discussion of rights as entitlements rather than claims or duties, see H.J. McClosky, 'Rights', *Philosophical Quarterly* (April 1963), pp. 115–27; Wringe, *Children's Rights*, pp. 23–30; J. Feinberg, 'Duties, rights and claims', in *Rights, Justice and the Bounds of Liberty* (Princeton University Press, 1980), pp. 130–43.
80 Cranston, *What Are Human Rights?* pp. 4–5. Cranston subdivides legal rights into five categories in his essay 'Rights, real and supposed', in *Political Theory and the Rights of Man* ed. D. D. Raphael (Macmillan, 1967), pp. 47–8.

81 J. Feinberg, *Social Philosophy* (Prentice Hall, 1973), p. 84. Feinberg divides moral rights into four categories: conventional, ideas, conscientious and exercise rights.

82 Cranston, *What Are Human Rights?*, p. 5.

83 Pinchbeck and Hewitt, *Children in English Society*, vol. 2, p. 347.

84 Freeman, *The Rights and the Wrongs of Children*, pp. 40–52. The framework which Freeman develops draws upon the work of Wald. See M. Wald, 'Children's rights: a framework for analysis', *University of California Davis Law Review*, 12 (1979), pp. 255–82 but especially p. 260.

85 Wald, 'Children's rights', p. 260.

86 Ibid., p. 261.

87 See, for example, the comment by Keith Waterhouse in *The Daily Mirror*, 21 January 1985, quoted by Emma MacLennan in chapter 6.

88 Geach and Szwed, *Providing Civil Justice for Children*.

89 Freeman, *The Rights and the Wrongs of Children*, p. 44.

90 Ibid., p. 45; Wald, 'Children's rights', p. 265.

91 Freeman, *The Rights and the Wrongs of Children*, p. 45.

92 Ibid., p. 48; Wald, 'Children's rights', p. 270.

93 Wald, 'Children's rights', p. 271.

94 Freeman, *The Rights and the Wrongs of Children*, p. 43; Wald, 'Children's rights', p. 261.

95 C. M. Rogers and L. S. Wrightsman, 'Attitudes towards children's rights: nurturance or self determination', *Journal of Social Issues*, 34, 2 (1978), p. 61.

96 Ibid., p. 61.

97 Farson, *Birthrights*, p. 165. The distinction is also made by P. Goodman in 'Reflections on children's rights', in B. and R. Gross (eds), *The Children's Rights Movement*, pp. 140–1.

98 Advisory Centre for Education (ACE), 'A draft charter of children's rights', *Where*, 56 (April 1971), p. 107.

99 This point is made by David Watson in *Caring for Strangers* (Routledge and Kegan Paul, 1980), p. 131.

100 B. and R. Gross (eds), *The Children's Rights Movement*, p. 7.

2

Children's Political Rights

Bob Franklin

In this chapter I wish to consider the arguments which are traditionally offered to justify the exclusion of young people from the possession of political rights, particularly the right to vote, and suggest that such arguments are ultimately unconvincing. I shall also argue that the exclusion of children from full political status is an enigma which democratic politics should not allow. Because of their age, children are, of course, denied many rights which adults consider to be basic human rights; the right to freedom from parental control and the right to own property are obvious examples. But their exclusion from political involvement is a more serious matter, since what is at stake here is not simply the denial of citizen rights but the right to be a citizen.

As a consequence of exclusion, children constitute a unique political grouping in democracies in two important respects. First, they offer a clear example of the violation of the democratic principle that no individual or group should be subject to laws which they have not participated in making. This violation is particularly acute when many political decisions – for example, the future deployment of nuclear weapons, or educational provisions – arguably have a greater relevance for young people than other members of the polity.

Second, they are the only grouping in a democracy whose political rights are entrusted to another group, to be exercised on their behalf without the restraint of any mechanism of accountability or democratic control. It is clearly worrying and 'dangerous for one class to have its interests entrusted to another'.[1] Dahl's claim that parents understand the interests of children and will seek to promote them on their behalf, because 'adults are closely tied to children by bonds of love', does little to allay fears and prompts difficult questions.[2] How are children's interests to be determined if they are not consulted? Are children's and parents' interests always identical? 'If not can parents be trusted to promote the child's interest?'[3] This exclusion from citizenship on the basis of chronology is both unjust and arbitrary. It is unjust because the individuals concerned cannot reasonably do anything, no matter how highly motivated, to alleviate or change the conditions that exclude them. If the grounds for exclusion were incompetence, and these might exclude many adults, this would be more acceptable, since the ignorant can learn and become educated and the stupid can become wise. However, a child, even if foolish enough to desire it, cannot grow old prematurely. In this way exclusion is a 'permanent' exclusion, since *all* children are denied rights simply because they are children and can acquire them only when they cease to be children. The exclusion is arbitrary, because the age at which full citizenship is presumed to commence has varied historically. In the Athenian democracies of ancient Greece a young person became a citizen, if they met certain other requirements, at the age of thirty. One writer suggested the transition to political adulthood occurs between the ages of twenty-seven and thirty-six.[4] while in the context of British politics the age qualification for citizenship has been lowered from twenty-one to eighteen.[5]

However, while it might be expected that such arbitrary, unjust and undemocratic treatment of children would give rise to controversy, discussion and a substantial literature, quite the reverse is true. Political theorizing has tended to give only 'a passing nod'[6] to the fact that the 'citizens of states without exception start off as children';[7] philosophy has been 'guilty of child neglect'.[8] The neglect is curious, since a discussion of children's rights touches upon many of the central concerns of political philosophy. It raises, for example, interesting and important questions about the nature of equality, the significance of reason and rationality in human affairs, the power of one group to control another and the ways in which such subordination is legitimated, as well as general questions about the nature of democracy: Who is a citizen, who is not and on what grounds are they excluded? Who has rights and who can participate in making laws?

One reason for the neglect of children's rights is the difficulty of getting people to take the matter seriously. Arguments have too frequently been dismissed rather than met, and few have shared Russell's view that 'no political theory is adequate unless it is applicable to children as well as to men and women'.[9] Dahl's remarks are typical when he suggests that 'no one seriously contends that children should be full members of the State's demos'.[10] What is important in all this is that the case for children's rights is dismissed, not by systematic, closely reasoned or coherent argument, but rather on the basis of implicit and taken-for-granted assumptions; a sort of

self-evident common sense which concludes the matter to be unworthy
of serious consideration and thereby precludes discussion. This should
not come as any surprise, since, with the benefit of hindsight, it is clear
that the case for the exclusion of different groups from full political
rights has never been cogently argued and could withstand no more
than cursory examination. Political history is littered with examples:
women, the propertyless, blacks and slaves have all been the victims of
common sense. It was argued that women lacked the rationality,
judgement and knowledge of the political world necessary to exercise
the obligations of citizenship, while those without propety had proved
their inability to direct their own affairs by their very propertylessness.
A similar circularity of argument excluded slaves. Slaves were
denounced by Aristotle – departing from his usual reflective, detached
and democratic theorizing and displaying all the prejudices of an
Athenian gentleman of his day – as unworthy of political rights since
they lacked intellect and were therefore less than fully human; the
circle is complete when he asserts that we know they lack such
qualities because they are slaves. This 'logic' has subsequently been
deployed by racists to exclude blacks from citizen rights in the
southern states of America and in South Africa.

Such beliefs are now recognized by most for the absurd
rationalizations they have always been, but they warn of the dangers
of excluding groups unless the grounds for exclusion are clearly stated,
supported with evidence and proven. In democratic states the
presumption must always be against exclusion, and the burden of
proof must rest with those who propose to disfranchise. However, if
coherent argument, serious reflection and detachment are abandoned
in favour of a resort to 'common sense', it is appropriate to be sceptical
and ask what is the substance of this common sense and whose
interests it serves. The answer, quite simply, is that it is no more than a
thinly veiled justification which functions to protect and promote the
interests and power of one social group against rival claimants – in this
instance, the power of adults over children. It is important to remember that the extension of political rights diminishes the power of those
who previously held such rights in monopoly, and history reveals that
no dominant group, whether based on gender, age, race or class, has
ever conceded its authority voluntarily. Since this justification is
therefore one means whereby adults seek to maintain the existing
pattern of power relationships, those who seek to expand the political
rights of children must challenge 'common sense' and subject it to the
closest reasoning.

The 'commonsense' exclusion of children from political rights
derives much of its content and credibility from an uncritical

acceptance of paternalism. In the following section I shall argue that paternalism offers no cogent grounds upon which to deny young people political rights, including the right to vote, but simply provides a justification for political elites. But if age cannot serve as a criterion to decide who should possess political rights, what can serve as substitute? In the second section I consider two different criteria for establishing voting competence and offer a third, more equitable, possibility. Finally, I assess the possible implications of changing the political status of children, moves towards the acquisition of political rights for young people in International Youth Year, and the limitations upon such political change.

Paternalism

Paternalism involves intervention in an individual's freedom of choice and/or action in an attempt to enhance or secure the best interests of that individual, even though the individual concerned may not recognize any advantage in such intervention or indeed may perceive it to be injurious. In Dworkin's classic discussion of paternalism it is understood to be 'the interference with a person's liberty of action, justified by reasons referring exclusively to the welfare, good, happiness, needs, interests, or values of the person being coerced'.[11] On this account, the adult exercise of children's political rights does not constitute any undemocratic procedure, as it would if any group other than children were involved, but is simply an attempt to secure the interests and welfare of young people.

Three reasons are traditionally offered to legitimate this paternalism. First, young people lack the rationality, knowledge and experience necessary for political autonomy. If they were allowed political self-determination, children would make disastrous and damaging mistakes. Paternalism seeks to protect children from the injurious consequences of their incompetencies. Since children are unable to choose for themselves, adults must make their choices for them. Second, as children mature, they will come, with hindsight, to see the wisdom of the decisions that adults have taken on their behalf and subsequently endorse them; paternalism in this instance is justified by a 'future-oriented consent'. Third, children are dependent on adults in many ways and are incapable of sustaining themselves without adult assistance; paternalism is justified here by the young person's inability for 'self-maintenance'. I wish to examine each of these three justifications for paternalism, although the first is by far the most important and will require lengthier consideration.

The most commonplace justification for paternalism runs something along the following lines. Children are presumed to be ignorant of political matters, insufficiently rational to make discriminating choices in the political sphere, incapable of any systematic and purposeful behaviour and thereby unable to fulfil the requirements and obligations of citizenship. Since these deficiencies are considered to be a direct consequence of age, every young person is to be excluded. As individuals grow older and acquire the competencies necessary to exercise political rights, they will be inducted into citizenship. Locke's judgement is typical:

> Children I confess are not born into this full sort of equality though they are born to it. Their parents have a sort of rule or jurisdiction over them when they come into the world . . . but it's a temporary one. The bonds on this subjection are like the swaddling cloaths they are wrapt in and supported by in the weakness of their infancy. Age and reason as they grow up loosen them till at length they drop off and leave a man at his own free disposal.[13]

On this account, freedom depends on maturity, which alone can bestow the ability to make reasonable discriminations. To cite Locke again, 'We are born free as we are born rational; not that we have actually the exercise of either; age that brings one, brings with it the other too.'[14] Two aspects of this argument are more problematical than appear at first glance and require closer scrutiny: the claim that children lack reason or rationality, and the assertion based upon this that, if granted political rights, they would commit errors and mistakes.

The assertion that children should be excluded from political citizenship because they lack rationality raises the problem that it is extremely difficult to ascertain exactly what is meant by rationality and whether it can be defined with sufficient precision to determine whether any individual or category of individuals possesses the capacity or does not. The question 'What is rationality?' has been answered in many ways. Rationality may be used to connote thoughts and actions which are conscious and in accord with the rules of logic and empirical knowledge. Or individuals may be considered rational to the extent to which they are able to infer the possible consequences of a choice. For Max Weber, actions could be purposively rational (*zweckrational*) where appropriate means are chosen to obtain some predetermined end, or value rational (*wertrational*) where actions are in accordance with the moral standards and values of the community. Again, rationality may be designated by the 'possession of a certain level of measured intelligence on some standardized IQ test'.[15]

This uncertainty of meaning raises problems for those who seek to distinguish children from adults on the basis of a presumption of a lack of rationality in the former group. Moreover, the uncertainty is not confined to philosophers, and those who have sought a more rigorous and precise definition in the work of psychologists have been disappointed. Piaget's work is often cited in this connection.[16] Piaget's theorizing on developmental psychology identified several stages in the cognitive development and moral growth of human beings. The highest stage, the stage of 'formal operations', begins at around the age of twelve and develops further during adolescence. At this stage,

> the adolescent's system of mental operations has reached a high degree of equilibrium. This means among other things that the adolescent's thought is flexible and effective. He can deal efficiently with problems of reasoning . . . can imagine the many possibilities inherent in a situation. Unlike the concrete operational child, whose thought is tied to the concrete, the adolescent can transcend the immediate here and now.[17]

However, this assertion that children mature through a succession of evolutionary stages, gradually developing their cognitive and moral capacities *en route*, has not been accepted unequivocally. Piaget's assumption that childhood is a single uniform and universal experience denies the credibility of much cultural, historical and anthropologial evidence.[18] If accepted as credible, Piaget's work generates as many problems as it resolves. Does this mean that other groups, especially adults, perhaps those who are retarded or becoming senile, who do not reach the stage of formal operations, should be excluded from political rights?[19] Even those who find justification for paternalism in Piaget's theories acknowledge that 'the evidence about older children is not so clear', and that, 'in both moral and cognitive development, many reach adult levels between twelve and fourteen'.[20] There are thus substantial difficulties in defining the term 'rationality' which must be faced by those who wish to use it as a criterion for distinguishing children from adults.

However, these difficulties are not acknowledged by everyone, and Scarre, with all the certainty, confidence and naïvety so characteristic of a utilitarian, offers the following account which is worth considering in some detail:

rational actions are those which are directed towards maximizing the expected utility of the agent. In addition, actions backed by rational decisions typically manifest themselves as elements of a systematic approach adopted by the agent for maximizing his good.[21]

Scarre develops his argument by presuming that which he is trying to prove: namely, that rationality is present in adults but absent in children. Adult rationality is manifest in

the ability to plan systematic policies of action . . . essential to solving the practical problems of living. Most adults, because they have lived a long time, have this ability, but children, because their mental powers and experience are alike inadequate, do not. Hence adults must impose a comprehensive 'system of purpose' on them.[22]

All this, of course, sounds reminiscent of Locke. The only problem remaining, at least as far as Scarre is concerned, is to establish a criterion which will distinguish the justified from the illegitimate imposition of such a 'system of purpose'. 'The paternalist', he claims, 'should intervene in an individual's affairs only when there is reason to believe his decisions are not based on rational calculations and that they are likely to result in a diminution of his stock of existing good or under-achievement of his possible stock of good.'[23] Scarre is offering here a classic statement of the case for denying children political rights on the basis of protective paternalism: children lack rationality, they will make unwise choices and mistakes, and therefore they should be subject to a protective paternalism. His argument requires closer consideration to reveal its many shortcomings.

First, in typically utilitarian fashion Scarre overstresses the presence and significance of rationality in human affairs. I consider myself to be a fairly cautious, thoughtful person who tries to assess the likely outcome and consequences of my decisions, although not necessarily in terms of 'maximizing my expected utility', but I am none the less constantly aware of how few of my decisions derive from rational considerations. In confessing this I do not feel condemned to solitude, since I doubt that many match Bentham's curious ideal-type individual who carefully, if not obsessively, estimates potential utilities on a complex felicific calculus.

Second, to be able to show – and this is what Scarre believes he can do – that adults have an understanding of the interests of children which is superior to that possessed by the children themselves is not sufficient to justify intervention in their affairs; it does not justify imposing a 'system of purpose' on them. As adults there may be many occasions in our lives, perhaps at times of great stress or emotional upset, when others such as close friends, colleagues or professional advisers and counsellors can, from a position of some detachment from our immediate affairs, gain a clearer picture in the short term of our interests and needs. As Schrag points out, 'might not my psychoanalyst . . . have a better understanding of my situation and its possibilities and limitations than I do?'[24] The important word in Schrag's question is *might*, since it is far from certain that such a 'better understanding' could be achieved. However, even if it were possible, what we would seek from friends would not be intervention in our affairs but guidance, suggestions and advice. As adults we are likely to be shocked by the elitism inherent in Scarre's assertion that others might be better placed than we are ourselves to make decisions regarding our own welfare. We must be equally shocked when such elitism is argued against children. Scarre's argument here is close to one of the principles offered by Dworkin to justify paternalism, which appeals to what would be chosen by fully rational individuals. Dworkin claims that 'since we are all aware of our irrational propensities, deficiencies in cognitive and emotional capacities . . . we may argue for and against proposed paternalistic measures in terms of what fully rational individuals would accept as forms of protection.'[25] Dworkin's position thus requires the construction of a rational will (i.e. the will which would be expressed by any fully rational being), its comparison with the actually existing will of the individual, and finally the substitution of the former for the latter in cases of mismatch. The elitist implications of such an argument are clear and raise obvious questions. Who is to construct this rational will and decide that it should prevail over actual wills? If, as Dworkin claims, 'we are *all* aware of our irrational propensities', are the decision makers exempt or, as he implies, as much in need of guidance as we all are? This advocacy of paternalism falls foul of Berlin's forceful critique in his *Four Essays on Liberty*

> The common assumption of these thinkers is that the rational ends of our 'true' natures must coincide, or be made to coincide, however violently our poor, ignorant, desire ridden, passionate, empirical selves may cry out against this process. Freedom is not freedom to do what is irrational or stupid or wrong.[26]

This leads to a third and related flaw in Scarre's case.

His justification for paternalist intervention is that there may be reason to believe that an individual lacks rationality; it is therefore the possession or not of certain characteristics and competencies which justifies intervention. However, if the argument for paternalistic intervention in children's affairs is based on their assumed incapacity for reasoned and rational thought, then it is not children as such who should be excluded but those incapable of rational thought. An absence of rationality does not distinguish children from adults but the irrational from the rational. Therefore, if Scarre is to be consistent, he mut intervene in the affairs of all those who, without regard to age, lack the relevant qualities necessary for autonomy. There are some obvious examples here, and Scarre himself suggests the case of the alcoholic whose behaviour and decisions, at least for much of the time, must be deemed less than rational. However, Scarre will not countenance interference in the affairs of the alcoholic.

> The reason why we cannot carry the alcoholic away for a fortnight's forcible cure, even though his drinking is harmful and not sanctioned by his reason, is that by doing so we should insult him by imposing our plans for his life on him when, as an adult, he has plans and policies of his own. Children do not have such systems of purpose of their own, so it does not infringe their rights to intervene on their behalf when their irrationality threatens their well being.[27]

Perhaps aware of his contradictory treatment of children and adults, Scarre has shifted the grounds of his argument: the justification for intervention now becomes the lack of any 'system of purpose'. However, what appears self-evidently true to Scarre again appears to me less certain and contentious. Is it really the case that children lack 'purposes' or the ability to formulate plans to achieve certain objectives and then the capacity to implement them. Watson is surely correct when he claims that children can and do plan things, 'and do them . . . from buying ice-cream to housebreaking'.[28] It may well be true that children's objectives and purposes are different from adult concerns, and some may even appear to adults to be trivial by comparison, but this is not the point. Scarre is claiming that children have no such 'plans and policies' at all.

The fourth objection to Scarre's case centres on his argument that, if left to their own devices, children will make mistakes which may be harmful, damaging and, in his terms, detracting from their utility. This is important, since 'the amount of a person's happiness or utility is the key consideration in determining whether he is to be subject to paternalism'.[29] Scarre's error here lies in confusing the right to do something with doing the right thing or, as Dworkin expresses it, 'someone may have the right to do something that is wrong for him to do.'[30] Indeed, Scarre himself wishes to defend the right of alcoholics to drink themselves ultimately to death. However, he seems to wish to deny children a right which adults have long enjoyed and exercised extensively – namely, the right to make mistakes. Adults have certainly not displayed any nurtured or obvious capacity to make wise judgement and avoid mistakes. A brief review of human history reveals a catalogue of blunders. It is adults who have chosen to pollute their environment with industrial, chemical and nuclear waste, fought wars, built concentration camps, segregated people because of the colour of their skin, and it is adults in developed countries who stupidly and insensitively eat their way to a premature death through coronary disease while many starve in the Third World. It is hard to imagine how this finely developed capacity for damaging incompetence could be exceeded by children. But, since we do not believe that adults should be denied rights because they make mistakes, it is both inconsistent and unjust to argue for the exclusion of children on this ground.

Harris makes the point squarely. If the 'justification of paternalism lies in the desirabilty of the reduction of vicious mistakes', then 'it would be absurd if one class could become licensed, by something as absurd as chronology, to make such mistakes and another not.'[31] As adults we consider mistakes to be something from which we learn rather than need protection. Children can also learn from their mistakes, and by giving them responsibility at an earlier age it may be possible to remove or at least reduce the more serious consequences of unwise choices. Errors are an inevitable part of the maturation and learning process. As Feinberg acknowledge's, 'Even children, after a certain point, had better not be "treated as children", else they will never acquire the outlook and capability of responsible adults.'[32] It is almost certainly true that in later life I will come to regret a number of the decisions I made in my youth, perhaps I will even come to consider them as mistakes, but this does not make a case for intervention. Everyone changes and develops new needs, attitudes, interests and purposes as they progress through life. But I cannot make current decisions in the light of how I might assess them in ten or twenty years' time, or try to take account of how my attitudes might have changed in the interim; current decisions must be based on current wisdoms and follies, no matter how limited. So why establish an arbitrary age of eighteen 'rather than 11 or 31',[33] below which attempts are made to protect people from the possibility of making mistakes and learning from them. It would be curious if, with the benefit of hindsight and the more thorough reflection which time allows, I could not see more possibilities and alternatives in my situation than were visible at the moment of taking the decision – whatever my age.

Scarre's view that paternalistic intervention in children's lives can be justified by reference to a presumed absence of rationality in young people, and hence the likelihood of their making harmful mistakes, is therefore seriously flawed in a number of ways. There is no agreed view concerning what constitutes rationality, even when the more rigorous and scientifically based discussions deriving from developmental psychology are invoked, and this clearly generates problems. Those who, like Scarre, try to put aside such difficulties offer unsatisfactory and in his case tautological definitions which stipulate a very narrow meaning for the term. Moreover, the presence or absence of rationality does not justify the exclusion of children from political rights but the exclusion of, if anyone, the irrational. This category may involve many adults who currently enjoy political rights; conversely, the yardstick of rationality may enfranchise many children. This confusion in turn leads to the employment of double standards. Confronted by the apparently irrational behaviour and mistakes of both adults and children, paternalism is deemed appropriate only for the latter group. Most important, paternalism, sanctioned on this ground, produces an adult political elite which, in the name of protection, interferes in children's lives and represses and damages their potential for learning and development by denying them the possibilities for growth.

Paternalism is traditionally supported on two further grounds: that of 'future-oriented consent' and that of 'lack of self-maintenance'. The argument centring on 'future-oriented consent' claims that parents have not only a right, but a duty, to restrict a child's freedom and take decisions on the child's behalf where it is necessary in order to promote the best interests of the child. However, the parental right to intervene is limited by the fact that the child must eventually acknowledge the wisdom and correctness of that intervention. Paternalism may therefore 'be thought of as a wager by the parent on the child's subsequent recognition of the wisdom of restrictions. There is an emphasis on what could be called future oriented consent – on what the child will come to welcome, rather than on what he does welcome.'[34] However, such a position raises the obvious logical difficulty that, if the justifiability of paternalistic intervention is really to depend on future consent, there is no way of knowing at the time of the intervention whether it is justified. But a more serious objection can be raised.

There is a danger that the consent to intervention which is achieved at some future date is itself the product of the process of intervention; that is, consent is manufactured, created or contrived by the very process of intervention.[35] Thus the child's later consent to intervention is not necessarily evidence of its legitimacy. To give an example, a child who is forced by parents to attend church, pray and read the Bible may indeed concur, if asked at some future date, that they now consent to the earlier parental wish that they should come to an understanding of God's love and compassion and enjoy a religious life. But what is the credibility of such consent when the hallmark of all processes of socialization, up to and including brainwashing, is that the person violated in this way should be happy in the acceptance of their newly acquired beliefs and values? Rawls has a forceful example:

> imagine two persons in full possession of their reason and who will affirm different religious or philosophical beliefs, and suppose that there is some psychological process that will convert each to the other's view, despite the fact that the process is imposed upon them against their wishes. In due course, let us suppose, both will come to accept conscientiously their new beliefs. We are still not permitted to submit them to this treatment.[36]

Despite Rawls's warning, the notion that it is acceptable to force children to do things which they currently object to doing, but which they will subsequently endorse, has proved popular with paternalists. Freeman, for example, defends compulsory education on the grounds of its ultimate desirability and unquestionable worth. 'A morally neutral theory of the good would', he believes, 'require adolescents to undergo education whether they wished to do so or not. That many would not is a sign that short term gains rather than lasting benefits were uppermost in their thoughts.'[37] Freeman, however, is really rigging the argument here to the extent where even disagreement with the argument is taken to be evidence of its correctness; those unable to see the benefits of education have clearly not received enough education. But some of us genuinely believe that much of the educational provision we received was a valueless waste of time and are not convinced that 'lasting benefits' are always to be preferred to 'short-term gains'. Not all are in agreement with Freeman's rather naïve and liberal view that it is through education 'that adolescents

acquire the capacity for full autonomy'.[38] Althusser[39] has argued
quite convincingly that education is one of a number of ideological
state apparatuses through which a dominant social class imposes its
conception of the world, thereby repressing possibilities for
rationality and generating precisely the contrived consensus which so
worries Rawls.

The third defence of paternalism, which has its origins in Kant's
work, claims that paternalism is justified by children's presumed
incapacity for self-sufficiency. In Kant's words, 'The children of the
house . . . attain majority and become masters of themselves . . ., even
without a contract of release from their previous state of dependence,
by their actually attaining to the capability of self-maintenance.'[40]
This view at first sight appears credible, since it seems reasonable that
those who are not self-sufficient will require and appreciate
assistance, support and protection from others. However, the
criterion of self-sufficiency fails to distinguish adults from children
and unless given greater precision could be used to justify a range of
further unwarranted interventions among adults as well as children.
The handicapped, the sick, the unemployed and the elderly all lack
self-sufficiency in the sense that they need various kinds of assistance
from others, on either a temporary or a permanent basis. It is a
dubious moral claim that anyone who lacks self-sufficiency must be
subject to the coercion and intervention of others in their affairs.
Morality aside, the important point for present purposes is that such
a claim does not serve to distinguish children from adults. Moreover,
in any society, all members rely on the expertise, competence and
capacities of others. Everyone at some time lacks the self-sufficiency
to mend a leaking tap, repair a broken television, heal a sick person,
remove an aching tooth.[41] We constantly depend on others for our
supplies of water, power, lighting, heating and food production and
distribution. Societies are by necessity built on the mutual
interdependence and communitarianism of their members, and children are not unique in needing assistance to survive and flourish. To
isolate one group within society and insist that they alone should
display the mythical qualities of latterday Robinson Crusoes, or else
be denied political rights, is unjust.

Criteria for establishing competence to vote

I have tried to argue that age cannot be related to competence in order
to provide a convincing citerion for distinguishing those who should
possess full political rights as citizens from those who should not. But,

if age cannot discern fitness for citizenship, how is the problem of political inclusion to be resolved? What skills, characteristics or knowledge are necessary to establish a claim to political rights? Schrag assesses the merits of allocating voting rights according to success in a test of electoral competence, while Harris, more generously, advocates voting rights for everyone who can be classified as 'a person'. I shall discuss these two options and offer a third solution to the problem of inclusion, which has its roots in John Holt's work.[42]

Schrag is unhappy with a specified minimum age qualification for voting. One alternative would require that 'any prospective voter must pass a fitness test to qualify', even though such a test might be considered 'unpalatable'.[43] Schrag's test would require potential voters to illustrate a knowledge of the respective ideologies and policies of the major political parties. The test would have certain affinities to a driving test, since the information upon which questions were based would be freely available to all citizens, in much the same way as the highway code.[44] Schrag offers a sample question: 'Is the following point of view more representative of the Republican or the Democratic Party? Government ought to see to it that old and poor people get good medical care.'[45] Schrag seems to disregard the fact that many adults are not always well informed about policies and that their knowledge is often an individual interpretation of parties' public pronouncements. He does however acknowledge a danger that some children might learn or memorize sufficient information to pass the test, without really understanding what they have learned (although he does not mention that adults might do likewise), but he considers that these technical problems in implementing the test can be easily overcome. Schrag appears, at least initially, to favour such a procedure. The test would discriminate against those who lack the capacity to vote, but would 'not directly discriminate against any other identifiable minority group'; whereas existing procedures 'discriminate against capable voters under eighteen'.[46] Schrag acknowledges that there are a number of objections to such an eligibility test, and these weigh so heavily with him that he concludes by endorsing the age qualification he has so successfully called into question. By arguing here against Schrag's objections to a fitness test, I seek not to endorse the test but to criticize his view that it is acceptable to revert to an age of majority. Three objections to a test seem particularly persuasive to him.

First, a fitness test would ensure an informed and competent but not necessarily responsible electorate which would 'take their vote seriously';[47] responsibility is a product of maturity and guaranteed with age. But, if adult voters 'take their vote seriously', why is rainy weather considered electorally good for the Conservative Party? Why did Harold Wilson change the date of the 1966 general election when he realized it clashed with the English football team's performance in the World Cup, and why did the Labour Party sponsor a 'Song for Europe' competition to generate interest in the 1984 elections to the European Parliament? The use of such tactics by politicians suggests they remain doubtful that the electorate can be both serious and responsible.

Second, Schrag claims that the age criterion does not favour any special interests or groups in society. An eligibility test may favour the well educated who, for Schrag, are synonymous with the rich. The age criterion, however, discriminates equally against all: 'the children of Republicans, or the affluent or whites and the children of Democrats or the poor or blacks are all equally excluded.'[48] But this, of course, is precisely the objection: all children are excluded from political participation. Children – like blacks, whites, rich or poor – constitute a group with a common characteristic; in this way, a coherent section of the community is unrepresented. This is not discrimination 'equally against all', but simply discrimination against children. Schrag's claim that the exclusion is 'temporary', inasmuch as children ultimately mature into adulthood, does not excuse the injustice. Schrag confuses the child as an individual with children as a group. Individual children grow and 'move up' into political enfranchisement but, as an excluded class, children remain permanently disfranchised and politically ineffectual.

Schrag's third objection to a fitness test is that it leaves the question of political eligibility 'within the realm of human control'.[49] Where this is so, there remains the fear that powerful groups will try to manipulate the test to exclude other groups; Schrag acknowledges that this was the case with southern racists who attempted to exclude potential black voters. What Schrag fails to acknowledge is that the age qualification is a human choice, which can be changed by human initiative and which by conscious human purpose 'illegitimately disfranchises a proportion of the electorate'.[50] Convinced of the absurdity of an age qualification, but timorous of the potential hazards of a fitness test, Schrag opts for absurdity. He concludes: 'one is confronted with a choice between a known or at least an estimable injustice on one side and an unknown risk of injustice on the other.'[51] Schrag is right to reject the elitism and dangers of the so-called 'fitness test', but wrong to resort to the injustices consequent upon a too narrow qualification for citizenship based on age.

Harris offers a different solution to the problem of political inclusion which, *contra* Schrag, is too broad in scope. His basic assumption is that everyone who is a person is deserving of full political rights. The traditional distinction between adults and children is unhelpful in deciding who should possess rights. It must be replaced by a distinction between 'persons' and 'non-persons'; this will, in turn, distinguish those deserving rights from others. The question which Harris must address becomes 'How then do we recognize beings as people?'[52] He lists a number of minimum requirements, chief among which is that persons must 'value their own lives', must have a conception of their life as their own – 'that they had a life to lead and valued leading it'.[53] This in turn requires a number of other faculties. The creatures must be self-concious and have an awareness of themselves as beings existing over time. It requires that they have decisions to take and plans to make, and this necessitates some intelligence and the ability to use language.

If these are the characteristics which define a person, and therefore someone deserving respect, dignity and rights, says Harris, then it is difficult to exclude children. Harris is quite correct. However, the problem with his formulation is that it is not only difficult to exclude children: it becomes as difficult to exclude anyone or, indeed, anything. If the prime characteristic of a person is that they 'value their own lives', few, except the suicidal, might be denied the title 'person'. Equally, if it could be agreed that the ability to take decisions and make plans did not require language, or if a broad definition of the term 'language' is accepted, then it would be quite difficult to exclude some animals from Harris's view of a person. Harris acknowledges, if somewhat reluctantly, this conclusion to his argument. 'Where we have reason to suppose that beings, while not possessing language (or not giving evidence of such a capacity), are nonetheless self-conscious beings, aware of themselves existing over time and valuing existence' (in Harris's terms a 'person'), 'then we will have reason to include these creatures as well.'[54] Harris's admirable desire for egalitarianism commits him to answer the question 'Who is a citizen?' in a way which few could accept as legitimate.

I would suggest that the most persuasive solution to the problem of political inclusion can be provided by resurrecting a simple proposal made by John Holt, which is endorsed by the research literature on political learning and childhood political socialization. Holt's prescription is as appealing as it is simple. He doesn't wish to lower the voting age incrementally but seeks 'the right to vote for people of any age. No one should be left out.'[55] Eligibility, on his account, is determined by awareness and interest in political affairs. Everyone should have the right to vote when their interest, knowledge and involvement in politics are sufficiently developed to motivate them so to do; as interest develops, so participation will increase. This does not mean that all children would vote, and it seems probable that very young children with only a marginal, if any, interest in politics would abstain. Holt considers that few six-year-olds would exercise their vote but that ten-year-olds would be different, since they 'seem to understand at least as much about the world and its problems as I or most of my friends did when we left college'.[56] Children themselves are enthusiastic about the possibilities of voting. Consider the following:

> We've got to vote. I mean, us children. We're not allowed to vote until we're eighteen, the Government said that. But I think we should have more say – in the Common Market and things. We might make the wrong suggestions, but at least we've tried to be more mature in our ways.[57]

The exchange quoted below emerged when two children were asked if there 'should be something like a children's vote? Or should you have an adult vote?'[58]

> Janet: Yes I think we should. Each family discusses it with their parents first, and then the parents give in the vote that we've all settled at together. Not just the parents saying: 'Right I'm voting for the Conservatives, right, that goes in . . .'

> Jamie: I think it should be a separate children's vote, not a family, because they'd all have different views about it, and what would they vote then? It should be a separate vote.[59]

The discussion cited here reveals not only a capacity to discuss quite complex and sophisticated problems but an ability to isolate and define potential problems if electoral arrangements were altered. Little wonder that the researcher who taped the interview queries whether 'children's abilities to handle abstract ideas contradicts much in our present assumptions about what nine year olds, and even eleven year olds can do.'[60] Moreover the exercise of franchise hardly places any intellectually onerous demands on adults. The whole process of voting has been consciously designed for simplicity. Not even basic literacy is a requirement to place an X against the chosen candidate. Holt's formula is attractive because it would allow those young people who are interested in politics, who do understand and are concerned about the issues involved in policy decisions, to help form those decisions. In addition, a franchise of this type could avoid the fatuous criticism which usually assumes the form 'I can just see my two-year-old voting.' Of course two-year-olds will not vote, since they are likely to be interested in things other than politics at this age. But whoever imagined they might?

Holt's suggestion, which might be termed 'participation according to interest', or a 'creeping franchise', mirrors adult electoral behaviour. Adults vote when they are sufficiently interested in the issues upon which the election centres. Accordingly, turnout varies substantially. The 1983 British general election attracted 72.7 per cent[61] of the electorate, while the elections to the European Parliament in June 1984 inspired only 30 per cent of the electorate to vote.[62]

Existing research on childhood political socialization and political learning suggests that Holt's advocacy of a revised suffrage would not make demands which were beyond children's competence. This research is concerned to answer questions such as 'How are political ideas and attitudes acquired?' and, more important for present purposes, 'When?' The answers are, of course, complex, but there is substantial agreement in some areas.

Political socialization is a long process which starts very early in life. Although political learning is continuous, it is accelerated and more rapid in certain periods of the life cycle, which makes such periods more important than others in the overall process.[63] Childhood years are such a period, since 'in childhood we find the roots of adult political life', and 'In many respects the pre-adult years are those when the most significant political learning takes place.'[64] The development of political knowledge and attitudes can be traced by dividing the pre-adult years into three phases: early childhood (ages five to nine), late childhood (ages nine to thirteen) and adolescence (ages thirteen to eighteen).[65]

Early childhood is a period of substantial learning when basic political attachments are established and children learn to identify themselves with a particular race, class, nation and political party.[66] Indeed, 'every piece of evidence indicates that the child's political world begins to take shape well before he enters elementary school and that it undergoes the most rapid change during these years.'[67] Along with these fundamental political identifications, the early childhood period, according to Greenstein, is when young people begin to form attitudes towards political authorities and leaders – monarchs, prime ministers, members of parliament and presidents. Children display a tendency to personalize political authorities and view them in an unduly benevolent fashion. Greenstein comments that the 'most conspicuous difference' between adults and children was in 'attitudes of cynicism and distrust towards politics. Virtually no children entertained these widespread adult views.'[68]

Late childhood from the ages of nine to thirteen is acknowledged by research findings, to be the most significant period for developing personal and social attitudes that are reflected in political choices.[69] Two aspects of the child's development are noteworthy. First, the basic identifications of early childhood are consolidated and reinforced by an increased political knowledge and information. Second, young people develop a more discriminating, critical and sophisticated attitude towards political matters. By the age of thirteen a person has acquired the 'major components of a mature political self. Basic political attachments and identifications are well established. . . . By early adolescence much of the political world has been mapped out.'[70]

Adolescence, the final phase of pre-adult learning, is a period when the existing view of politics is refined and the capacity for abstract thought develops.

Two comments about these research findings seem appropriate. First, people learn political identifications, knowledge, awareness of political problems, the capacity to discuss them, assess them and make decisions about them, at a much earlier age than popular opinion imagines. Second, the pace of political learning is, at least in part, a product of that popular opinion. If adults acknowledged young people's capacities to discuss political issues, those capacities would be nurtured, enhanced and, perhaps, show signs of even earlier or accelerated development. An obvious question needs to be asked. If political skills develop at such an early age, and if young people appear to possess similar capacities to adults in this respect, would the granting of political status to children make any difference to the outcome of elections? The answer, of course, is no. For self-evident reasons, there are difficulties in marshalling evidence to support such a view. What can be done is to compare the voting behaviour of the youngest section (eighteen to twenty-two) of voters with that of other age groups. This is a useful comparison, because, prior to the lowering of the age of citizenship from twenty-one to eighteen in 1969, the majority of these young voters would not have enjoyed suffrage. In the 1983 general election young (eighteen to twenty-two) voters' support for the three major political parties was 41 per cent for the Conservative Party, 29 per cent for the Labour Party and 30 per cent for the Liberal/SDP Alliance.[71] The overall result of the election gave the Conservative Party 42 per cent, the Labour Party 29 per cent and the Liberal/SDP Alliance 25 per cent of the total vote.[72] The political allegiances of young voters with the exception of support for the Alliance seem to be a very close reflection of the general voting pattern for all age groups. There is a need for caution here because turnout of eighteen- to twenty-two-year-olds in the 1983 election was only 53 per cent and the trend, first evidenced in 1979, for young people to move away from Labour support continued in 1983. The myth of a radical, left-wing, young electorate remains sadly just a myth or perhaps it is simply that young people do not consider the Labour party to be radical? Whichever is true, there is no reason to believe that, if the age of citizenship were lowered to fifteen, there would be any critical difference in the outcome of an election. Young people, like any generation or age group, are heterogeneous in composition, displaying differences of gender class, race, wealth and educational attainment, and it is these attributes rather than age which become evident in a diversity of political allegiance. Extending the franchise to children would not radically change the electoral support of any particular party. If research in political learning is correct, the differences of political opinion evident between children are simply a portent of adult political divisions. As Greenstein notes, 'differences in the political participation of adults of different social class background and of men and women are clearly presaged by similar differences among preadolescent children.'[73]

Holt's case for extending the suffrage to children has much to recommend it, but I envisage four immediate objections; three may be dealt with briefly since they have, in part, been met before, but the fourth deserves lengthier consideration.

First, it will almost certainly be claimed that young people are ignorant of political affairs – 'that they would not know a good policy from a bad one'.[74] If this is true, then it is a truth which extends to adults and we must take care not to use double standards. In a political system where voters' ignorance of issues is readily acknowledged, and where 'no amount of ignorance, misinformation, or outright delusion will bar an adult from voting',[75] it is a weak argument to suggest that a presumed ignorance of political affairs is sufficient grounds to exclude children from citizenship. The major point here is that arguments about ignorance are spurious. People should possess a vote, not because they are specialists in some area of government or because they have detailed knowledge of some aspect of political life, but because it is a matter of justice that they do.[76] Democracy requires that everyone should have the right to participate in making political decisions which will affect their lives.

A second, related claim is that children should not be considered responsible electors and may cast their vote frivolously. While there is no evidence to support such a view, there is substantial literature which suggests that adults are less than responsible in their electoral motives. Harrop and Hague lament that 'By and large . . . hopes have been dashed' that voters will 'cast their vote in an informed and intelligent way',[77] while McLean suggests humorously that many voters appear to have a predisposition to vote for the first candidate on the ballot paper. Since candidates are arranged alphabetically, it is not surprising that this habit 'benefits politicians whose names begin with the letter A', or produces a preponderance of twentieth-century prime ministers with surnames beginning with A, B or C.'[78] As with the first claim, dual standards are unacceptable. If voters are to be excluded when it can be shown that they may vote frivolously, then this proposal would disfranchise many adults.

Third, it might be argued that children are more likely to vote on the basis of the personality of the party leader than on the policies of the party. It is true that children tend to have an extremely benevolent and uncynical view of political authority which political leaders could exploit to their advantage, but these attitudes exist only in the period of early childhood and are transcended around the age of nine. Adults too are not indifferent to personalities when making electoral choices. 'Leaders, party policy, self-interest and sheer partisan loyalty' all influence voters to some degree, and 'disentangling precisely their separate effect is impossible'.[79] Moreover, the different personalities of the party leaders are relevant considerations which any voter might wish to take into account when assessing a party's potential for successful government and the achievement of its objectives.

Finally, it could be argued that there is a danger that parents might seek to exert influence upon children and coerce them to vote according to their preferences. This not only would render childhood suffrage meaningless, but would confer political advantage on those with children. This objection can be met in a number of ways. First, if children had the right to vote and enjoyed a greater autonomy and responsibility for their affairs, they would be likely to be much less readily influenced by adults. Children would probably value their own judgement and grow in independence so that parental influence would diminish. Holt makes a related point when he claims that a society which had changed its attitude towards children sufficiently to acknowledge their right to vote would be a society in which adults would not seek to coerce young people, or, if they did, such interference would be frowned upon.[80] Second, a secret ballot ensures the child's autonomy, since no adult could discover the child's electoral choice. Third, the argument must be conceded in a special sense. The most influential determinant of our political allegiance is the political preferences of our parents. If I had to guess the party for which a particular individual voted and I could ask only a single question (excluding 'Which political party do you vote for?'), I would be advised to ask 'Which political party do your parents support?' Butler and Stokes's study revealed that 89 per cent of Conservative voters have parents who are both Conservative voters and 92 per cent of Labour supporters have parents who both support the Labour Party. The children of 'politically mixed' marriages divided 48 per cent Conservative and 52 per cent Labour.[81] These data are, of course, complicated by the emergence of the SDP/Liberal Alliance, but such evidence suggests that, whether we are ten, thirty or sixty when we vote, the electoral behaviour and preferences of our parents are a powerful and lasting influence; to exclude only young people because of parental influence is therefore unjust.

Conclusions and prospects

In this chapter, I have tried to argue that the denial of political rights to children offends fundamental democratic principles and that the division between citizens and non-citizens, based upon age, is incoherent and cannot be sustained. I have tried to develop a different proposal which is more positive in its appraisal of children's capacities and their political interest and potentials. This would give rights to all young people but presumes that the majority of very young children, given their probable lack of concern for political affairs, would not utilize their franchise. There is, of course, a problem of abuse with such a procedure, although I consider it to be less substantial than might be imagined. Moreover, the potential danger of a few children voting who perhaps should not is far outweighted by the actual injustice involved when large numbers of children who are interested and informed about politics and wish to vote are excluded from so doing. The scale of the current exclusion of 12½ million children is massive and somewhat akin to denying voting rights to everyone in Greater London. Giving children the right to vote has distinct advantages over other proposals aimed at the protection of their rights. Various institutional devices have been suggested, such as an ombudsman for children, a minister for children, a select committee on children as well as a children's council and children's congress discussed in the Deakin Report.[82] The advantage derived from enfranchising children is that the responsibility for securing the best interests of children and protecting their rights would reside with children themselves. For the first time, children could deploy their vote to guarantee the enjoyment of their rights and the prosecution of their interests; child perceptions would replace adult interpretations of children's rights.

Research evidence suggests that the party political implications of change would be minimal, with no party finding its support disproportionately enhanced. But the abolition of age-related rights would lead to change in at least three areas.

First, it would be reasonable to speculate that all political parties would give higher priority and emphasis to policies relating to youth affairs than at present. There would be a new section of the electorate to be wooed which, if disappointed, could hold the parties to account.

Second, it could lead to the democratization of the whole range of educational, social and welfare institutions of which young people are currently the major consumers. If, for example, education were not compulsory, it is hard to imagine that many teachers could attract an audience for their tedious diet of rote learning and inconsequential knowledge. Young people would probably demand greater participation in all aspects of the operation of their school community, from issues of uniform to curriculum design. Similarly, the acquisition of suffrage would possibly initiate substantial reforms concerning children's rights in care and within the juvenile justice system.

Finally, I believe that the absence of all age qualifications, not simply political (dis)qualifications, would mean that young people could develop skills and potentials at a much earlier age across a variety of activities. If young people's efforts were taken seriously, criticized, evaluated and assessed in the way that as adults we assess each other's work in a dialogue between equals, then children's skills and intellectual achievements could be enhanced to a degree which, by existing standards, would appear precocious. Firestone makes this point when discussing the early life of Louis XIII, who grew up at a time when there was little division between childhood and adulthood. At seventeen months the Dauphin played the violin. At three he learned to read, at four to write. By five he was a keen archer who enjoyed chess and card games. The Dauphin was no exceptional genius; indeed, he proved 'himself to be no more intelligent than any average member of the aristocracy'.[83] Political equality would require adults to take young people more seriously and abandon patronizing attitudes which systematically underestimate and indicate disrespect for their abilities. If these are some of the possible implications of the extension of franchise to young people, I welcome them.

But what is the likelihood of such political reform? 1985 was International Youth Year (IYY), which, although a good deal less successful than its predecessors for women and the disabled,[84] served to some extent to focus attention on the problems facing young people and prompted a number of initiatives to extend their rights. Two are especially worthy of mention.

First, a private member's bill, the Youth Charter as it became dubbed, was introduced on the first parliamentary day of IYY by Jim Wallace (Liberal), the youngest member of the House. The purpose of the charter was to 'establish rights and create a framework within which young people could participate more fully in the affairs of the community'.[85] The charter offered three specific proposals. First, the voting age should be lowered to sixteen. Second, young people should be represented on a range of local committees including health councils, local education authority committees, the Police Authority and local MSC committees. Finally, democratically elected youth councils should be established, to 'ascertain, coordinate and express to the local authorities for its area, and to public authorities, the views of the young people it represents'.[86] The charter's status as a private member's bill, coupled with its contentious proposals, meant that its chances of success were slight. A second reading was deferred from 19 April to 5 July, when it was placed twenty-third in order of business; in the language of parliament, it had fallen.

The Youth Charter was a laudable, if small, step in the direction of achieving representation for young people, but it was rather naïve in its recommendations and could be criticized on two grounds. First, to give young people rights is of little use unless they also achieve an understanding of how to exercise them. The mere possession of rights without this knowledge can lead to the worst sort of tokenism, with young people being manipulated by more experienced participants. Second, meaningful participation must be participation on a genuinely equal basis, and age is only one obstacle to the achievement of such an objective. The discussions of girls' rights and black children's rights, in later chapters, illustrate quite clearly how discrimination on the basis of gender and race systematically undermine the capacities of girls and black children to participate equally, in many areas of their lives, where the right to equality of opportunity and equal participation are formally guaranteed by law. Similarly, the inequalities and advantages which derive from the possession of wealth, a high level of income or a superior educational background, which make effective participation a sham for so many adults, must also be confronted. These problems, however, are more resilient to change. Reforms of political rights guarantee no magical panacea for equality unless they are made in tandem with economic, social and attitudinal changes.[87]

A more significant development for children and their political rights in IYY was the emergence of the Youth Trade Union Rights Campaign (YTURC). In 1985 YTURC organized strikes in oppositions to the government's proposals to make Youth Training

Schemes (YTS) compulsory for all school-leavers without a job. On 21 March 20,000 schoolchildren went on strike in Glasgow. This was followed by a national half-day strike on 25 April which, because it involved 200,000 children, was the largest demonstration by children in British history. Four thousand attended a rally in Liverpool, a thousand marched in each of the cities of Belfast, Cardiff and Manchester, there were strikes in sixty other towns and cities, and children were arrested in Reading and Stoke-on-Trent as police tried to stop the children's protest.[88] Leading members of all the major political parties condemned the day of action. The TUC General Council, Neil Kinnock and the majority of the Labour Party National Executive Committee spoke out against YTURC and evicted it from Labour Party headquarters in Walworth Road. Some Labour MPs supported the strike with Tony Benn urging the party to identify with it, insisting that if the Labour Party wished to attract young people to its ranks it was not enough 'to encourage school children to listen to Billy Bragg protest songs'.[89]

Despite the derision of adult politicians, YTURC's claims reveal a sophisticated and radical understanding of youth training. YTURC want training schemes at trade-union rates of pay, guaranteed jobs upon completion of training, and no use of YTS labour to substitute for someone previously working at a proper rate for the job. What is significant about the emergence of YTURC is that it illustrates young people's capacities to analyse political issues that concern them and to initiate and organize themselves politically without assistance from adults. They understand that conventional party politics currently largely ignores their demands and offers few possibilities for change. The joint president if IYY commented:

We've got to bypass the existing channels because they're not listening anymore. . . . It's down to young people . . . to seize their own power.[90]

However, any organized attempt by children to secure their rights faces a unique set of obstacles which the campaigns to secure black and female suffrage, for example, never had to confront. There is the problem of lack of money. Most children have no independent access to cash and receive only trivial sums, usually from adult sources. There are the difficulties involved in producing leaflets, organizing meetings, or mounting a systematic campaign, which arise from the fact that children's organizational, administrative and formal education skills are less well developed. Children are also under the constant surveillance and control of adults both at home and at school. In both environments they can legitimately be subjected to emotional or physical punishment for behaviour which does not meet with adult approval. Children organizing for political rights will probably be treated initially with ridicule and derision, and then with misunderstanding and perhaps eventually violence if the experience of the struggle for women's suffrage is any precedent. Undoubtedly the greatest obstacle to be overcome is the adult refusal to acknowledge that children suffer political discrimination and exclusion. Adults do not perceive children as a minority group but as helpless, inexperienced, defenceless young people who need protection. Adult paternalism seeks to protect and if in this process it curtails freedom, truncates potentials and destroys civil liberties this is taken to be incidental. The belief in the legitimacy of paternalism justifies and cements the existing power relationships between adults and young people. This attitude must be confronted, challenged and refuted if young people are to secure their political rights.

Notes

1 F. Schrag, 'The child's status in the democratic state', *Political Theory*, 3, 4 (1975), p. 445.
2 R. Dahl, 'Procedural democracy', in *Philosophy, Politics And Society*, ed. P. Laslett and J. Fiskin, 5th series (Blackwell, 1979), p. 128.
3 For an attack on what they term 'the child's best interest syndrome', see H. Geach and E. Szwed, *Providing Civil Justice for Children* (Edward Arnold, 1983).
4 H. S. Harris, *Hegel's Development: towards the sunlight, 1770–1801* (Oxford University Press, 1972), p. 265.
5 Representation of the People Act (1969).
6 G. Haydon, 'Political theory and the child: problems of individualist tradition', *Political Studies*, XXCII, 3 (September 1979), p. 405.
7 Ibid.
8 Scarre notes that there is a more substantial literature dealing with the rights of foetuses, animals and even plants: G. Scarre, 'Children and paternalism', *Philosophy*, 55 (1980), p. 117. There are remarkably few discussions of children's political rights. See Haydon, 'Political theory and the child'; Schrag, 'The child's status in the democratic state', and the reply by C. Cohen in *Political Theory*, 3, 4 (1975), pp. 458–63; J. Harris, 'The political status of children', in *Contemporary Political Philosophy: radical studies*, ed. K. Graham (Cambridge University Press, 1982), pp. 35–59; T.M. Reed and P. Johnston, 'Children's liberation', *Philosophy*, 55 (1980), p. 263–6; V. Worsfold, 'A philosophical justification for children's rights', *Harvard Educational Review*, 44 (1974), pp. 142–57.
9 B. Russell, *Principles of Social Reconstruction*, 15th edn, (Allen and Unwin, 1971), p. 100.

10   Dahl, 'Procedural democracy', p. 120.
11   G. Dworkin, 'Paternalism', in *Morality and the Law*, ed. R.A. Wasserstrom (Wadsworth Publishing Co., 1971), p. 108.
12   The phrase and the argument belong to Kant. See I. Kant, *The Philosophy of Law*. tr. W. Hastie and W. Clark (Edinburgh, 1887), p. 118.
13   J. Locke, *Two Treatises of Government*, ed. P. Laslett (Cambridge University Press, 1964), section 42, p. 321.
14   Ibid., section 61, p. 326. Political theorists, when they have considered children at all, have always entertained a pessimistic view of their potential for political activity. See J.S. Mill, *Utilitarianism*, ed. M. Warnock (Fontana, 1969), pp. 135 and 211; T. Hobbes, *Leviathan* (Fontana, 1967), pp. 299 and 197; J.-J. Rousseau, *The Social Contract and Discourses*, Everyman (Dent, 1968), p. 234; Spinoza, *Ethics*, Everyman (Dent, 1963), p. 193; *Kant on Education*, tr. A. Churton (Heath, 1906), pp. 93 and 51. G.W.F. Hegel, *Hegel's Philosophy of Mind*, tr. W. Wallace and A.V. Miller (Oxford University Press, 1971), p. 60.
15   Worsfold, 'A philosophical justification for children's rights', p. 146.
16   See J. Piaget, *The Moral Judgement of the Child* (Routledge and Kegan Paul, 1968). Among those who have tried to use Piaget's work as a justification for paternalism are F. Schrag, 'The child in the moral order', *Philosophy*, 52 (1977), pp. 171–2, and M. D. A. Freeman, *The Rights and the Wrongs of Children* (Frances Pinter, 1983), p. 46.
17   H. Grinzberg and S. Opper, *Piaget's Theory of Intellectual Development: an introduction* (Prentice-Hall, 1969), p. 181, quoted in Schrag, 'The child in the moral order', p. 172.
18   P. Ariès, *Centuries of Childhood* (Jonathan Cape, 1962), especially pp. 15–137; M. Hoyles, *Changing Childhood* (Writers and Readers, 1979); J. Walvin, *A Social History of English Childhood, 1800–1914* (Penguin, 1982).
19   Aiken argues, for example, that if rationality is the criterion for inclusion then such categories as those who are becoming senile must be denied political rights. See H.D. Aiken, 'Rights, human and otherwise', *The Monist*, 52 (October 1968), p. 513.
20   Freeman, *The Rights and the Wrongs of Children*, p. 46.
21   Scarre, 'Children and paternalism', p. 123.
22   Ibid.
23   Ibid.
24   Schrag, 'The child in the moral order', p. 171.
25   Dworkin, 'Paternalism', p. 120.
26   I. Berlin, *Four Essays on Liberty* (Oxford University Press, 1969), p. 148.
27   Scarre, 'Children and paternalism', p. 123.
28   D. Watson, *Caring for Strangers* (Routledge and Kegan Paul, 1980), p. 123.
29   Scarre, 'Children and paternalism', p. 123.

30 R.D. Dworkin, *Taking Rights Seriously* (Duckworth, 1977), pp. 188–9.
31 Harris, 'The political status of children', p. 54.
32 J. Feinberg, 'Legal paternalism', in *Rights, Justice and the Bounds of Liberty: Essays in Social Philosophy* (Princeton University Press, 1980), p. 110.
33 Schrag, 'The child in the moral order', p. 171.
34 Dworkin, 'Paternalism', p. 119.
35 See J. G. Murphy, 'Incompetence and Paternalism', *Archiv für Rechts und Sozialphilosophie*, 60 (1974), p. 482.
36 J. Rawls, *A Theory of Justice* (Oxford University Press, 1972), p. 249.
37 Freeman, *The Rights and the Wrongs of Children*, p. 4.
38 Ibid. This view is shared, however, by Amy Gutman, 'Children, paternalism and education: a liberal argument', *Philosophy and Public Affairs*, 9, 4 (1980), pp. 338–58.
39 L. Althusser, 'Ideology and ideological state apparatus', in *Lenin and Philosophy and Other Essays* (New Left Books, 1977).
40 I. Kant, *The Philosophy Of Law* (T. and T. Clark, 1887), p. 118, quoted in Schrag, 'The child in the moral order', p. 173.
41 This point is made by Harris, 'The political status of children', p. 42, and H. Cohen, *Equal Rights for Children* (Littlefield Adams, 1980), p. 60.
42 J. Holt, *Escape from Childhood* (Penguin, 1975), ch. 17.
43 Schrag, 'The child's status in the democratic state', p. 452.
44 Ibid., p. 452.
45 Ibid., p. 457.
46 Ibid., p. 453.
47 Ibid., p. 453.
48 Ibid., p. 454.
49 Ibid., p. 454.
50 Ibid., p. 454.
51 Ibid., p. 47.
52 Harris, 'The political status of children', p. 47.
53 Ibid., p. 47.
54 Ibid., p. 55.
55 Holt, *Escape from Childhood*, p. 118.
56 Ibid., p. 122.
57 O. Stevens, *Children Talking Politics* (Martin Robertson, 1982), p. 28.
58 Ibid.
59 Ibid.
60 Ibid., p. 29.
61 B. Jones and D. Kavanagh, *British Politics Today* (Manchester University Press, 1983), p. 184.
62 *The Times*, 18 June 1984, p. 1.
63 R. Hague and M. Harrop, *Comparative Government: an introduction* (Macmillan, 1982).
64 R. E. Dawson, K. Prewitt and K. S. Dawson, *Political Socialization* (Little, Brown, 1977), p. 49.

65 This threefold division of pre-adult learning belongs to Dawson, Prewitt and Dawson, *Political Socialization*, pp. 49–63.

66 F. Greenstein, *Children and Politics* (Yale University Press, 1974), p. 8.

67 D. Easton and R. D. Hess, 'The child's political world', *Midwest Journal of Political Science*, VI (1962), pp. 237–8.

68 Greenstein, *Children and Politics*, p. 31.

69 Dawson et al., Political Socialization, pp. 53–4; Easton and Hess, 'The child's political world', pp. 237–8; Hague and Harrop, *Comparative Government*, p. 51; Greenstein, *Children and Politics*, p. 1.

70 Dawson et al., *Political Socialization*, p. 56.

71 I. Crewe, 'The disturbing truth about Labour's rout', *Guardian*, 13 June 1983.

72 Jones and Kavanagh, *British Politics Today*, p. 184.

73 Greenstein, *Children and Politics*, p. 155.

74 Watson, *Caring for Strangers*, p. 131.

75 Holt, *Escape from Childhood*, p. 128.

76 Ibid., p. 118.

77 Hague and Harrop, *Comparative Government*, p. 122.

78 I. McLean, *Elections* (Longman, 1976), p. 28.

79 I. Crewe, 'How Labour was trounced all round', *Guardian*, 14 June 1983.

80 Holt, *Escape from Childhood*, p. 129.

81 H. Elcock, 'Young voters 1988: will they break the mould?', *Youth and Policy*, 2, 2 (Autumn 1983), p. 30.

82 N. Deakin, *A Voice for All Children* (Bedford Square Press/NCVO, 1982), pp. 31–7.

83 S. Firestone, *The Dialectic of Sex* (Bantam Books, 1972), p. 84.

84 'Will Youth Year be wasted on the West?', *The Times Higher Education Supplement*, 19 April 1985, p. 11.

85 Youth Charter Bill, no. 55, 9 January 1985, Hansard.

86 Youth Charter, section 3 (2).

87 The Labour Party also introduced *Labour's Charter for Young People* (Labour Party, July 1985). This was not a bill but a statement of its policy intentions in the area of youth affairs. A similar 'Charter' was introduced in the European Parliament by Kyriakos Gerontopollos in July 1985. See *European Parliament Working Documents*, no. A2–71/85, 2 July 1985, and *European Parliament News*, 67 (July 1985), p. 1.

88 *Guardian*, 26 April 1985, and *The Times* 25 April 1985.

89 *The Times*, 25 April 1985.

90 'Rise, rise, protest and rise', an interview with Paul Weller, *Sanity*, 4 (April 1985), p. 19.

Further reading

G. Dworkin, 'Paternalism', in *Morality and the Law*, ed. R. A. Wasserstrom (Wadsworth Publishing Co., 1971).

F. Greenstein, *Children and Politics* (Yale University Press, 1974).

J. Harris, 'The political status of children', in *Contemporary Political philosophy: radical studies*, ed. K. Graham (Cambridge University Press, 1982).

G. Haydon, 'Political theory and the child: problems of the individualist tradition', *Political Studies* XXCII, 3 (September 1979).

J. Holt, *Escape from Childhood* (Penguin, 1975).

G. Scarre, 'Children and paternalism', *Philosophy*, 55 (1980).

F. Schrag, 'The child's status in the Democratic State', *Political Theory* 3, 4 (1975).

O. Stevens, *Children Talking Politics* (Martin Robertson, 1982).

3

Children's Rights at School

Tony Jeffs

The British education system is undergoing a major restructuring. Progressivism, with its emphasis on child-centred learning, more open access, less authoritarian style of pedagogy and a more liberal curriculum, has, as a movement, been halted and on a number of fronts reversed. Increasingly the emphasis is upon such nebulous concepts as discipline, traditional values and a return to basics. Not merely in governmental circles but to an extent throughout society, it is felt that our schools and colleges have failed both their clients and the nation. As the 1985 government White Paper *Better Schools* put it, 'the high standards achieved in some schools throw into relief the shortcomings, some of them serious, of others. Nor are the objectives which even the best schools set themselves always well matched with the demands of the modern world.'[1] As a result, according to government thinking, teachers need to be more rigorously trained, supervised and inspected; schools must be made more accountable to parents, the needs of industry, the taxpayer and the Department of Education and Science (DES); parents are hectored to take an even greater role in the control and regulation of their offspring; and finally the young are to be more thoroughly disciplined, schooled and vocationally trained.

These ideological shifts and their accompanying policy changes are, of course, taking place against a wider backcloth of financial restraint, public expenditure cuts and privatization of significant parts of the public sector. The inescapable end-product of this is that the material quality of the education system deteriorates by the day and by the hour. The curtains in the school hall become visibly shabbier, the textbooks if available become tattier, the playing fields more overgrown and the schools dirtier and less inviting than a decade ago. Even the government's own inspectorate have been prompted to protest. They reported in 1985 'that much of the nation's school building stock is now below an acceptable standard'[2] and 'that the present state of repairs in schools was judged to be less than satisfactory or poor in over half of all local education authorities (LEAs)'.[3] Further, a lack of equipment, textbooks and suitably trained teachers was causing serious concern in all sectors, with inevitably 'marked disparities of provision between schools serving affluent and poor areas'.[4] This was not merely a spacial divide. As the scale of unemployment has grown alongside a fall in real incomes for many in employment not least those employed within the education sector itself, so poverty has disadvantaged even greater numbers of young people. Education cannot isolate itself from the backwash of this. Evidence exists that children are now more frequently being kept from school because of poverty. More children are likely to arrive at school hungry and, as a result of cuts of over a third in the schools meals budget since 1979, are likely to leave still hungry.[5] Family poverty is obliging more each year to terminate their education at the earliest possible date in order to earn a wage, acquire a YTS allowance or draw supplementary benefit.[6] The right of young people to a free education has been seriously eroded in recent years. Schools and LEAs have often illegally introduced charges for books, equipment and even specialist tuition. This, coupled with the withdrawal of clothing and equipment grants, transport subsidies and the dragooning of parents to carry out essential repairs to the fabric of the schools themselves, is undermining the principle set out over a century ago in the Newcastle Commission Report that, in the case of compulsory education, 'no duties rendered to the state by individuals should involve pecuniary loss to such individuals'.[7]

No contemporary discussion concerning young people's rights in the setting of the school can ignore these new 'realities'. To do so would lay oneself open to the charge of addressing the issue in a purely academic fashion. The changing ideological terrain and the deteriorating economic and social environment mean that the debate has to be located in a new context – a context markedly different from that which coloured the thinking of those who produced much of the most influential literature on young people's rights within the school of the recent past. The optimism of Duane barely a decade and a half ago, when he described the school of the future as having only 'certain superficial resemblances to schools that we see today',[8] seems to have largely evaporated. New school building has virtually ceased, and we appear to be 'stuck' with the buildings we now operate for the indefinite future. This is a depressing prospect, because many reforms such as curricular development, wider community involvement and more flexible modes of teaching depend upon the creation of new educational environments, as has been amply demonstrated not only

in the primary sector but also at secondary level. Equally, the optimism
has been curtailed by the growing tyranny of the exam system and the
narrow vocationalism of the MSC's intervention via the Technical
and Vocational Education Initiative (TVEI) into the secondary
curriculum.

Yet I do not believe the case for a radical extension of young
people's rights and autonomy within the school has been weakened by
the changing educational environment. Rather, the continued denial
of many basic rights in this setting remains wasteful of human
resources, damaging to the long-term health of the body politic and
can only be justified or explained by inertia and a blind refusal to
accept that young people have the right to be treated with the same
respect as other people – inside the school as well as outside.

In terms of their powerlessness, young people are treated with
remarkable similarity within and without the school, although to a
degree they are less well protected in the former; the NSPCC, for
example, will not take action against teachers for ill-treatment, only
against parents. Under section 36 of the 1944 Education Act it is the
'duty of the parent of every child of compulsory school age to cause
him to receive efficient full-time education suitable to his age, ability
and aptitude, either by regular attendance at school or otherwise'.
Given that few parents have the resources of income or time to give the
'otherwise', in reality this means the transference of responsibility for
the child to a local authority school for what will eventually amount to
over 15,000 hours. More than the child is transferred. Parental control
is also handed over to the educational institution and enshrined in the
notion of *in loco parentis*. The leading case defining this remains that
of Williams *v.* Eady and the judgement of Mr Justice Cave handed
down in 1893, which stated that 'The duty of a schoolmaster is to take
such care of his boys as a careful father would take care of his boys.'[9]
LEAs do have a duty to 'determine the educational character of each
school and its place in the local education system',[10] but their powers
are severely limited. The courts have, for example, upheld the right of
a teacher to inflict moderate and reasonable corporal punishment,
even where LEA regulations forbid its use.[11] Indeed, Keith Joseph has
argued for legislation to curtail the power of LEAs to interfere in
matters relating to the internal discipline and management of the
individual school.[12] School governors have a vague right to intervene.
However, it is so nebulous that as presently constituted in terms of
their formal powers 'there does not seem to be any overwhelming
justification for their existence'.[13]

Such a view needs to be set in the context of events since the 1980
Education Act gave parents the power to elect their own repre-

sentatives to sit on school-governing bodies. Experience has shown that the impact of such a change has been varied and that, without a desire on the part of the headteacher to give the parents a real influence, and by the LEA to ease its dominance of such bodies, many parents have found their role to be little more than tokenistic.[14] What these changes have not altered is the extent to which the headteacher still retains virtually unfettered control over the daily management of the internal affairs of the school. Legalism and tradition demand that, in any conflict over policy or style, headteachers 'must win or cease being heads',[15] and the new managerialism abroad in education is increasingly teaching them how to win more effectively. The law does not provide for corporate responsibility, and ultimately, until this is changed, any fundamental extension of children's rights in the educational setting is effectively blocked.

By administrative and legal design it is ensured that the first 'community' the child enters outside the home is one organized and managed on hierarchical and authoritarian lines. A pattern is set which encourages young people to accept as natural and inviolable 'a degree of powerlessness with which they will be faced as mature workers'.[16] In the early years of schooling the imposition of this power relationship upon young people presents few problems; given their relative inexperience and youthfulness, they offer minimal resistance. Yet, even at this stage, teachers are aware that their professional standing and their right to a measure of autonomy within the classroom are primarily dependent upon their ability to 'keep order' and the class 'under control'. All teachers operating in the school system as presently structured know they must always win the battle for control or 'they cannot remain a teacher'.[17] At the primary end of the educational spectrum, the battle for control to a considerable extent entails conflict with the child's parent(s), who may resent the unbridled power of the school to set and seek to impose standards and norms of behaviour which do not match those of the 'home'. At many schools, parents are 'taught' their place by being kept at the school gate to collect and deposit their children, however inclement the weather. Even when contact is made between the school and the parent(s), the rules of the discourse are firmly set down by the school and designed overwhelmingly, whatever the rhetoric of the progressives, to cool out parents interference. Parents learn quickly that they are welcome, if at all, only on the school's terms. One researcher found that many parents made such comments as 'I went once. I felt that I was back in my own school. They made me feel so ignorant, so ashamed of myself, that I'll never go back there again.'[18] Thus the majority of parents learn the futility of intervention and young people the irrelevance of turning to parents as potential mediators in disputes with the school.

In the face of the apparently unfathomable power of the teacher in the classroom and the head in the school, survival for the young person appears to be dependent upon learning certain arts: for example, how to lie convincingly to those in authority, the skill of ingratiating oneself with the powerful, the art of securing anonymity in a crowd and perhaps, as the school career progresses, the most important art of all – the ability to make networks of friendships that will provide support and a sense of individuality. Schools are rarely happy places for those who fail to master these skills or who can be easily scapegoated by their peers or by teachers, some of whom purchase a dubious popularity by ridiculing those pupils who stand apart as different. The ethos of all but a tiny minority of schools is sadly one that is conducive to bullying at all levels, and it is hardly surprising that over a quarter of mothers of eleven-year-olds in one survey knew that their children were victims.[19] The protestations of teachers that they are wholeheartedly opposed to all manifestations of bullying are as empty and hypocritical as those of army officers. For the structures of the organizations they operate within are based upon the denial of basic human rights to those who occupy the lower echelons. The survival of both organizations in their present form is dependent on the arbitrary use of force. The genteel camaraderie of the staffroom and the officers' mess is a carefully elaborated charade providing a temporary retreat from the harsh and often brutal world of the playground and lower decks.

The principle of *in loco parentis* and the traditional powers of the headteacher which predated it have encountered severe difficulties in adjusting to the changes wrought upon the educational system by the successive lifting of the school-leaving age. The extension of compulsory schooling at the end of the 1914–18 war aroused the opposition of employers' representatives. Prior to that, in Britain as a whole, the average attendance rate had risen from approximately 60 per cent in the 1880s to over 80 per cent from 1906 onwards. This was achieved only after a prolonged struggle to overcome the widespread resistance of many working-class children and their parents, which expressed itself in the form of truancy, classroom unrest, refusal to learn and a significant number of school strikes.[20] Post-1945 legislation to raise the minimum school-leaving age, along with policies designed to lower the age of first admission, has not aroused similar parental or employer opposition. Indeed, it is conceivable that any future resistance to a further extension of compulsory schooling might well be primarily located within the teaching profession itself. An indication of this is to be found in the widespread support expressed at the 1985 conference of the National Association of Headteachers for a proposal to campaign for a lowering of the school-leaving age to fourteen. Although the motion was eventually defeated, it is remarkable that such a suggestion could seriously be discussed in a period when falling school rolls already threatened the job security of many of those present, and when the government expressed a tentative interest in the proposal, prior to the conference, on the grounds of its cost-cutting potential. It should not be imagined that the motion, and the widespread support one suspects it could garner outside the conference, represented within the teaching profession a conversion to libertarian values. Quite the reverse. It constituted a public acknowledgement by a significant number of headteachers that the presence of disaffected young people in their schools amounted to a serious threat to their authority.

This oppositional behaviour by young people towards the school, as already noted, is not a recent phenomenon. However, the extension of the length of compulsory schooling has probably contributed to the growth in its virulence. The resistance of pupils to their compulsory incarceration within schools takes many forms. The most obvious is the growth in truancy among young people as they mature and approach school-leaving age. The work of Grimshaw and Pratt found that truancy is predominantly a secondary school problem. It increases from the second year onwards (age thirteen), peaking in the final year when, in their survey, they found that 9 per cent missed over half their schooling for the final term and over 5 per cent half of the whole school year.[21] Truancy rates, however, are notoriously difficult to calculate. First, because it is illegal and can result in the prosecution of the parent(s) and/or the young person being taken into care, it is in the self-evident interests of both to conceal it from the authorities. Second, truancy takes a number of forms. A common variant is for a pupil to register and then leave the school premises for part or the whole of a session often with the unspoken collusion of a teacher, or even the school, who is relieved to see the departure of a 'disruptive' or 'deviant' pupil. Nevertheless truancy is widespread, with surveys showing an average school non-attendance rate of between 15 and 82 per cent nationally of which, according to the National Association of Chief Education Welfare Officers' survey between 20 and 40 per cent were 'avoidable'.[22]

Truancy should not be viewed as a mere reflection of the pupils' inadequacy. Galloway found that it is misleading to see truants as under-achievers avoiding school as an escape from academic failure, because persistent absentees tended to be better readers than other pupils in their class.[23] Similarly, to view truancy as an indication of criminal intent is equally simplistic, for the linkage of truancy to school-time delinquency is not sustained by the evidence. Given the socio-economic backgrounds of the young people most likely to be absent, the proportion with recorded criminal offences is barely above the norm.[24] The majority, it seems, absent themselves because they view school as unpleasant or irrelevant, or for the simple reason that they have something more important to do, which for many thousands, some as young as four, may entail caring for disabled relatives.[25] Further, they do so with the knowledge of their parent(s), as few as 15 per cent were what we might normally understand as truants, and the majority are 'quite indignant at the suggestion that they wagged school: they regarded staying at home with their parents in quite a different light'.[26] Research relating to truancy, however, tends to be totally unambiguous in identifying the school as the major variable. How the school treats the young person is crucial. High truancy rates occur in those schools that operate according to a custodial orientation, where primitive and unbending rule enforcement is found, where excessive controls are exercised over the pupils, and where the school management tends to isolate itself from contact with pupils and parents.

Truancy is not, of course, the sole indication of disaffection. The existence of disruptive behaviour within the school is another litmus test. The difficulty besetting any discussion of disruptive behaviour is that, like any form of deviant activity, the definition is problematic and to a large extent contructed in the eye of the beholder. Among the types of behaviour listed by Lawrence as falling in this category are 'blank defiance, rejection of reasoning, unacceptable noise levels, physical violence between pupils, threats to teachers or pupils, theft, extortion, graffiti and vandalism, verbal abuse, lack of concentration, boisterousness, lack of consideration to others.'[27] Given this breadth of definition, measuring the extent of disruptive behaviour is clearly impossible. Nevertheless in a recent survey over half the teachers reported experiencing a problem with disruptive behaviour.[28] Failure to 'control' such behaviour is potentially very threatening to both the individual teacher and the school. The former, as Woods notes, finds the stakes high, for 'What is at risk is not only his physical, mental and nervous safety and well-being, but also his continuance in professional life, his future prospects, his professional identity, his way of life, his status, his self-esteem.'[29] The school is similarly at risk from such behaviour, for it may acquire a 'reputation' and be labelled in educational parlance 'a sink school'. With falling school rolls and the advent of parental choice in the selection of a school for their child since 1980, such a reputation can seriously threaten the very survival of an institution.

As with the incidence of truancy, the level of disruptive behaviour is a reflection, to a great extent, of the treatment of the school students by individual teachers and the school. The issues are complex, but research indicates that the more repressive the regime within the classroom, and the lower the level of respect accorded to the young person, the greater the potential risk of conflict leading to incidents that are likely to be labelled disruptive. As Benson argues, schools organized along hierarchical and strongly bureaucratic lines 'tend to alienate both teachers and students',[30] yet the overwhelming majority of schools cling to this model. The possibly exaggerated picture drawn by Atkin of the United States school system serves as a dreadful warning of what might be. American schools are increasingly 'sites for individual and group conflict', both teachers and pupils being subjected to physical assault to a degree 'unimaginable twenty or thirty years ago', with 'police patrolling corridors and doors locked to keep out ex-students'.[31] The fear that such a reality may already have come to pass in a society from which we seem to inherit so much at second hand prompts not a search for new and more imaginative approaches to school management, but an ever more frantic scurrying backwards towards the lumber-room of Victorian values, to seek the key to a mythical tranquillity that we convince ourselves our forebears possessed. Atkin's picture does appear to many to describe a future that awaits our school system, but this is not unavoidable like rain at a test match. If it comes to pass, it will be because we have allowed a particular view of education to remain dominant – a view that sees education as a war of attrition between the students and the institution, one that inevitably fosters the arts of war, which are, to quote William Morris, 'briefly trickery and oppression',[32] rather than those of harmony.

The rigid hierarchy of our schools that reflects the vision of the factory and the military camp, rather than the community of scholars, is embodied within the role of the headteacher – a position defined as long ago as 1909 by Norwood and Hope as 'an autocrat of autocrats'[33] and not substantially altered with the passing of the years. The headteacher still has the power to define the objectives and values of the school, to determine the bulk of the curriculum, to control the shape of the internal organization, to manage the distribution of funding, to choose staff (although this may be shared with the governors) and to determine the prospects of promotion for the teaching staff. The inequalities in this relationship mean that, as one ex-headteacher has commented:

It becomes very difficult for a Head to be sure when a teacher is being completely honest and frank with him, not saying what he thinks the Head wants her to hear, and it becomes difficult for the teacher behaving in that way to retain self-respect, which is the main reason for the usual isolation of the Head: the staff find it easier not to speak to him too often.[34]

Schools offer teachers few opportunities to participate in decision-making, and 'hierarchical control over assigned tasks, an abundance of rules, and rigid enforcement of rules'[35] all lead to high levels of teacher alienation and a stifling of creativity, producing 'that peculiar blight which affects the teacher's mind, which creeps over it gradually, and, possessing it bit by bit, devours its creative resources'.[36] Even where the rhetoric of teacher participation does enter the school, it rarely amounts to more than a 'legitimating strategy'. Because teachers have so little say in the management of 'their' schools, it is hardly surprising that they are indifferent to suggestions that parents and pupils might acquire rights of participation.

A school's power to impose rules and regulations upon its students is immense. Almost universally such rules relate to dress and appearance, times of arrival and departure, attendance, access to the school building, norms of behaviour which will refer to matters such as bullying, fighting and rowdiness, homework, sports equipment and apparel, the manner of addressing members of staff and visitors and the consumption of food on the premises. In addition to these, of course, are the rules enforced within the classroom which constrain movement, speech and behaviour. Yet the tradition of allowing teachers relative autonomy behind the closed door of the classroom means that great variations in interpretation and implementation coexist within any school. Indeed, survival for teachers in the classroom may depend upon negotiating a temporary or even permanent negation of certain school rules in the interests of social 'harmony' and the completion of academic tasks.

School rules commonly exceed the bounds of acceptable interference and would not be tolerated by adults outside 'closed' institutions such as prisons or the armed forces – neither of which should surely serve as models upon which we should base the setting for the education of young people. For example, there is the continuing obsession of so many schools with matters of pupils' appearance and the imposition of school uniform. It is still a widespread practice to demand the wearing of a specified uniform as a condition of attendance. Failure to conform, no matter how expensive or embarrassing the uniform might be, can lead to suspension, ensuring that young people up to the age of eighteen can effectively be denied an education. Abundant evidence exists to show the quite gratuitous financial burden which the need to provide school uniform places upon low-income families,[37] and it is a sad reflection on the crass insensitivity of many teachers that they still insist on adding to the hardship of such families. The implementation of uniform regulations can reach ridiculous extremes. For example, I have seen the girls of a secondary school being led after assembly into changing rooms so that it could be ascertained that they were wearing the regulation underwear. At another, girls whose hair fell below their collars were issued with elastic bands to put them into 'bunches', while others were ordered to remove jewellery and earrings apart from sleepers. It is almost commonplace to recall boys being sent home for hair too long or too short, and Hargreaves reports an incident (later hushed up by the LEA) of a member of staff cutting boys' hair to match the regulation length.[38] Compulsory sports are often a point of conflict, with boys forced to do gym in underpants if they forget their shorts and pupils of both sexes, despite acute embarrassment, being ordered to shower with their peers and in front of strangers.

The imposition of these rules and regulations leads to often quite unacceptable punishments being inflicted indiscriminately on the innocent as well as the guilty. At one school where I taught, the doors were removed from the toilets for a term after an outbreak of graffiti – ostensibly for them to be sanded down. At another, soap was taken out of the washrooms to prevent misuse. Always, though, the overriding memory is of the incalculable hours of valuable time lost upon such activities as practising how to walk into assembly, close hymn books, line up in the corridor and walk into a classroom silently, stand up when a teacher enters the room without scraping the chairs, shut desk lids inaudibly, walk along corridors in twos and eat meals in unnatural silence. Not surprisingly, then, research has shown that teachers devote a quite disproportionate amount of classroom time on non-instructional matters, disciplining, organizing and striving to maintain order. In a survey carried out in New York, Deutsch discovered that teachers spent between 50 and 80 per cent of class time upon such activities,[39] while a later study by Gump put just 'admonishing, giving permission and dealing with deviant behaviour' at 23 per cent of class time.[40]

To this must be added the absence of any mechanism by which school students can effectively influence the curriculum. The content, balance and emphasis of this is exclusively in the hands of the staff, although in some cases this means merely the power to select the

external exam syllabus. For school students, except at the most
marginal level – which book to choose from the reading table or
which group CSEs or O levels to opt for – the content of the lessons is
beyond their control. Not only does the student have almost no room
to manœuvre, but no agency exists through which dissent or even
preference can legitimately be expressed in an effective or collective
manner. Inevitably dissatisfaction is often channelled into partial or
total rejection of school, or disruptive behaviour, much of which is
selectively directed towards particular subjects or members of staff in
a way that is damaging for the wellbeing of all parties.

The rules imposed by our schools upon their students are
profoundly undemocratic, and yet those who create and implement
them rarely see the need to justify them to either parents or pupils.
This is not because those responsible for them feel unable to do so,
but because they are viewed as an ingredient of the education system
as essential as the school building itself. Even the most irrelevant rules
will produce their advocates. Much of the support may be mindless
and purely deferential, as one of the teachers put it to Hargreaves
during a discussion over a pupil's hair: 'I don't care a damn over his
long hair, but if that's the school policy it's OK by me.'[41] However,
more substantive defences are thrown up. A major one rests upon the
inevitability of the need for rules and order in an institution as
complex as a school. This is argued by Strawson in lucid but familiar
fashion as follows:

> It is a condition of the existence of any form of social
> organization of human community that certain expectations of
> behaviour on the part of its members should be pretty regularly
> fulfilled; that some duties, one might say, should be performed,
> some obligations acknowledged, some rules observed.[42]

Circumstances and design make schools special cases, and it is
questionable whether they have the right to demand or even expect
their students to accept this formulation. As school students by law
and practice have no power, right or mechanism by which they may
involve themselves in the creation or administration of those rules,
they can never be viewed as citizens in miniature. Consequently, as
Marshall points out, they 'cannot be morally obliged to follow those
rules . . . if they are obliged to follow such rules then the obligation
must be similar to that of the coerced slave.'[43] Support for such
coercion is, of course, inevitably forthcoming. It is primarily based
upon the notion that school students are so deficient in maturity that
they might well, indeed probably would, exercise their rights in a way

that would damage themselves and others; that the school as a school could not function if the students were granted sufficient democratic rights to overcome the objections voiced to coercion by Marshall. This point is made by Dunlop when he claims it 'would necessarily alter the fundamental hierarchical relationship between teachers and taught, and lead to countless unforeseen changes, making the cultural tasks of education, especially the passing on predominantly by example of values, unformalized skills, appreciations, ways of behaving and so on, virtually impossible.'[44]

The case for the denial of rights to school students on the grounds of their assumed immaturity is, I believe, as weak in the school setting as Bob Franklin has argued it is in the political arena.[45] Surely it cannot be acceptable that the rules of schools should be allowed to operate in a way that stands outside the principle that 'the individual should be treated not as a means to others' ends but as an end in himself',[46] or that headteachers and teachers be allowed to act in ways that 'express contempt for the values of a free society'.[47] Yet we currently endorse such behaviour and allow it to go unchallenged because the victims are judged to be below an artificially constructed age of majority. Worse, we allow the schools to reinforce the image of their students as immature by denying them the opportunity to exercise mature judgements.

Dunlop is, of course, correct in his analysis that the school in its present form would be unlikely to survive an injection of 'genuine rather than merely game-like democratic participation'.[48] However, that must prompt the question whether our schools in their present form are worth saving. Are the benefits to the students and society so substantive that we should allow those who control them to continue to act in ways that run counter to the values of a democratic society? I think not. The record of the contemporary system is less than encouraging. The majority of pupils, despite the improvements in standards achieved since the 1944 Act, still leave with a reading age inferior to their chronological age. A majority still leave having failed to achieve the elusive exam results required to negotiate a career as opposed to a job. Worse, our school system has totally failed, despite the best efforts of reformers, to alter the class, regional, ethnic and gender gradients of inequality in educational achievement. The waste of 'talent' is as acute today as it was when the need to staunch the loss prompted the Robbins Report to advocate the substantive expansion of higher education two decades ago. Of course it would be somewhat dishonest to lay the blame for the failure to reduce social and educational inequality solely at the door of the school system, although some educationists do invite such admonishment by making

grandiose claims for schools as the 'engines' of social reform. Even in
the arena of social education the evidence is at best anecdotal, and to
claim for schools a major civilizing role is as unjustifiable as Margaret
Thatcher's prejudiced accusation that lack of 'teacher discipline' is a
cause of juvenile crime.[49] The truth is that we know very little, but
strong evidence does indicate that the more authoritarian, less liberal,
less sensitive the school is to the needs of the individual student, the
worse the problems within the school and the greater the probability
of deviant behaviour outside it.[50]

Equally worrying is that the compulsory nature of schooling and its
alienating effects produce, in a considerable segment of the
population, a lifelong resistance to education and the cultural values
they perceive it to represent. The adventure of learning and schol-
arship, having been reduced to a grind and chore by the school, is
understandably rejected by the 'free' adult. Also, for the majority,
education represents a degree of failure. In a highly competitive
education system such as ours, in which the majority are from an
early age streamed and examined, more must fail than succeed. Few
will actively seek to revisit the experience of failure, and consequently
those who fail – the majority – tend in later life to avoid educational
institutions or experience great difficulty in re-entering them as
mature students. Thus as presently constituted even adult education
and 'second-chance' programmes end up, despite their good
intentions, reinforcing rather than eroding class differentials in
attainment.[51] The removal of compulsory attendance might lead
many of those who currently fail to opt out earlier, to avoid the
stigma of failure. Moreover, given the current need for schools to
maximize their numbers in order to survive falling school rolls, they
might reassess their curricula and ethos better to meet the educational
needs of those they currently ignore.

As well as compulsory attendance, our schools in their present
form seem to require inhumane types of punishment, such as corporal
punishment, to control many of their students. A series of cases in the
European Court appears to threaten its legality. The attempt by the
British Government to find a compromise, designed to allow schools
to beat young people with the permission of their parent(s), has at the
time of writing been thrown out by the House of Lords. None the less
the use of physical punishment remains widespread. Bennett found
that in the primary schools he researched, despite the discouragement
of the LEA and NUT, 'over half the teachers admitted to smacking'
pupils.[52] In the secondary sector an estimated 80 per cent of schools
still use the cane, although, as would be expected, wide variations are
found in the frequency with which it is employed.[53] In many schools

it is still gratuitously 'dished out' for minor offences, but the most commonly listed offence is fighting or bullying, the caners apparently believing that 'they can teach children not to be violent by beating them'.[54] The use of corporal punishment also tends to be more prevalent during the early years of secondary education. Pupils learn quite correctly that the smaller and weaker you are, the more likely you are to be beaten. The bigger and stronger, and presumably the more likely to strike back or refuse the cane, the greater the possibility of being suspended or consigned to the growing number of educationally dubious special units or sin-bins, to which transfer can be made without the permission of either the parent(s) or pupil.[55]

The continued use of corporal punishment in our schools, long after its abolition in every other European country, is an amazing testimony to the inefficiency of many of our teachers and schools and the callous disregard of school students' rights by our legislators. It is also anachronistic, since its use in the penal system was ended after the Cadogan Committee (1983) concluded that the levels of recidivism among those birched was at least as high, if not higher, among those offenders who had not been so punished. The retention of corporal punishment in the school setting, along with the widespread acceptance of violence against pupils in the form of pushing, hair pulling, poking and other manifestations of physical intimidation by teachers, is clearly a cause for major concern and denies all the long-established principles of justice. Royce illustrates this in an account of the 'treatment' of a pupil who is accused of an act of impertinence towards a teacher. The teachers not only perceive themselves as the victims but frame the rules, police them, act as witness, prosecutor, judge, jury and eventually gaoler/probation officer. The pupils have at best only another teacher to appeal to if they feel aggrieved by the outcome.[56] The end result is that the rules of natural justice are ignored as a matter of course within the school system, and not merely with the use of humiliating and degrading punishments. It is only when the process is spelt out in this fashion that the accepted, everyday treatment of young people in the school setting can be grasped in terms of its traditional negation of their basic rights. If the schools do require such a diet of rules and punishment, as the clear majority of teachers maintain, that does not justify such practices but rather constitutes a 'prima facie indictment of the arrangements or possibly of the institutions themselves'.[57]

The denial of rights to school students effectively excludes them from the power to influence the shaping of school policy and serves as a serious block on the road to reform. It allows incompetent teachers and schools to survive much more easily while flagrantly teaching their students that they are inferior as citizens and can be treated as objects rather than persons deserving respect. The ending of compulsory schooling would fundamentally redraw this relationship, giving school students a clear right to decide whether to attend or not, what institutions to affiliate to and which subject units to study. In terms of overall attendance it would possibly make little difference. Those who currently do not wish to attend largely do not, but it is likely that some of these would attend on a part-time basis if the compulsion was removed. Finally, given the focus of the school as a social as well as an educational centre for young people – Thompson found, for example, that 90 per cent of friendships were formed at school[58] – we have no basis for assuming that the removal of compulsion would lead to a mass rejection of education. However, this should not be misinterpreted as a crude argument for education to be offered to young people on a purely 'take-it-or-leave-it' basis. The ending of the school's right to demand attendance on pain of punishment must be tied to a shift in resources from the school and classroom, to the wider community and home. Those responsible for educational services need to learn from the health service and in particular health education. For example, the health visitor needs to be complemented by an education visitor offering the parent(s) support, guidance and practical help in matters educational. It is amazing that so little support is given in the vital area of language formation and during the crucial pre-school years. Yet we know from innovatory projects in this area that the benefits to the young person and parent(s) can be substantial. Equally, a more imaginative and responsive use of resources might be engendered, enabling provision to be made in a wide variety of settings such as youth centres, sports halls and at home, for those young people who find the battery-house atmosphere of the school unpleasant and inhibiting. Potentially the removal of compulsion could liberate education as much as the young people themselves.

The removal of compulsion would amount to a significant first step towards giving citizenship a meaning for young people in the school setting. However, in itself it would not be sufficient. Within the management and administrative structures of our schools, space has to be found for meaningful participation by students. It might be argued that we are well on the way to achieving this, now that over a third of all LEAs allow pupils' representatives on governing bodies, and nearly 20 per cent grant speaking and voting rights.[59] This argument ignores, first, the inherent weakness of such bodies to act in more than an advisory capacity and, second, the fact that apart from one LEA which allows students to be full governors at fourteen this is a reform which applies to those largely beyond the statutory leaving age. For many people to have rights within the school, a much more far-reaching extension of democratic practices is required. Schools would require something along the lines of councils made up of pupils, teachers, ancillary staff and other users, such as adult students. These would possess the right to meet in school hours, to discuss all relevant issues, to determine rules and to have full representation on the governing body. Alongside this, students would need to be granted the right to organize their own union if they so desired without let or hindrance. The hostility directed towards the National Union of School Students (NUSS) by so many educationists and politicians speaks volumes about their contempt for the rights of oppressed groups to organize themselves and their profound ignorance of the NUSS. For what is remarkable is not their wild radicalism or 'dafty' leadership but their measured moderation. By no stretch of the imagination would even the most hostile reader of their literature and policies be able to portray them as either anti-teacher or anti-education. They are, however, pro-pupil.

The key reform is probably none of these, although the value of them all should not be lightly dismissed. As Handy noted in his study of the management of schools, they 'are different because of the children',[60] and therein lies the root of the problem. Most urgently of all we need to rethink the very structure of our schools that allows their particular isolation as factories for the young. What would transform the average school and classroom as nothing else would is the presence of adults who wanted to learn. It would revolutionize the behaviour of teachers and improve standards rapidly, as well as altering the tenor of the school itself, as some have already discovered.[61] Once the idea is accepted that education and schools are no longer merely for 'children', the problem of securing the rights of children within them becomes that much less intractable, for children will have to be treated in an identical fashion to other users, or the institution will encounter severe managerial problems. Despite the resistance of headteachers and their colleagues, falling school rolls, financial restraint and community demand for resources are making the all-age, open-educational institution a growing probability, giving grounds for optimism that children's rights within the school will become a live issue after all.

Notes

1 *Better Schools*, Cmnd 9469 (HMSO, 1985), p. 1.
2 *Report by Her Majesty's Inspectors on the Effects of Local Authority Expenditure Policies on Education Provision in England, 1984* (DES, 1985), p. 8.

3   Ibid., p. 26.
4   *Report by Her Majesty's Inspectors on the Effects of Local Authority Expenditure Policies on Education Provision in England, 1981* (DES, 1982), p. 10.
5   See C. Glendinning and P. Dixon, 'School meals', in *Thatcherism and the Poor*, ed. D. Bull and P. Wilding (CPAG, 1983), pp. 48–52.
6   L. Burghes and R. Stagles, *No Choice at 16* (CPAG, 1983).
7   G. Sutherland, *Policy Making in Elementary Education, 1870–1895* (Oxford University Press, 1973), p. 186.
8   M. Duane, 'Freedom and the state system of education', in *Children's Rights*, ed. P. Adams et al. (Elek, 1971), p. 240.
9   *Williams* v. *Eady* (1893), 10 TLR 41, CA.
10 Model Articles for School Management, quoted in D. E. Regan, *Local Government and Education* (Allen and Unwin, 1979), p. 64.
11 P. Newell, *Corporal Punishment in Schools* (STOPP, n.d.), p. 16.
12 Reported by S. Bayliss, 'Governors to have greater freedom', *The Times Educational Supplement (TES)*, 25 May 1984.
13 D. A. Howell, 'The management of primary schools', appendix 13 of *Children and their Primary Schools* (Plowden Report) (HMSO, 1967), vol. II, p. 611.
14 See, for example, S. Parker, 'Voting with their feet?', *TES*, 5 October 1984.
15 G. Cortis, *The Social Context of Teaching (Open Books, 1977), p. 140.*
16 S. Bowles and H. Gintis, *Schooling in Capitalist America* (Routledge and Kegan Paul, 1976), p. 265.
17 W. Waller, *The Sociology of Teaching* (Wiley, 1932), p. 196.
18 N. Fruchter, 'The role of parent participation', *Social Policy* (Fall 1984), p. 33.
19 J. and E. Newsom, 'Parents' perceptives on children's behaviour at school', in *Disruptive Behaviour in Schools*, ed. N. Frude and H. Galt (Wiley, 1984), p. 104.
20 S. Humphries, *Hooligans or Rebels?* (Blackwell, 1981).
21 R. Grimshaw and J. Pratt, 'School absenteeism and the education crisis', *Youth and Policy*, 10 (1984), pp. 16–19.
22 NACEWO, *These We Serve* (NACEWO, 1975).
23 D. M. Galloway, 'A study of persistent absence from school in Sheffield', PhD thesis (Sheffield Polytechnic, 1979), p. 184.
24 Ibid.
25 Report of Association of Careers Research, *The Times, 14 November 1984.*
26 D. M. Galloway, '*Only the tail wags*', *TES*, 15 February 1985.
27 J. Lawrence et al., *Dialogue on Disruptive Behaviour: a study of a secondary school* (PJD Press, 1983), p. 5.
28 R. Dierenfield, 'All you need to know about disruption', *TES* 29 January 1982.
29 P. Woods, 'Teaching for survival', in *School Experience*, ed. P. Woods and R. Hammersley (Croom Helm, 1977), p. 274.

30 J. Benson, 'The bureaucratic nature of schools and teacher job satisfaction', *Journal of Educational Administration*, XXI, 2 (1983), p. 137.

31 J. M. Atkin, 'Education accountability in the United States', *Educational Analysis*, 1 (1979), p. 12.

32 W. Morris, 'Work in Factory as it Might Be. III' in *William Morris Artist, Writer, Socialist*, ed. M. Morris (Blackwell, 1936), vol. 2, p. 139.

33 C. Norwood and A. H. Hope, *The Higher Education of Boys in England* (1909), p. 213.

34 J. Watts, *Towards an Open School* (Longman, 1980), p. 94.

35 W. K. Hoy, R. Blazovsky and W. Newland, 'Bureaucracy and alienation', *Journal of Educational Administration*, XXI, 2 (1983), p. 118.

36 Waller, *The Sociology of Teaching*, p. 391.

37 D. Bull, *What Price Free Education?* (CPAG, 1980), pp. 21–3 and 35–8.

38 D. Hargreaves, *Social Relations in a Secondary School* (Routledge and Kegan Paul, 1967), p. 138.

39 M. Deutsch, 'Minority groups and class status as related to social and personality factors in scholastic achievement', in *The Disadvantaged Child*, ed. M. Deutsch et al. (Basic Books, 1967).

40 P. V. Gump, *The Classroom Behaviour Setting* (University of Kansas Press, 1967).

41 Hargreaves, *Social Relations in a Secondary School*, p. 139.

42 P. F. Strawson, *Freedom and Resentment* (Methuen, 1974), p. 30.

43 J. D. Marshall, 'John Wilson on the necessity of punishment', *Journal of Philosophy of Education*, 18, 1 (1984), p. 103.

44 F. Dunlop, 'On the democratic organization of schools', *Cambridge Journal of Education*, 9, 1 (1979), p. 53.

45 See chapter 2.

46 C. B. Macpherson, *Democratic Theory: essays in retrieval* (Clarendon Press, 1973), p. 56.

47 K. Strike, *Liberty and Learning* (Robertson, 1982), p. 147.

48 Dunlop, 'On the democratic organization of schools', p. 53.

49 Hansard, 14 March 1985.

50 See, for example, M. J. Power et al., 'Delinquent schools', *New Society*, 10 (1967), pp. 542–3.

51 K. Jackson, 'Foreword' to J. L. Thompson (ed.), *Adult Education for a Change* (Hutchinson, 1980), p. 17.

52 N. Bennett, *Teaching Styles and Pupil Progress* (Open Books, 1976), p. 44.

53 Quoted by Newell, *Corporal Punishment in Schools*, p. 5.

54 P. Temperton, 'A sordid and futile business', *TES*, 17 July 1981, pp. 16–17.

55 P. Marsdon, *Law Centres: a guide for young workers* (NYB, n.d.), p. 9.

56 R. J. Royce, 'School-based punishment', *Journal of Philosophy of Education*, 18, 1 (1984), pp. 86–7.

57 Ibid., p. 94.

58 DES, *Young People in the 1980s: a survey* (HMSO, 1983), p. 62.

59   Advisory Centre for Education Survey, *ACE Bulletin*, 6 (1985), pp. 1–2.
60   C. Handy, *Taken for Granted? understanding schools as organizations* (Longman, 1984), p. 25.
61   See B. Moon (ed.), *Comprehensive Schools: challenge and charge* (NFER/Nelson, 1983), especially ch. 3.

Further reading

Better Schools, Cmnd 9469 (HMSO, 1985).
S. Bowles and H. Gintis, *Schooling in Capitalist America* (Routledge and Kegan Paul, 1976).
M. Deutsch et al. (eds), *The Disadvantaged Child* (Basic Books, 1967).
C. Handy, *Taken for Granted? understanding schools as organizations* (Longman, 1984).
J. Lawrence et al., *Dialogue and Disruptive Behviour: a study of a secondary school* (PJD Press, 1983).
J. D. Marshall, 'John Wilson on the necessity of punishment', *Journal of Philosophy of Education*, 18, 1 (1984).
R. J. Royce, 'School-Based punishment', *Journal of Philosophy of Education*, 18, 1 (1984).
J. Watts, *Towards an Open School* (Longman, 1980).
P. Woods, 'Teaching for survival', in *School Experience*, ed. P. Woods and R. Hammersley (Croom Helm, 1977).

4

The Rights of Children in Care

Gerry Lavery

The purpose of this chapter is to highlight some of the ways in which the rights of children in care are violated. Specifically I shall consider certain legal and administrative procedures which serve to deny children coming into care, and those already there, an effective voice in decision-making processes of direct relevance to their affairs. Reforms of such procedures, including the need to prevent admissions to care in the first place, are then discussed. It is, however, equally important to assess the role of care in society and in particular its relationship to structural inequality and poverty. The chapter concludes by suggesting strategies for change.

But how many children are in care and what institutional forms can care assume? Most children in care are there through no fault of their own, and many of those whose presence is connected to their apparent culpability are there, it has been argued, unnecessarily.[1] Reasons for admission apart, the process of entry into care invariably takes place through the courts or through voluntarily negotiated agreements between families and local authority social services departments (SSDs). On 31 March 1982 there were 93,200 children in care in England and Wales or, looked at another way, for every 1000 of the population below the age of eighteen years, 7.5 are in care.[2] About 5000 children in local authority care are placed in homes or foster homes run or organized by voluntary organizations.[3] Normally it is possible for children to remain in care until they are eighteen, but in some circumstances the upper age limit is nineteen.[4] Although a child may be described as being 'in care', this does not necessarily denote a placement in physical care, since it is possible to be the subject of a care order but be placed 'home on trial'. 17,200 children in care are under the charge of a parent, guardian, relative or friend.[5] Such children would, however, also normally be under the supervision of a social worker and, in theory at least, still be subject to the powers of a care order. However, most children in care are either boarded out with foster parents or placed in residential care of

some form, and it is these two groups that will be the main focus of
our attention, since it is their rights which are most frequently and
comprehensively denied by the state.

Four observations are appropriate at the beginning. First, one of
the major difficulties in ensuring the rights of children in care is
the limitations of the law. Section 18 of the Child Care Act (1980)
states:

> In reaching any decision relating to a child in their care, a local
> authority shall give first consideration to the need to safeguard
> and promote the welfare of the child throughout his childhood
> and shall so far as practicable ascertain the wishes and feelings
> of the child regarding the decision and give due consideration to
> them, having regard to his age and understanding.

Such a vague and limited general duty upon local authorities invites a
tokenism where a child's views may be sought but then promptly
ignored. In practice, violation of section 18 is discernible from the
point of entry into care and those newly placed can be unwillingly
thrust into a variety of settings without much say in the matter. This
has led the National Association of Young People in Care (NAYPIC)
to call for a say in the choice of placements.[6] Residential care can take
several forms, all of which may be experienced in the course of a
'career' in care. Most children are accommodated in community
homes of various sorts. Of those in residential care, 16,200 are in
community homes such as small group homes; 12,300 are in
voluntary homes, hostels and other accommodation such as boarding
schools; 4600 are in observation and assessment centres (O and A
centres); and 4200 are in community homes with education (CHEs)[7]
– CHEs are the successors to approved schools. This leads to a second
point.

Some forms of residential care, particularly O and A centres and
CHEs, have been criticized in terms of their purpose, structure and
effectiveness. Professor Norman Tutt and others have forcefully
argued that the assumptions underlying the official policy for O and
A centres are highly questionable.[8] Such centres are frequently used
as an initial placement for older children entering care and juvenile
offenders held on remand pending a full court hearing. The
assessment component of their task is seen as: first, describing the
problem as 'presented or experienced by the child'; second, making a
judgement about the nature of the child's referring problem; and,
third, recommending an appropriate form of intervention if any.[9]
Tutt argues that such an approach is mistaken beause it assumes that

human behaviour is constant and it ignores the centrality of structural factors, while overstating the importance of individual pathological factors, in explanations of the problems which have brought young people to O and A centres. 'It should be obvious', he concludes, 'that any remedial intervention directed at the child must be doomed to failure if the child is returned to an unchanged hostile environment which still retains criminogenic factors'.[10] Furthermore, as NAYPIC maintains, young people can spend unnecessarily long periods in O and A centres – a view endorsed by the House of Commons Social Services Committee (HCSSC).[11] There is a growing body of opinion, therefore, which recommends a move away from O and A centres to more community-based assessments as a more appropriate way to ascertain the needs of children entering care. Indeed, some local authorities, like Bradford, have already made moves in this direction by establishing initiatives, such as community assessment teams.

CHEs have been criticized on the grounds of the considerable confusion about their role. Although they developed as successors to the old approved schools, there is no evidence that CHEs have contributed to a significant drop in conviction rates. About half the residents of CHEs are offenders.[12] CHEs have also tried to develop a more therapeutic orientation and, coupled with the more punitive approved school legacy, this led the HCSSC to comment: 'At present CHEs seem uneasily poised between their essentially punitive past and supposedly therapeutic future'.[13] The committee had doubts about what CHEs offered children.

A third point is that there are difficulties with fostering in its present form. As some aspects of fostering are discussed later in the chapter, suffice it to say for now that children placed with foster parents[14] are likely to experience a breakdown of their placement and may also experience problems concerning access to their natural parents. The questions of payment, support and training of foster parents are also important considerations in the provision of an effective service,[15] as is the requirement that SSDs recruit foster parents whose ethnic origin or culture meets the needs of those who are fostered.[16] More recently there has been a growth in the practice of advertising children in order to recruit suitable foster parents; this requires a more sustained comment.

The difficulty of placing black children, brothers and sisters wishing to stay together, some adolescents and children with mental or physical handicaps with foster parents has led in recent years to the advertising of children on television and in the press. Rick Rogers has pointed to a number of difficulties with advertising.[17] First, there are no guidelines from the Independent Broadcasting Authority (IBA) or the Advertising Standards Authority (ASA). Second, there can be problems with 'poor photographs' and 'crass copy'. Third, there is a lack of consultation about the content of advertisements which can stereotype children, make them out to be 'really pathetic' and disparage natural parents. Fourth, while there is some evidence that television advertising has met with success, there are no reliable statistics for success rates of adverts in papers and journals. If advertising continues to be widely used there is a need for legal safeguards and, as Rogers argues, perhaps for the implementation of more discreet techniques, such as photo listing services.

Finally, although the cost of keeping children in care is perceived as relatively expensive (in 1981–2 the average weekly cost per child was £197);[18] this does not guarantee the provision of an adequate service. One of the difficulties here is the pay, conditions and training of residential social workers. They receive considerably less pay than field social workers, are expected to work longer hours, often in difficult circumstances, and less than 20 per cent of them are qualified.[19] The long campaign waged by residential workers, sometimes involving industrial action, for improvements in their lot has met with little positive response from their employers.[20] The HCSSC in their report on children in care was concerned about the turnover of dissatisfied residential staff and recognized that their training should be 'a priority in improving the long-term standard of care for children'.[21]

Keeping these four general observations in mind, let us move on to consider some specific aspects of life in care which deny rights to children and young people.

Decision-making

Once a child or young person has been placed in care, various processes are used to make important decisions and to check on her or his progress; the most central of these is the review. The practice of some SSDs in this area has been found wanting and provides good examples of how the letter and spirit of section 18 is abused. The Children and Young Persons Act (1969)[22] lays a duty on local authorities to review the cases of all those children in care every six months, and as part of the review they should consider whether to apply for the discharge of a care order where one is in force. This provision would, of course, include children returned home on trial from care. The Secretary of State also has the power to make regulations governing the form, content and timing of reviews.[23] For children in foster care, reviews differ slightly in that they are covered by the Boarding-Out Regulations (1955), which lay down the minimum standards for those boarded out, and, as well as being a little more specific, they are also covered by some limited guidelines. However, the DHSS found from an examination of foster children's files that in only eleven out of twenty-eight SSDs studied 'were reviews carried out regularly within the statutory limits'.[24]

The present lack of regulations means there is no agreed definition of the purpose of reviews. Nevertheless many SSDs plan and monitor the progress of those in care during reviews, even though these functions receive variable priority across different authorities. Given the *de facto* importance of the review, it is crucial that those in care have the right to attend and participate fully in them. However, despite the desire of many in care to take part,[25] a survey conducted by the Children's Legal Centre (CLC) reported that only fifteen out of sixty-three SSDs invited children in their care to review meetings.[26] Although age and immaturity are reasons for partial or total exclusion, the most common is the risk of imparting information sensitive to the child or someone else. As the CLC argue, if information affects someone in care, then he or she has the right to know and should be given appropriate support and preparation in such circumstances.[27] Bob Franklin has argued earlier in this book that the present age limitations on the right to vote cannot be sustained, and similar reasoning suggests there is no case for the exclusion of certain age groups from participation in review; the Family Rights Group (FRG) recommends participation at ten years and NAYPIC at thirteen years.

If encouragement is to be given for attendance at reviews, a simple invitation may not be enough. Review meetings may be attended by SSD managers and others, barely known to children, creating feelings of lack of any control of the situation and resulting in only their passive participation. As someone in a NAYPIC survey on reviews observed: 'it is not very fair to be discussed amongst a bunch of strangers.'[28] NAYPIC therefore advocates that those in care should be consulted about who attends reviews and that their wishes should be made known to the meeting; a young person should also be able to choose someone they trust to help them put their point of view.[29] Reviews are often imbued with professional ideology, and the CLC discovered that foster parents and natural parents had a lower status than professionals at reviews.[30] To ensure the attendance of those traditionally more marginal participants, it is also important to give thought and care to the timing and venue of reviews.

The poor conduct of reviews is also a serious concern. Their seeming lack of purpose has been noted by some children in care and is perhaps best summed up by one who replied to the question 'What is a review?' by saying: 'Where people discuss your future and come to no definite conclusion'.[31] Reviews could be more purposeful, in the absence of regulations, if more care and attention was paid to review forms, often the central focus of the review meeting. These are not standardized, as the CLC points out, and vary enormously.[32] The case for comprehensive review forms is well made by the CLC,[33] and such forms should cover major decisions and important aspects of a child's progress as well as containing the opportunity for written contributions from participants in order to ensure yet further accountability, NAYPIC rightly advocates a complaints system to be used where there are disagreements or, as sometimes happens, when review decisions are not implemented.[34]

The variable and inadequate practices relating to reviews demands greater standardization and effective regulations, but the DHSS has traditionally dragged its feet on this. The fact that those in care are not full participants in their own reviews is unjust, and NAYPIC's disappointment over the HCSSC's failure to make stronger recommendations on this is understandable.[35] If the more general position on reviews is to be altered, then significant legal, administrative and attitudinal changes are required. However, the continued absence of such changes suggests that official attitudes are caught firmly in the paternalist trap of leaving adults to act in the child's best interests.[36]

As well as reviews, case conferences can be important areas of decision-making. It is fair to say, however, that case conferences are seen by many authorities as being less concerned with those actually in care than the need to discuss suspected child abuse cases. They also differ from reviews in that they involve several agencies. Nevertheless, the CLC discovered that case conferences are sometimes used to determine a child's future following a period of observation and assessment or to discuss single issues and unforeseen problems.[37] The CLC were rightly alarmed that some SSDs saw case conference as having more power than reviews. But reviews are statutory – and may be called as often as needed – whereas case conferences are discretionary and should not, therefore, relegate reviews to an inferior status. Without effective review regulations, SSDs could easily – and perhaps do at times – use reviews as exercises in token participation, with the real decisions being taken at case conferences from which significant actors may be excluded.

A prerequisite to effective participation in the decision-making process of care is access to information, particularly to files. This area also raises the issue of a child's right to know her or his background, since the developments of self-identity can be crucial.[38] Again, as with sensitive or painful information at reviews, support and preparation may be needed. The completion of life-story books is particularly useful in providing information to younger children and indeed, in the experience of the author, an increasing number of social workers appear to be using this technique.

Everyday matters?

What often distinguishes the experience of state care from life in a family is the stigmatizing effect that the former has upon its consumers. Nowhere is this more evident than in the rules and administration of everyday concerns such as money matters, privacy, school, punishment and discipline experienced, particularly by children in residential institutions and, to a lesser degree in foster homes.

The attempts to make care resemble family life more closely through the expansion of fostering and the development of small group homes are often thwarted by, among other things, forms of local authority administration. The system adopted by some SSDs for buying clothes for children in care uses the order book or clothing voucher scheme. Although this practice has been phased out in many areas, it remains in others.[39] It has obvious shortcomings. First, the use of the order book can make those in care feel like the recipients of charity and different from other children. Second, the system restricts choice, since only certain stores accept vouchers. Third, the order book denies these young people any idea of the value of money or experience of using it. The abolition of the order book system is therefore long overdue and it should now be replaced by cash allowances for clothing and other items fixed at realistic rates.

Another important area of campaigning by 'in care' groups has been to demand the right to privacy. There are at present no specific regulations governing privacy, but the day-to-day practice of many residential homes denies it. As someone in the *Who Cares?* study complained:

> The trouble with care is there is no place to sulk. If you are upset, perhaps something has gone wrong at home, or for whatever reason, there's no place to have a sulk, the staff pop up wherever you go. Perhaps you might want to be left alone but they'll say 'Go up to the table tennis room' but there are other kids there so you go out of bounds to get some privacy.[40]

The invasion of privacy pervades many aspects of life in a children's home: 'There is no question of locks on bathrooms and toilets, in some children's homes the locks are hanging off and the staff just barge in and put you in an awkward position'.[41] The lack of privacy is also acknowledged at official levels.[42]

Closely related to the right to privacy is the right to communication by letter and telephone (the issue of contact with parents, etc., is explored later in the chapter). Mail is sometimes censored or at least read by residential staff: 'in our place the staff read our letters the ones we get and the ones we write.'[43] Despite the fact that contact by relatives and friends (where access has not been severed) is governed by regulations, the CLC has reported attempts by residential establishments to prevent such contact.[44]

The differential position of children in care with regard to education is acute, and those concerned with the rights of children have signalled several major difficulties in this respect. First, many children in CHEs and O and A centres receive education within their institutions, which effectively fall outside the education system's network of responsibilities, support, inspections and other safeguards.[45] Such children, having been failed by the mainstream system, find themselves in 'educational limbo'. Their situation is therefore in need of urgent review. Second, as many children in care have special educational needs, there should be an attempt to clear up the confusion over who is defined as the parent (the local authority, the natural parent or the SSD?) for the purposes of the 1981 Education Act which regards parental involvement as 'essential' in assessing special needs. A wide interpretation of the term 'parent' would ensure a full assessment from several sources. Third, schools can stigmatize those in care. As a participant in the Life in Care Conference (1981) stated: 'Recently a teacher said to me in front of everybody "I hear you're doing much better in a home". This made me feel like walking out of school.'[46] Fourth, and related to the last point, social workers can often share with a teacher information of which someone in care is unaware, even though it concerns them. Finally, although local authorities have the power to support young people in care through further education, they do not always exercise this power. While the list is far from exhaustive, the above represents some of the major ways in which the state denies important rights to those in care in the pursuit of their education.

A further aspect of care which has received considerable attention in the literature relating to children's rights concerns the issues of discipline, punishment and control. Perhaps of most concern here are the following: the use of corporal punishment; the use of secure accommodation; the use of drugs as a means of control; and the withdrawal of parental contact as a means of punishment.

Corporal punishment is still permitted by some local authorities for children in their care. As a former social worker, I have never been able to resolve the apparent contradiction between the vigilance and decisiveness of the state when it comes to parental ill-treatment of children and the official and unofficial barbarity, in both its physical and its emotional manifestations, which may be imposed on those very same children – and others – once they have entered the state care. The HCSSC's equivocation on corporal punishment is quite remarkable. In its reports it merely recommends the DHSS 'to incorporate regulations in quite specific policy towards corporal punishment in community homes'.[47] The case for abolition has previously been recognized at the DHSS[48] and should now be acted upon.

Apart from corporal punishment, another means of control is the placement of children in secure accommodation. On 31 March 1984, 241 children were locked up in care.[49] SSDs may place children in care in secure accommodation if there is a danger of their absconding; but the child must have a history of absconding *and* be likely to abscond from other accommodation *and* be likely to be at physical, mental or moral risk. Lock-up accommodation may also be used if there is a risk of injury to the child or others.[50] When a child has been placed in secure accommodation for seventy-two hours, the case must be reviewed by a court which has the power to extend a placement for up to three months. The court review is a recent enactment following concern about abuses expressed by the CLC. Six months after the implementation of the new legislation, the CLC conducted a survey and discovered that, out of 182 court reviews studied, 178 were successful in favour of local authorities. This suggests that 'magistrates are rubber stamping the local authorities' applications – possibly because the child's lawyer is insufficiently vigorous'.[51] It should be noted that children under ten cannot be placed in secure accommodation without the prior consent of the Secretary of State.

The research into secure accommodation and difficult children points not only to their ineffectiveness but also to the shortcomings of more open forms of residential care. A DHSS report concluded: 'save in a small number of severe cases, troublesome behaviour in an institutional setting is produced by the institution rather than being an attribute of the individual.'[52] It is instructive to consider that in another CLC survey four local authorities said they did not run or make use of secure accommodation and one of them stated that they preferred to consider more positive ways of dealing with troublesome children.[53] In advocating the complete abolition of lock-ups,

NAYPIC exposes the contradictions involved when they juxtapose the position of those in care with those out of care.

> Why should young people in care be locked up, when those not in care can only be locked up if they commit a serious criminal offence or are so mentally ill they have to be 'sectioned' for compulsory medical treatment?[54]

In the light of the available evidence about difficult children and secure accommodation, it is hard to argue with NAYPIC's demand.

The use of drugs or 'the liquid cosh' to control children in care is not unknown, although its precise extent is difficult to gauge. Certainly individual cases can be cited.[55] Recent concern about the forcible injection of a young person in care with major tranquillizers prompted the DHSS to issue guidelines for their use in secure accommodation. The relevant circular restricts the use of tranquillizers to situations where there is a danger of harm to others or self-harm. Care and medical staff must agree, however, after a full assessment, that such a danger exists to the point where medication can be justifiably given to avert it.[56] Drugs can be used to medicalize difficult behaviour problems and, as Ron Lacey has pointed out, their side-effects can be downright dangerous.[57]

Other forms of control can be symptomatic of the failings of open institutions. The practice of transferring children from one care setting to another is an example. In such circumstances there is a real danger of inculcating a sense of failure in children as well as risking the harmful effects of experiencing too many placements in care – a lack of security being an obvious but vital one. It is worth noting, however, that a change of placement can be brought about by the closure of a community home, and section 18 can be used to some effect in such cases. When objections were raised to the closure of Richmond House in Solihull, for instance, it was argued in court that such an action was not consistent with section 18. Solihull Council was forced to think again, by finding suitable alternative placements for residents, even though ultimate closure of the home was not prevented.[58]

Other degrading forms of punishment can be imposed, particularly after initial attempts to abscond. For example, in one local authority where I worked, it was a common punishment to make children wear pyjamas to deter further attempts to abscond. In the same authority, the denial of home leave to parents was also used as a form of punishment. Apart from being a gross infringement of a child's rights, such a practice is hardly conducive to early rehabilitation to parents.

Parental contact

A child's contact with parents may be prevented in other ways. Recent shifts in the child care policies and practices of SSDs have resulted in trends towards child rescue and permanency planning (i.e. the early placement of children entering care with substitute families if speedy rehabilitation with natural parents is not possible); this is often thought to be in the best interests of the child. This process may – and often does – involve the severing of the child's ties with natural parents in favour of long-term fostering with a view to adoption or indeed an immediate placement for adoption. There are cases where parental contact is undesirable: for example, in situations where there is real danger to the child or where the child does not want parental contact. The choices, however, may be far from clear cut in all cases.[59]

Administrative and legal procedures can be used to powerful effect to support rescue and permanency. Where children have been admitted to voluntary care (section 2, Child Care Act (1980)) and rehabilitation to natural parents is thought to be unlikely or undesirable, a local authority social services committee can assume parental rights (section 3, Child Care Act (1980)). Parents, particularly single parents, may place their children in voluntary care in stressful situations for reasons quite beyond their control. None the less an increasing proportion of those admitted to voluntary care in recent years have become the subject of a parental rights resolution.[60] This is an administrative procedure carried out by SSDs and their committees to which neither parents nor children are parties. Once a resolution has been passed, parents are informed *afterwards* and while they have the right of appeal to a court few parents actually exercise it.[61] Even in cases where parents successfully appeal, it is not unknown for local authorities to instigate wardship proceedings in the High Court (Family Division) to prevent a child's removal from care. In such circumstances, wardship would give an SSD care and control, while custody would remain with the court until it decided on the child's future. As such decisions can take months, an SSD could persuasively argue against a child's return home because she or he could be well settled in a foster home by the time of a final court hearing. Parental rights resolutions have their roots in the Poor Law and, as recommended by the HCSSC, such powers should only be dispensed within the formal legal procedure of a court.[62]

Place of safety orders (POSOs) (section 28, Child and Young Persons Act (1969)) are a frequent means used by SSDs to remove children from home. Removal is permitted up to a maximum of twenty-eight days on application to a single magistrate before recourse to a full court hearing is required. There was a dramatic increase in POSOs from the early to mid-seventies after the death of Maria Colwell and, although it is difficult to identify the same trends (the figures have been compiled on a different basis since 1976), 'it would seem this increase has been maintained'.[63] POSOs are a major route into care, and the CLC believes that, in the absence of a more immediate appeal for child and parent than twenty-eight days, the law on POSOs is actually in breach of the European Convention on Human Rights.[64]

Once a child has been compulsorily detained in care, parental access may be terminated by a local authority or, in the case of wardship, by the High Court. Parents have the right of appeal (section 12 Health and Social Services and Social Security Adjudication Act (HSSSSA) (1983), and a local authority must give notification to the parent that it has terminated access, but, in order to avoid any appeal, the Authority could simply grant minimal access. Furthermore, under the current legislation (section 12(F), HSSSSA (1983)) children are not a party to the proceedings unless the court so orders it.[65]

Legislation has attempted to afford greater protection to children in parental rights resolution cases, care proceedings and access hearings. In 1984 section 103(1) (2) of the Children Act (1975) was eventually implemented and gave courts the power to appoint guardians *ad litem* to generally safeguard and promote the welfare of the child in these various proceedings. However, the rules involved are a source of potential conflict between the guardian *ad litem* and the child. For example, the guardian *ad litem* could advise the court that a child's welfare would be best served by being in care, while the child, through a solicitor, could argue the very opposite. Such situations are, as the CLC has commented, 'an illustration of the difference between the child's welfare approach (independent assessment by a benevolent adult) and the child's rights approach (advocacy of the child's wishes)'.[66] It is quite possible in these more cautious days for a court to overturn the expressed wishes of the child.

A growing body of opinion has begun to question the tendency towards permanency as it has been developed by SSDs. Greg Kelly, for instance, in a discussion of relevant theories and research, has argued that continued parental contact may well be beneficial to the emotional adjustment of children in care and in accordance with many of their wishes, even though rehabilitation may not be immediately possible.[67] Social work practice can be crucial in encouraging or discouraging parental contact after a child's admission to care. The fact that contact lapses in the first place is associated with the exclusivity of some models of fostering, i.e. where foster parents cannot cope with or have not been prepared for the child's contact with natural parents.[68] Social workers, argues Celia Atherton, can use their powers to give financial support for natural parents to contact their children as well as moral support. In her experience, however, some do not.[69] In the light of the high rates of marital breakdown (one in three marriages break down; and one in five children have divorced parents) and foster parents breakdowns (this can be as high as 50 per cent in long-term foster care); *permanent* alternative placements cannot always be guaranteed.[70] In a series of placement breakdowns, a natural parent may be a child's only consistent figure. An appropriate direction for child care would therefore be towards more open, democratic and shared forms of care between natural parents and the state.

Leaving care

For those who leave care, difficulties can be encountered at almost every important level of their lives. We are referring here principally to those whose time in care comes to an end at the age of eighteen or nineteen. In 1982, 9800 people in these age groups left care, and in recent years this annual total has not altered much.[71] The current statutory responsibilities of local authorities are far from satisfactory. Sections 27, 28 and 29 of the Child Care Act (1980) empower local authorities to give financial help, particularly to assist with accommodation and/or further education, as well as powers to 'advise and befriend' those who have left care. As the HCSSC commented, the present law is 'diffuse', 'misleading' and 'discretionary rather than obligatory', as well as being open to wide interpretation by local authorities.[72]

The shortcomings of the present law and deficiencies in practice can have quite devastating consequences for young people once they have left care.[73] They are likely to be ill prepared for independent living and to lose contact with their previous carers and social workers. It is probable that they will have experienced a number of placements during care and have been in care a long time. There is a good chance too that they will experience uncertainties about their personal identity. These difficulties may be further compounded by a lack of employment, suitable accommodation and educational opportunities. There will be a risk of isolation and a lack of support.

As the National Children's Centre pointed out to the HCSSC, adolescent girls with young babies who have left care are in a particularly vulnerable position.[74] The status of those leaving care is, then, highly marginal and very much a legacy of poor experiences in care. This position is not likely to be helped by current official thinking. At the time of writing, the rather tentative recommendations of the HCSSC[75] on leaving care are likely to be watered down even further because of lack of resources.[76] However, it seems that, to overturn the present very worrying state of play, fundamental shifts in law and child care practice, together with a significant increase in resources, are needed – and as a matter of urgency.

The role of care

While there are denials and violations of the rights of children in care at many levels, these problems cannot be simply related to present administrative, legal and professional deficiencies. It is only by understanding something of the role of care that we can begin to understand how it imposes such limitations on its consumers. In the remaining space, therefore, I shall consider the following questions: who comes into care and why; whether care is preventable; and, finally, in the light of this, what can be done to defend and improve the rights of children in care.

Historically, the development of state care has been inextricably bound up with the control of the poor. The harsh regime of the Poor Law in the nineteenth century, for instance, was concerned to separate children from their parents and tried 'to cut pauperism at its roots, by ensuring for the children in its care moral and industrial training'.[77] The re-education of the children of the poor was a common theme in the workhouses and behind the expansion of boarding out. Rescue and separation were the order of the day. A cardinal principle of boarding out, an early inspector reminds us, was to help the child 'to forget its alien birth and to merge it in the foster family'.[78] Another strategy, encouraged by the Poor Law with the help of voluntary organizations, at this time was the rescue of poor children and their subsequent emigration on a quite massive scale.[79] Permanency planning with a vengeance! It was not until after the Second World War, with the passing of the Children Act (1948) and subsequent legislation, that there was a move away from rescue towards rehabilitation, and preventive work with families. However, in discussing the recent re-emergence of the rescue approach, Kelly suggests that American studies have given legitimacy to permanency in this country, although he points to the methodological weakness of these studies because of differences in legal framework between here and the USA. He also cites the added pressure on social workers not to take risks because of child abuse tragedies as well as the pressure to adopt as further reasons for the trend. Finally, he suggests:

> A tentative political point – 'child rescue' philosophy in child care or 'only the fittest parents survive' was at its pinnacle in the UK when politics and economics were dominated by 'laissez-faire' philosophy that almost despised public expenditure and State intervention on behalf of the poor. This same philosophy has come back to us, in part at least, from across the Atlantic where it has survived the twentieth century almost untouched. Readers will have their opinions of how closely Britain's governing philosophy has moved from the philosophy of the Welfare State back to those of the Victorian era that were so punitive to the poor in general and to the parents of children in care in particular.[80]

The poor undoubtedly remain the main recipients of state care and, as Robert Holman has shown, the children of the poor are disproportionately represented in state care.[81] He has pointed out that those most susceptible to care are likely to come from families with the following sorts of characteristics associated with social deprivation: single-parent families; large families; families of low social class and low income; and families living in inadequate housing.[82] Of those in care on 31 March 1982, 2300 were in care from single-parent families, 8800 because of unsatisfactory home conditions and 1100 because of homelessness.[83]

The centrality of poverty as an explanation for the presence of children in care can be obscured, however, by a process of ideological mystification. Such a process tends to rely more on the individual pathology of those in care and/or their families as an explanation of their predicament rather than on the impact of crucial structural factors. In his study of child abuse, for example, Parton argues that the influential 'disease model' of child abuse, by 'focusing exclusively on the abusive parent . . . has legitimated practices which "blame the victim"'.[84] (At the last count 18,400 children were in care because of neglect or ill-treatment.[85]) He goes on to argue that child abuse can only be adequately explained in relation to the social structure of age, class and gender, and that families with a low socio-economic status are over represented in cases of child abuse.

The process of ideological mystification blinds us to child abuse at other levels:

> the activities of schools, institutions, unemployment, social security systems, racial discrimination, class differentials have more deleterious effects upon the life chances and development of children than the traditional concerns of the child abuse literature, policy and practice. For example, the higher rate of neonatal mortality among social classes IV and V is not seen as abuse, nor is the pharmaceutical industry seen as having complicity in the maiming of children from poorly tested antidepressants or contraceptives.[86]

There are, of course, many other ways in which the poor are blamed for their plight.[87] If Michael Freeman's belief that children have a moral right not to come into care[88] means anything, then tackling poverty must be an essential feature of any strategy designed to prevent care. The implementation of an effective anti-poverty programme is therefore essential and Peter Alcock has recently outlined such a programme. It would have to include a major shift in resources from the rich to the poor. Alcock argues that the effect of present government tax policy to benefit the better off would have to be reversed, while low wages might be tackled by the introduction of a national minimum wage. Although effective strategies to tackle unemployment are crucial, full citizenship needs to be restored to those who cannot work, by scrapping the stigmatizing and confusing present system of benefits. Instead, it could be replaced by a system of paying benefits close to the level of a minimum wage to those men and women out of work without means-testing and contributions conditions. Benefit could also be paid to those in part-time work on an appropriate proportional basis.[89] The recommendation of the HCSSC – 'that the long-term rate of supplementary benefit be extended to unemployed families with children'[90] – is hardly adequate.

The provision of adequate day care for children under five is also important in preventing receptions into care. Devon Social Services Department, for example, noted the low rate of care admissions in those areas with most day care provision, while the reverse applied in those areas with a low provision.[91] Nationally, day care provision is wholly inadequate: it has been estimated that 145,000 places are needed just to cope with the requirements of one-parent families.[92] If children are really to be accorded priority, then we need to think differently about the nature and purposes of day care.[93] At present, day care has to be fitted round employment rather than the other way round. The old sexual divisions of labour around childrearing need to be broken down, so that men and women are enabled to make a public and private commitment to their children, free from economical and emotional restraints, with non-patronizing forms of education for parental responsibilities available to all. Decentralized and democratically run day care services would give more control to local people to fit the needs and wants of their children and themselves. As local authorities are not under a statutory obligation to provide day care, its universal provision, organized along demo-cratic lines, is an essential part of a strategy to prevent care.

While structural changes of the kind described are important, the priorities and practices of SSDs (and their local authorities) can also be structured more towards preventive work. At present, the extent and distribution of resources does inhibit such developments: in 1982–3, for example, the cost of services to children in care was £400 million, while only a little under £15 million was spent on preventive work of various kinds.[94] Under Section 1 of the Child Care Act (1980), SSDs have a duty to promote preventive work and have the power to give 'assistance in kind or, in exceptional circumstances, in cash'. Some authorities interpret the latter part of section 1 very narrowly.[95] There is a need, therefore, to give it broader scope and the power to compel SSDs to use 'assistance' where applicable, as well as the need for expansion in resources.[96] SSDs can also make their services more relevant and accessible to consumers by devel-oping more community-oriented preventive forms of service delivery. One social services area team, reorganized along such lines, reduced the number of its statutory cases by about half in six years.[97] A lot more could be done to prevent care because of homelessness. It is remarkable, not to say punitive, that within the same local authority the housing department can declare a family intentionally homeless, while the SSD has to make arrangements to care for the children or pay to accommodate the family in bed and breakfast.

Juvenile offenders could also be the focus of greater preventive input. At present, about 12,500 are on care orders for offending.[98] The role of SSDs in preventing admission to care on this basis can be crucial both in developing community-based alternatives and by giving greater thought to the court process, particularly the prepara-tion of social enquiry reports.[99] Non-attenders of school should also be the subject of alternatives to care. Around 4000 children are in care as a result of non-attendence of school[100] and almost half are over the school-leaving age! As Tony Jeffs argues elsewhere in this book, the fact that truancy occurs at all may be due more to particular schools than to the pathology of individual truants. It is unlikely, therefore, that the resolution of such problems is to be found through the care system.

The preventive strategies we have outlined are only some of the ways in which care might be prevented or avoided. The central point is that SSDs – even in the absence of relevant structural change – are in a position to restructure their practice more towards prevention. As the HCSSC commented:

> Examination of individual cases cannot but prompt the question as to whether care was or should have become necessary: more help from one agency or another sometime before, a slightly different set of decisions and a child might still be living with his natural family.[101]

Conclusion

In its attempt to act in a child's best interests, the state's treatment of children in care rests uneasily, if not ambiguously, between its functions of care and control. The result is that the state behaves in some strange, if not positively harmful, ways and, invariably, with paternalism as its hallmark. Its target always seems to be the poor. Clearly, a lot more could be done, as we have seen, to prevent admissions to care (and control) in the first place but, even when admission proves inevitable, the state often seems reluctant to share care with parents, despite the fact that this may be important to a child. The many moral rights of children in care find little expression in law. To change the position of children in care, large-scale legal, administrative and attitudinal changes are needed. Children need a more effective say in their conditions of care. If adult society is to be consistent about protecting children from harm, there is a need to acknowledge the adverse effects of state care by establishing an effective and independent complaints procedure along the lines suggested by NAYPIC.[102]

Michael King has argued that the outlook for children's achieving their rights is bleak, since the power to grant such rights lies with adults, who have so far denied room for children's self-determination. He comes to the pessimistic conclusion that, 'unless and until children are able to gain some access to economic and political power, it is difficult to see how their situation within the legal and welfare systems is likely to change'.[103] His position, however, may be in danger of overlooking the power of the ideology espoused by some adults with a commitment to children's rights, as well as the possibilities of consciousness-raising and collective action. King's position could lead to resignation and fatalism but, as Peter Leonard has argued:

> The fact that it is possible ... to make headway, through collective action, in overcoming some of the psychological obstacles produced by subordinacy – deference, fatalism, self-destructive anger – is surely evidenced in the growth of the Women's Movement and black anti-racist movements.[104]

There are certain adults, particularly social workers (a crucial part of the welfare system!), who can be valuable allies to children in care. While the latter's experience of social workers can be contradictory, no doubt reflecting the differences between social workers, valuable allies are to be found among them, as NAYPIC reminds us:

> The most impressive moves forward have come from individuals within the social work system itself who have challenged and changed the old concept of maintaining control which leads to meaningful 'care'. Within some residential homes workers have sought ways to share the decision making with young people and in some cases have given up the concept of 'control' altogether.[105]

For those involved in state welfare work, there is obviously scope to emphasize the more progressive possibilities of their roles in collaboration with children in care. As we have seen, the role of social workers is vital in key decision-making processes. In the earlier days of campaigns around the rights of children in care, some social workers actively supported the formation of local groups such as 'Who Cares?'. The possibility of links between organizations like NAYPIC and social workers' trade unions, such as the National and Local Government Officers' Assocation (NALGO), are some of the ways in which even broader alliances can be forged.[106] Alliances also need to be formed with sympathetic members of the legal profession and organizations like the Family Rights Group (FRG). NAYPIC, although a young organization, has made its presence felt and, given that most children in care are in the older age groups, its potential for new members and greater influence is considerable.

The pay-off from traditional pressure-group politics can be valuable but limited, however. Structural inequality – such a crucial factor in the entry of young people into care – will not, of course, be effectively tackled only by the sorts of practices and alliances described so far. Years of piecemeal social reform have not altered the divisive social relations which place so many in a subordinate position. It is only by connecting with the struggles of other progressive movements in the wider struggle for the socialist transformation of society that structural inequality will disappear. But, in order to achieve the sorts of social relations we would like to see, we need to start developing them here and now.[107]

Notes

1 D. H. Thorpe, D. Smith, C. J. Green and J. H. Paley, *Out of Care: the community support of juvenile offenders* (Allen and Unwin, 1980).
2 DHSS, *Children in Care in England and Wales* (DHSS, 1982), p. 5.
3 Ibid., p. 30.
4 Children and Young Persons Act (1969), sections 20(3) and 21(1).
5 DHSS, *Children in Care*, p. 9.
6 NAYPIC, *Sharing Care* (NAYPIC, 1983), p. 10.
7 DHSS, *Children in Care*, p. 9.
8 N. Tutt, 'Observations and assessment', in *Providing Civil Justice for Children*, ed. H. Geach and E. Szwed (Edward Arnold, 1983); L. Taylor, R. Lacey and D. Bracken, *In Whose Best Interests?* (Cobden Trust/Mind, 1980).
9 N. Tutt, 'Observation and assessment', p. 164.
10 Ibid., p. 204.
11 NAYPIC, *Sharing Care*, p. 10, and The House of Commons Social Services Committee, HMSO, *Children in Care* (second report) (HMSO, 1984), p. lxxx.
12 HMSO, *Children in Care* (Second report), vol. I, p. lxxxvi.
13 Ibid., p. lxxxvii.
14 On 31 March 1982 there were 38,700 children in foster care: DHSS, *Children in Care*, p. 9.
15 National Children's Bureau, Highlight No. 56 Feb. (1983); see also *Children in Care: Second Report* (HMSO, 1984), vol. III, HC 360–III, p. 413.
16 HMSO, *Children in Care* (Second report), pp. cxxi–cxxii.
17 R. Rogers, 'Advertising children', *Childright*, 3 (January 1984), pp. 21–4.
18 HMSO, *Children in Care* (Second report), vol. I, HC360–1, p. x.
19 National Joint Council, *Residential Staff's Joint Inquiry 1984, Final Report* (National Joint Council for Administrative, Professional, Technical and Clerical Services, 1984).
20 Ibid., pp. 83–4.
21 HMSO, *Children in Care* (Second report), p. cxv.
22 Section 27 of the Children and Young Persons Act (1969), as amended by schedule 3(11) of the Child Care Act (1975).

23 Ibid.
24 *A Study of the Boarding Out of Children* (DHSS, 1982), p. 13.
25 M. Stein and S. Ellis, *Gizza Say?* (NAYPIC, 1983), p. 3.
26 CLC, *'It's My Life not Theirs'* (Children's Legal Centre, 1984), p. 26.
27 Ibid., p. 31.
28 Stein and Ellis, *Gizza Say?*, p. 4.
29 NAYPIC, *Sharing Care*, p. 18.
30 CLC, *'It's My Life not Theirs'*, p. 13.
31 Stein and Ellis, *Gizza Say?*, p. 2.
32 CLC, *'It's My Life not Theirs'*, pp. 33–5.
33 Ibid., pp. 34–43.
34 NAYPIC, *Sharing Care*, p. 18.
35 L. Parker, 'Damned by faint praise', *Community Care*, 7 June 1984.
36 Recent consultations between the DHSS and relevant organizations
    hold out little hope for the implementation of effective regulations.
    The proposed regulations are restrictive, infer that reviews are not
    central in decision-making and are to be implemented at no extra cost.
    See *Childright*, 14 (February 1985), p. 4.
37 CLC, *'It's My Life not Theirs'*, pp. 10–11.
38 M. Stein, 'Leaving care: a personal and political issue', *Youth and
    Policy*, 2, 3 (Winter 1983–4), p. 11.
39 NAYPIC, *Sharing Care*, p. 26.
40 R. Page and E. A. Clark (eds), *Who Cares?* (National Children's
    Bureau, 1977), p. 26.
41 NAYPIC, *Sharing Care*, p. 17.
42 *Residential Care for Children in London* (DHSS, July 1982), as
    quoted in *Children in Care: the need for change* (CLC, 1983), p. 34.
43 Page and Clark (eds), *Who Cares?*, p. 26.
44 *Childright*, 11 (October 1984), p. 4.
45 'The 1981 Act and children in care', *Childright*, 18 (June 1985), pp.
    16–17.
46 NAYPIC, *Sharing Care*, p. 24.
47 HMSO, *Children in Care (Second report)*, vol. I, p. lxxxv.
48 CLC, *Children in Care*, p. 43.
49 *Childright*, 16 (April 1985), p. 3.
50 Section 21 (A) Child Care Act (1980), as amended by section 25,
    Criminal Justice Act (1982). See also the Secure Accommodation
    regulations (DHSS, 1983).
51 *Childright*, 6 (April, 1984), p. 5.
52 DHSS, *Research Report No. 5*, 1979. Children referred to closed
    units as quoted in CLC, *Locked up in Care* (CLC, 1982), p. 8.
53 Ibid., p. 4.
54 NAYPIC, *Sharing Care*, p. 14.
55 See *Childright*, 1 (October 1983), p. 4, and Taylor et al., *In Whose
    Best Interests?*, pp. 80–4.
56 *Childright*, 5 (March 1984), p. 13.
57 Ibid., pp. 12–13.

58 *Childright*, 3 (January 1984), p. 4.
59 N. Parton, *The Politics of Child Abuse* (Macmillan, 1985), p. 124.
60 DHSS, *Children in Care*, p. 5.
61 HMSO, *Children in Care (Second report)*, vol. 1, p. lviii.
62 Ibid., p. lix. It has been recommended that parental rights resolutions for those at risk if removed from voluntary care, should be replaced by fairer, simpler care proceedings. These would also govern other children. If children are already in voluntary care but not at risk of positive harm, then the use of private law, such as adoption, is recommended. See DHSS, *Review of Child Care Law* (HMSO, 1985), pp. 28–9.
63 Parton, *The Politics of Child Abuse*, pp. 122–3.
64 CLC, *Children in Care*, p. 21. The DHSS has recommended legal changes concerning POSO's which includes renaming them Emergency Protection Orders and limiting their duration to a maximum of eight days. DHSS, *Review of Child Care Law*, pp. 25–7.
65 It has been proposed that there should be a presumed right of access, that parents should be able to apply to the courts to have access defined and, interestingly, that children should have the right to apply for access, to parents and others. DHSS, *Review of Child Care Law*, pp. 39–40.
66 *Childright*, 7 (May 1984), p. 8.
67 G. Kelly, 'Natural parent contact – a theory in search of practice', in *Permanent Substitute Families: security or severance?* (Family Rights Group, 1984).
68 R. Holman, 'Exclusive and inclusive fostering', *Fostering Parental Contact* (Family Rights Group, 1984).
69 C. Atherton, 'Permanency planning for children in care', in *Permanent Substitute Families*, p. 22. The DHSS has recommended that the expenses of a child wishing to visit a parent or some other person should also be met. DHSS, *Review of Child Care Law*, pp. 20–1.
70 Ibid., p. 28.
71 DHSS, *Children in Care*, p. 13.
72 HMSO, *Children in Care* (Second report), vol. I, p. cxvii.
73 M. Stein, 'Leaving care', pp. 10–12.
74 HMSO, *Children in care* (Second report), vol. I, p. cxvi.
75 Ibid., pp. cxvii–cxix.
76 See DHSS, *Review of Child Care Law*, p. 22.
77 J. Heywood, *Children in Care* (Routledge and Kegan Paul, 1959), p. 68.
78 Ibid., p. 87.
79 Kelly, 'Natural parent contact', pp. 12–13.
80 Ibid., pp. 18–19.
81 R. Holman, *Inequality in Child Care*, Poverty Pamphlet 26 (CPAG and FRG, 1980).
82 Ibid., pp. 15–16.
83 DHSS, *Children in Care*, pp. 16–17.

84 Parton, *The Politics of Child Abuse*, p. 149.
85 DHSS, *Children in Care*, p. 16.
86 Parton, *The Politics of Child Abuse*, p. 168.
87 Holman, *Inequality in Child Care*, pp. 31–3; see also C. Jones, *State Social Work and the Working Class* (Macmillan, 1983).
88 M. D. A. Freeman, *The Rights and the Wrongs of Children* (Frances Pinter, 1983), p. 150.
89 P. Alcock, 'Welfare State – safety net or poverty trap', *Marxism Today* (July 1985), pp. 13–14.
90 HMSO, *Children in Care* (Second Report), p. xxi.
91 *Children in Care – Portsmouth* (Social Services Research and Intelligence Unit, 1975).
92 R. Simpson, *For the Sake of the Children* (National Council for One-Parent Families, 1980).
93 M. E. David, 'Motherhood and social policy – a matter of education', *Critical Social Policy*, 12 (Spring 1985), pp. 28–43.
94 *Childright*, 8 (June 1984), p. 2.
95 HMSO, *Children in Care* (Second Report), p. xxii.
96 Initial government response to the HCSSC report suggests that the words 'in exceptional circumstances' may be deleted. See *Childright*, 17 (May 1985), p. 5.
97 M. Cooper, 'Community social work', in *The Political Dimensions of Social Work*, ed. R. Jordan and N. Parton (Blackwell, 1983), p. 159.
98 DHSS, *Children in Care*, p. 17.
99 R. Allen, 'Social workers and the juvenile court', *Youth and Policy*, 11 (Winter 1984–5), pp. 46–8.
100 DHSS, *Children in Care*, p. 17.
101 HMSO, *Children in Care* (Second Report), vol. I, p. xvii.
102 NAYPIC, *Sharing Care*, pp. 29–30: The DHSS endorse the need for a complaints procedure but does not wish to specify the form it should adopt. DHSS, *Review of Child Care Law*, p. 20.
103 M. King, 'Welfare and justice', in *Childhood, Welfare and Justice*, ed. M. King (Batsford Academic, 1981), p. 134.
104 P. Leonard, *Personality and Ideology* (Macmillan, 1984), pp. 205–6.
105 NAYPIC, *Sharing Care*, p. 3.
106 S. Bolger, P. Corrigan, J. Docking and N. Frost, *Towards Socialist Welfare* (Macmillan, 1981), p. 103.
107 See, for example, London to Edinburgh Weekend Return Group, *In and Against the State* (Pluto Press, 1980).

Further reading

Children in Care: Second Report from the Social Services Committee, vol. I, HC360–1 (HMSO, 1984).
Childright (Journal of the Children's Legal Centre).
M. D. A. Freeman, *The Rights and the Wrongs of Children* (Frances Pinter, 1983).

H. Geach and E. Szwed, *Providing Civil Justice for Children* (Edward Arnold, 1983).

R. Holman, *Inequality in Child Care* Poverty Pamphlet 26 (Child Poverty Action Group and Family Rights Group, 1980).

NAYPIC, *Sharing Care* (National Association of Young People in Care, 1983).

R. Page and G. A. Clark (eds), *Who Cares?* (National Children's Bureau, 1977).

N. Parton, *The Politics of Child Abuse* (Macmillan, 1985).

Permanent Substitute Families: security or severance? (Family Rights Group, 1984).

L. Taylor, R. Lacey and D. Bracken, *In Whose Best Interests?* (Cobden Trust/Mind, 1980).

DHSS Report, *Review of Child Care Law* September 1985.

5

Juvenile Justice and Children's and Young People's Rights

Robert Adams

In the last thirty years, professionals, the lay public and the media have keenly debated the problems of juvenile crime and the best ways of responding to them. Proposed solutions range from tougher custodial measures or even corporal punishment at one extreme, to radical, or some would say *laissez-faire*, non-intervention at the other;[1] in between range a variety of supervisory or treatment schemes in the community.

Although in one sense these controversies are not new, many observers see young people in our era as uniquely disruptive.[2] Since the late 1960s the younger generation is supposed to have undergone a liberating, even permissive, revolution which it is often said combines with a lack of parental discipline to exacerbate youth crime problems.[3] It is a sobering fact that, despite the varied proposals to deal with delinquency, none has proved to be particularly effective. Recent legislation, such as the Children and Young Persons Act (1969) and Criminal Justice Act (1982), has been no more capable of curbing youth crime than are the activities of the major parts of the juvenile justice system themselves – police, probation and social services departments, juvenile courts, custodial institutions and their community alternatives.

Meanwhile, the centre of gravity of discussion about juvenile justice remains not just professionally but adult-dominated. This is a fact which this chapter acknowledges but, like books on children generally, does little or nothing to dislodge. Nevertheless, the discussion which follows attempts to address some of the major issues concerning rights in juvenile justice. But this is best undertaken in the third part of the chapter, after a review of the rights of children and young people in different parts of the juvenile justice system has been set in the context of youth crime problems and policies.

Youth crime problems and policies

Nowhere is the paradoxical position of youth in society more vividly illustrated than in and around the juvenile justice system. Demographically, children and young people are on the decline, but in the media and in the eye of public attention they represent a growing problem. In 1980 there were 6.3 million teenagers in Britain and by 1994 there will be just over 4.5 million. In some parts of the country, the consequence of this demographic trend in the 1980s has been declining school rolls and falling numbers of young offenders appearing in courts.[4] Yet, in the longer term, recorded juvenile crime has increased and at the same time, whenever public attention has turned to the issue of rising crime, the focus of discussion has tended to be upon youth crime, and especially upon crimes of violence committed by young people. The puzzling feature of this is that while the increase has been marked – a 30 per cent increase in recorded juvenile crime in the past twenty years – it is no more than the increase in recorded adult crime. Even these increases are as much the reflection of policing practices and statistical methods of recording as any certain measure of the actual nature and incidence of crime itself.[5]

Ironically, children and young people in trouble may be seen as convenient scapegoats for many of the shortcomings of an unequal society which until recently failed to recognize, let alone guarantee, their rights to justice. By a strange inversion of logic, those who call stridently for harsher punishments or more effective treatment speak as though ignorant of the social conditions contributing to youth crime. The juvenile justice system itself manifestly fails to reduce delinquency,[6] while parts of the system actually create more crime.[7] Young offenders lose out whether they are held responsible for, or excused, their offences. Either way, they have little real direct voice or choice in what happens to them. Adults have shaped the contemporary circumstances which offer children the certainty of relative powerlessness, class, ethnic and gender inequalities, the likelihood of scholastic failure, poor or nonexistent jobs and ultimately the possibility of nuclear extinction. Paradoxically, when young people respond to these conditions by misbehaving, disrupting the classroom, running riot on the football terraces or otherwise breaking the law, adults often react as though young offenders are either inherently bad or as if they are acting out deep-seated personal problems.

The contemporary context in which youth crime policy is produced and administered is fraught with the same kinds of conflicts and controversies that characterize the making of other social policies. But, for whatever reasons, youth has often assumed the centre of the stage in post-war moral panics about the crisis of order in our society.[8] It is not surprising to find controversy wherever one looks in the juvenile justice system, from the harsher aspects of post-war legislation as exemplified in the development of detention centres,[9] to the more progressive spirit of social democracy displayed in the Children and Young Person's Act (1969)[10] and the subsequent retrenchment of the Criminal Justice Act (1982).

Professionals working in and around the juvenile justice system – social workers, probation officers, youth workers, institutional staff, police, magistrates, and so on – are not insulated from the problems and conflicts generated around youth crime, but experience these in the uncertainties and constraints of their own jobs. But if professionals involved in juvenile justice face difficulties and dilemmas in day-to-day decision-making, children and young people with whom they are working face them with even greater intensity. For children and young people the situation is doubly difficult, because they are not only offenders but young as well. Many people would assert that by the very act of committing a crime a young person forfeits even those limited and precarious rights and privileges which are held by other young people.

Commentators on youth crime policy are not exempt from the problems of uncertainty which afflict young people and those who work with them. But what emerges from reviewing the literature on juvenile justice is the way in which most commentators have become fixated upon its professional dilemmas, contradictions and shortcomings. So not only are the circumstances of lay, professional and consumer participants in juvenile justice riven with the kinds of contradictions and constraints permeating the system itself, but it is difficult to find commentators who, subject as they may be to the same circumstances, have been able to stand back from the process of juvenile justice and view it both knowledgeably and critically. In 1979 it was noted with concern that until the late 1970s even the radical critiques of juvenile justice remained largely confined to the realms of theory and rhetoric, detached from both the providers and the consumers of the system.[11]

It is very hard to reconcile the way many adults react to delinquents with the realities experienced by the young people themselves. Perhaps this is partly because the contradictions embedded in official responses to youth crime express societal ambivalence towards delinquents and potential delinquents. On the one hand, children in trouble and at risk are seen as victims of their circumstances in need of help, yet, on the other hand, they may be pictured as though they are capable of bringing sociey to a state of collapse. In the early 1970s West Yorkshire police campaigned against vandalism and associated crime. They used a poster depicting an unshaven, close-cropped, ape-like young man bearing a hammer, with the motto 'COMBAT THE URBAN GORILLA'. At that very time, the police were co-operating with youth, probation and social services departments and voluntary agencies to produce intermediate treatment schemes for the care and support of what one presumes were essentially the same children and young people.

Official and professional focuses on delinquency are distinctive also for their areas of omission and neglect. Women and girls suffer particularly in this male-dominated area.[12] It seems likely that girls experience responses to their deviance differently from boys. This reflects longstanding gender-linked divisions in society, often expressed in protectiveness towards girls and punitiveness towards boys.[13] But gender difference may exert a more subtle and sinister influence over the treatment of deviants. In school, Lynn Davies[14] has found that embedded constructs of 'normal' behaviour are biased towards expectations of male misbehaviour. So when girls misbehave they are much more likely than boys to be seen as behaving atypically and therefore in a disturbed or extreme way. A further paradox is that, while girls may attract particular attention when they offend, their deviance is likely to be reviewed more sympathetically than boys' offences. Perhaps the truth is that many females remain so to speak 'invisible' as offenders largely because their behaviour can be explained as symptomatic of emotionalism, women's irrationality, the time of the month, or whatever. It is true that activities for female young offenders in custody are geared towards home-making and domestication. But the most glaring recent illustration of the above processes is the way in which during the 1970s the redevelopment of the prison at Holloway, with its women and baby and young offenders' accommodation, has witnessed the medicalization of women's crimes. That is, official policy shifted towards viewing the prison as a hospital and putting a medical officer in charge. Perhaps such policy shifts can be dismissed as superficial or shortlived, but it is undeniable that in the past decade the women's movement had to fight against the philosophy of the new Holloway. Their argument for women's right to be considered bad, rather than sick, has echoed through the prisoners' rights movements in the penal system of many Western countries.

Has the context and character of youth crime policy always been such a vexed question? On the whole, the answer is yes. Comment-

aries in the liberal mainstream of social administration have tended
to write in an evolutionary way of the steady, if slow and uneven,
progress which has been made in the juvenile justice system towards
a better deal for children and society over the past 150 years.[15] It is
true that some areas of progress can be noted, but these vary
according to the vantage point of the observer. Thus the welfarist
lobby may see progress as synonymous with the growth of
professional intervention in the juvenile court by social workers,
while the advocates of justice may view this as a step away from
meeting the requirements of the natural rights of the child.[16] Further,
a critical view of social policy is likely to express reservations about
whether change is necessarily progress.[17] Criminologists may tend to
amplify these doubts with more specific concerns. Is the juvenile
justice system more caring, more humane, more just, more effective
than it used to be? Does the system guarantee more than hitherto the
rights of children and young people? Many would give a negative
answer to these questions.

But it is as inaccurate to dismiss any claims that significant change
has occurred since mid-Victorian days as it is to assert that change is
synonymous with progress. The latter part of the nineteenth century
saw tremendous efforts made in many spheres of the education, work
and leisure of children as a whole, and working-class children in
particular, to protect them from the worst excesses of hardship and
exploitation. As far as young offenders were concerned, Mary
Carpenter's campaign to have children treated separately from, and
less harshly than, adults was symbolized in the achievement of the
Reformatory Act (1854). The Children Act (1908) further segregated
juvenile from adult procedures of criminal justice and exemplified a
drift towards welfare in a system which has remained poised uneasily
for a hundred years now between preoccupations with justice for, and
the welfare interests of, the child. In general, in Britain and the USA,
the dominant theme of this period has been child rescue rather than
justice for children.[18] More specifically, it can be argued that in
Scotland the Social Work Act (1968) shifted the balance even further
towards welfare. In the Republic of Ireland the spirit of the 1908 Act
still holds, while in England and Wales the Children and Young
Persons Act (1933) and (1969) have produced a situation somewhere
between these two.[19]

If it is true that the roots of the theme of justice in Britain lie far
back in Magna Carta and the Bill of Rights, with their attempts to
protect the individual from the exercise of arbitrary power, then in
more recent times the preoccupation with welfare may be traced, at
least in part, to the growing influence of the professions which have

their rationales in the emergent disciplines of psychology and psychiatry. One consequence of the 'psychiatric deluge' in social work and allied professions so graphically described by Kathleen Woodroofe[20] may have been the tendency to subordinate children and medicalize the explanation and treatment of their problem behaviour which has been illustrated in the Children and Young Persons Act (1969).

In summary, the context in which youth crime policy is produced and operates both reflects and reinforces the problematic situation of youth in society. It also produces difficulties in reaching any consensus about how much consideration should be given to young people when they commit offences. Quite apart from the vexed question of whether an irreducible core of a young offender's rights should always be defended, different issues concerning rights are prominent at different stages of the criminal justice process. It is not possible to identify a clear correlation between particular preoccupations and different parts of the system. But some comments can be made about issues which arise in specific settings. These need looking at in more detail.

Rights in the juvenile justice system

There is a lack of literature discussing the rights of children and young people in the juvenile justice system. In part, this reflects the low status of juveniles, the principal parties, but also it may be linked with the extraordinary difficulty of arriving at a universally agreed statement of what rights are held, or what rights should be held. Behind this lies the further problems of the theoretical position from which rights are conceived.

Short-circuiting detailed examination of these difficulties here, the most helpful conceptualization has been provided by Dworkin,[21] who argues convincingly against a narrow legalistic approach to the charting of rights. He points up the limitations of a positivist conception of law as a fixed set of legal rules, independent of its social and political context. He prefers the search for statements of rights to expose at the outset the moral and political assumptions which underlie the principles on which they are based in particular settings. Once these principles are unearthed, it is possible to address much more constructively the question of, say, the rights of young offenders in custody. Of course, this does not mean that decisions about their rights will be arrived at easily. Dworkin's argument is that specific rights may be clarified only after 'hard cases' have gone through the courts. But he insists that this admittedly difficult struggle, often producing no single agreed or unambiguous statement for all time, will be much more likely to serve the interests of the parties concerned. Further, the worst excesses of moral panics and media sensationalism may be mitigated, since the judgements in such cases will refer back to principles already established rather than to the vagaries of current popular opinion.

So advocates of children's and young people's rights may be well advised to advance their cause, not through legal change alone, but with reference to principles concerning the injustice or unfairness of treating people in a particular way.

Turning now to specific parts of the juvenile justice system, the entire way in which a young offender is processed after apprehension potentially cancels his or her rights. Intrinsically, these processes are depriving. Many are concerned with at best requiring young people to give information, make statements, confess, promise to repay, undergo 'voluntary' treatment, live in a 'specified environment', or carry out a 'specified activity' for a prescribed period (Children and Young Persons Act (1969), section 12).

The organizational and institutional structures which buttress these processes and provide rationales for professional intervention are essentially coercive. This is not simply to imply, as Salaman does, that organizations in a capitalist society are concerned fundamentally with control.[22] The reality of the power vested in police, penal staff and others in similar positions is that in the last resort they can deploy it physically to force offenders and suspects to do as they are told. But, while an examination below of policing, the courts, custody and community alternatives confirms the general tenor of these pessimist statements, it also reveals the complexity of the processes of juvenile justice, which makes it impossible to stereotype them as mere social control, or to dismiss them altogether, at the stroke of a pen.

Policing

Over a decade ago, commentators on juvenile justice noted that police powers were growing,[23] and this trend continues with the Police and Criminal Evidence Act (1984). This affects young people particularly in the following areas: powers to stop, search and arrest without a warrant; powers to detail suspects, carry out intimate searches, interrogate suspects and delay access to legal advice for up to thirty-six hours. These measures contain certain safeguards of the rights of young people, but the cumulative effect is to increase police powers so as to restrict those rights. Expert opinion predicts that relations between children, young people, their families and the police will deteriorate as a consequence.[24]

A groundswell of criticism of police activities has increased in parallel with the extension of their powers. It has come from many sources, including professional bodies and pressure groups, as well as official reports. The Scarman Report, following the 1981 riots, identified racial discrimination as a major source of social tension,[25] and Shahin and Keith Popple in their discussion of black children's rights show how young black people received more severe policing than their white counterparts. In evidence to the Royal Commission on Criminal Procedure, the National Youth Bureau drew attention to numerous areas of encroachment by police on the rights of suspects and offenders.[26] Moreover, concern was expressed about the fact that many young people were uncertain about their rights when detained in a police station – which obviously affected adversely their ability to exercise them.[27]

The police are prominent gatekeepers of the juvenile justice process. Yet police forces, with their paramilitary discipline, are administratively and ideologically detached from other agencies such as education, probation and social services, which are also key components in the juvenile justice system. One effect has been that, since the Children and Young Persons Act (1969) legitimated multi-agency juvenile liaison as part of the decision-making about whether juveniles should be prosecuted, forces have developed differing practices, leading to wide variations in cautioning rates in different areas.[28] Some police forces pursue a justice approach to cautioning, simply considering the nature of the offence and the offender's criminal history, while others bring welfare considerations into all stages of decision-making.

But in many localities probation and social services negotiate delicately with the police, aware of the reality that the juvenile justice system is not a system so much as a jumble of loosely yet unavoidably linked agencies, and aware of the role of policing in 'shaping and editing the whole flow of cases which eventually come before the court'.[29] Of current concern is the tendency for police in some areas to pursue instant cautions for first and some second less serious offenders, largely as an expedient cost-saver, thus bringing within the net of official intervention many juveniles who would have escaped with a ticking-off. Further, recent Home Office guidelines (HO Circular 14/1985), suggesting that informal warnings should be considered where possible rather than formal cautions, have been incorporated by some police forces into 'no further action' procedures. This tends to reduce the opportunities for preventive activity on a multi-professional, but informal, front.

Finally, there is a virtual lack of any formal liaison between the police and groups of children and young people themselves, as part of the juvenile liaison process.[30] In addition, despite circulars urging consultation with children and families (HO Circular 70/1978), there seems to be little sign in individual juvenile liaison proceedings of the interests of the child being independently represented, save through the inevitably partisan voices of the professionals already participating.

Courts

The twin but opposed themes of justice and welfare have been present in juvenile justice since the mid-nineteenth century, when children began to be sharply distinguished from adults in the penal system. But since the Children Act (1908) justice has been softened increasingly by a concern for the individual offender. Given the legitimation of welfare or treatment in child care in both the Children and Young Persons Act (1969) in England and Wales and the Social Work (Scotland) Act (1968), only in the Irish Republic was much of the ethos of the old 1908 Act extant by the 1970s. The offenders' rights movement in general and children's rights movement in particular have attacked the welfare and treatment assumptions of this recent legislation. It is argued that the welfare emphasis on needs contradicts the client's rights by professionalizing aspects which previously and properly lay beyond professional understanding. King has amplified these criticisms. Primarily, he maintains that professional activity all too often reifies children's behaviour, regarding it as a characteristic of them rather than as arising from their circumstances. Further, there is in court a disproportionate emphasis on the past, whereas it is a child's future which is at stake. Similarly, there is a tendency to view children's behaviour in a deterministic way, with heredity playing an unduly prominent role, and to focus on the pathology of children and families to the neglect of other influences, including agencies.[32]

It has been argued that in England and Wales the welfare theme has permeated the adult criminal justice system sufficiently to leaven its justice orientation and could safely be abandoned in the juvenile court if, simultaneously, the minimum age of criminal responsibility was raised from ten to twelve and the minimum age for prosecution was raised in keeping with the school-leaving age. Above that age young people would be tried in the adult court, with the minor qualification that the names and other details of those under twenty-one would be withheld from media reporting.[33]

Whatever reforms of courts for juveniles are considered, there is clearly as much room for critical scrutiny of the context and structure of the judicial setting as for technical improvements in its procedures. The issue of indeterminacy in sentencing is dealt with later in this chapter. For the present, some of the more general questions raised by recent research into courts are discussed.

In his study of two juvenile courts, Anderson found wide variations in sentencing policy, courtroom procedure and the way different professionals made their contributions, not least in social enquiry reports. The wide discretionary powers of social workers emerged as questionable in circumstances where it seemed generally difficult for social workers to represent simultaneously the interests of clients and the bench. The impediments to establishing a straightforward accountability of social workers in the juvenile court seemed to be rooted in part in the ambiguity of the aims and philosophy of the court and partly in the history and culture of professional social work itself. All too often, social workers have tended to act on behalf of children rather than on the basis of children's active participation in the decision-making process in and out of court.[34]

But it is important to realize that the ambiguities and moral and professional dilemmas inherent in the court process should be faced but may not be resolved. In an important study of how juveniles actually receive juvenile justice, Parker shows how diverse local outcomes may be for those involved in similar circumstances and the consequent injustice of this. He reaches a depressing conclusion in his comparison of a city and a county area of Merseyside: 'Criminal-juvenile justice is at its best not concerned with social justice. Criminal-juvenile justice, at its worst, may not even be concerned with the minimal safeguards of natural justice.'[35]

As for those young offenders who are dealt with other than in the comparative informality of the juvenile court, Carlen's work demonstrates how the drama of the courtroom illustrates the monopoly by professionals over judicial proceedings. This rigid control is exercised through the physical setting of the magistrates' court, which underpins the relative powerlessness of non-professionals, enforces the social arrangements of the adversarial system and 'atrophies defendants' abilities to participate in them'.[36]

In summary, the view of many rights-oriented critics of juvenile court practice in England and Wales is that a shift towards justice, equality of treatment for like offences and demystification of proceedings would all be positive.

Custody

The custodial sector illustrates contradictory societal attitudes to crime, simultaneously seeking to deprive and punish while also treating and rehabilitating. The institutional rules and procedures tend to protect the interests of staff, the establishment and the state rather than the rights of children and young people. In prisons, any clash between staff and prisoners, the prisoners' constitutional rights are likely to be suspended.[37]

Rules governing penal institutions in general have been drawn up by the Home Office and are concerned with the maintenance of inmates according to conditions of minimal acceptability, in terms of physical, educational, medical or recreational provision. They tend to be too flexible and vague at the point of implementation to be much use to anyone concerned about a specific aspect of the quality of life in an institution.[38]

Despite a vociferous literature of protest, the Official Secrets Act still protects penal institutions from unwary comments by staff and critical external scrutiny. Also, staff in local authority or voluntary community homes may feel informal, but no less real, pressure to watch what they say about their establishments. Secrecy is not a Home Office monopoly.

The contracting community home system apart, many institutions in the rest of the custodial sector are bursting at the seams, despite a large building programme. Penal institutions not designed to stretch beyond 40,000 people increased their numbers to 44,500 in April 1984, 46,000 in spring 1985 and 48,000 in July 1985.[39] The Home Secretary's response is not to take a progressive initiative and give early release to 11,800 short-term prisoners under the Criminal Justice Act (1982) but to turn the remand centre at Wetherby, Yorkshire, into an adult gaol. The transfer of 230 young men at Thorp Arch to the adult prisons at Hull and Leeds, where top-security prisoners[40] are also held, reverses a 150-year trend towards separate treatment of young offenders in the penal system. The safeguarding of rights of remand prisoners for many years has been a hit-and-miss affair. Ten years ago, researchers found limited scope for those on remand to exercise their right to have their cell privately furnished, to choose whether or not to work, or to have newspapers, books and other items supplied, or to have exemption from haircutting or shaving.[41]

It is an oversimplification that, remand prisoners apart, a well-demarcated distinction generally exists in England and Wales between adult and young offenders in custody. Tens of thousands of Borstal trainees have habitually in the past suffered 'storage' in warehouse Borstall allocation wings of Strangeways and Wormwood Scrubs adult prisons. And under the Children and Young Persons Act (1933) children convicted of grave offences may be incarcerated for years cheek by jowl with adults in prisons.

So, given that delinquents cannot expect segregation from adults in custody, or custody as a last resort in institutions which are open to public scrutiny and likely to stop them reoffending, what rights may they reasonably expect to exercise? The depressing answer is that they can anticipate possessing only very few, and then probably only after a struggle. It is no surprise that the Home Office largely ignored Cohen and Taylor's recommendation that a prisoners' charter of rights should be established, including for each prisoner access to all files and case records on him or her and access to all rules and regulations concerning prison life (apart from matters of security).[42] Further, the general overcrowding of penal institutions means that daily living conditions fall far short of what prisoners might expect as a right. In the old Victorian local prisons, the majority of prisoners are locked up, two or three to a cell, twenty-three hours a day, with no sanitary arrangements beyond a chamber pot.

In Juvenile justice in particular, campaigns have focused on conditions in custody, the safeguarding of rights on remand and before and after sentence. Symptomatic of the defensiveness and secretiveness of penal institutions in Britain, however, is the issue of access of children and young people to independent, external legal advice and representation in any matter arising during custody. These rights are underwritten by the European Convention on Human Rights (article 6, 1975).

Few aspects of the way inmates are dealt with in penal establishments have received as much criticism as the conduct of disciplinary proceedings. Although in practice often claimed to be inadequate, the Prison Rules (Home Office 1964, 49.2), in stating that any inmate charged with an offence shall have the right to present his or her own case, express two principles of natural justice: that nobody should act as the judge on behalf of their own interest in a case (*nemo judex in causa sua*) and that both sides of a case should be heard (*audi alteram partem*).[43]

But practical difficulties stand in the way of the implementation of these principles. First, despite pressure from reformers, the authorities display a longstanding reluctance to allow external judicial bodies to adjudicate on matters internal to a custodial establishment. Second, the authorities tend not to accede to claims from outside parties that particular judicial decisions within an establishment should be reviewed by external bodies. Third, the case law of attempts by inmates to make prison adjudications more judicial is equivocal. Not only is it generally not possible to claim that breaches of institutional discipline are criminal offences against society at large and should be investigated as such, but also the European Commission of Human Rights has been known to deny the assertion that all prison adjudications should fall within the scope of article 6.[44]

Rather than attempting to survey the change from Borstal to youth custody provision as well, we shall take the changes in detention centres in recent years as exemplifying the current retrograde trends in custodial regimes for young offenders. If detention centres were originally the experiment which could not be allowed to fail,[45] the new army glasshouse-style regime introduced in two centres in 1979 and extended to all eighteen centres on 6 March 1985 reaches the high peak of illogical penal policy. It simply ignores current evidence that tougher regimes are no more effective than their less tough counterparts. The officially commissioned evaluation by the prison service's own psychologists concluded that the pilot tougher regimes had 'no discernible effect on reconviction rates'.[46]

But more disturbing from the vantage point of young offenders and their rights is the increasing evidence that the centres may well harm young offenders suffering from any weakness in their health, and that the official, but unpublished, guidelines for police surgeons assessing the fitness of young men aged fourteen to twenty for detention are 'improper and inhumane', in the words of one doctor.[47]

Also worrying are the conclusions of an official report to investigate unusually high suicide rates at one of the Scottish detention centres. It found that the grim and largely isolating routine adopted for observing potential suicides was 'a form of gross deprivation rather than treatment and should be abolished'.[48]

Children in care

The situation of children in care is dealt with in chapter 4 by Gerry Lavery. Suffice it to say here that the present position regarding secure accommodation for children in care varies from the unsatisfactory to the positively alarming.[49] The legislative framework is confused and very complex,[50] and increasing numbers

of children and young people are being locked up in these units in the
face of evidence that they produce the very behaviour problems they set
out to curb.[51] According to the DHSS itself, the practice of placing
children in secure accommodation without their having committed a
criminal offence, without any judicial proceedings, without any
opportunity to represent against it or any independent advocacy,
contravenes natural justice[52] and the European Convention on Human
Rights (article 5, paragraph 4; article 6). There is an undoubted and
urgent need for a total overhaul of child care law in this area.[53]

Community alternatives

Non-custodial alternatives include a variety of disposals, such as
conditional discharge, fines and intermediate treatment (IT). The
example of IT highlights the major concerns in this area.

The reality in many local authorities is that harrassed,
overworked practitioners navigate the turbulent waters of the
relationship between society and themselves as society's agent, the
offender and, sometimes, the victim. However bold and clear-cut
the 'community alternatives' aim of local juvenile justice policy may
be, the process of implementing it is not at all straightforward.
Implicit in the philosophy of IT as a community alternative to
custody is the ambiguous role of the social work supervisor of the
child or young person in trouble. He or she is required to befriend
the offender but also to represent society's disapproval of
wrongdoing. Beyond this is the perennial dichotomy between the
role of carer and controller, whose familiarity does not make it
easier to manage. More significant from the standpoint of rights,
however, is the option practitioners face of adopting either a
treatment approach or acting as the advocate of the offender. This
may seem to be nothing much more than a reformulation of the
'befriend or disapprove' dilemma, but it may acquire much more
significance. Some practitioners find the question of whose side they
are on much more problematic than do others.[54]

The abiding impression left by this brief review of the juvenile
justice system is of considerable diversification in post-war provision
and the consequent difficulty of making general prescriptions to
guarantee children's and young people's rights within and around
the system, let alone translating these into specific procedures or
arrangements. Informed opinion among commentators on judicial
efforts to improve the status of prisoners in custody in general

acknowledges the limited ability of individual case activity to achieve significant change in the penal system.[55] Further, the dispersed and disparate nature of struggles for rights in other settings raises the disturbing possibility that reformist activity has been concentrated on the surface, the visible consequences of state responses to youth crime, rather than penetrating to the nature of state power itself as expressed in the structuring of institutional and community arrangements to deal with delinquents. This is discussed further towards the end of this chapter.

Perspectives on rights in juvenile justice

This final section examines six ways of approaching rights in juvenile justice: protection, proceduralism, exemptionism, effectivism, liberation and reconstruction. These terms are convenient descriptive labels for approaches each of which has a particular emphasis and illustrates certain theoretical assumptions. But none of them has an exclusive claim on one theoretical position, and neither do they represent together an exhaustive typology. The limited objective of this discussion is to evaluate the relative merits of different responses to the question of rights. Pat Carlen's paper on rights in the penal system in general[56] has helped the thinking in this section. But Carlen's discussion of strategies is especially relevant to the adult sector of the penal system, while the discussion below takes account of concerns which apply particularly to the juvenile justice system.

Protection

The twentieth-century growth of protectionism is fed by the twin nineteenth-century impulses of child rescue and welfare. The central concern of protectionists is to shield youngsters from harm within the juvenile justice system. The assumption is that children and young people are immature and weak and therefore dependent on adults, who act in their best interests. Protectionism may draw heavily on developmental psychology of a more or less psychoanalytic kind. In the past, campaigners for the rights of children have been concerned with saving them from poverty, urban corruption, delinquency, Godlessness, or all of these. The contemporary reworking of protectionist beliefs and practices still leaves clearly visible their paternalism. Protectionists may see the child's developmental interests as paramount, but at the same time they assume they know what is in the best interests of the child.

To the extent that protection may be identified with the defects of welfare, it is possible to dismiss it out of hand. Again, if juxtaposed simply with a libertarian position, protectionism seems to be anachronistic and not at all the approach to advocate in a book on children's rights! But it should be noted that in many parts of juvenile justice – in the police station or in the penal institution – young people may need all the external protectiveness they can get! The achievements of protectionism are not to be belittled. Many substantial reforms have been effected by philanthropists acting on behalf of children. A further strength of protectionism is that it emphasizes the need for accepting the validity of children's rights – to autonomy, for instance – without at the same time leaving them to it. The weakness of protectionism is its rationale, which may foster a benign condescension towards youth. Arguments commonly advanced on the grounds of children's relative lack of experience, wisdom, competence, maturity, foresight, judgement and irrationality are all subject to the criticism that many children possess these qualities to a greater degree than many adults.

The problem with paternalism is that it easily creeps into situations where decisions are allegedly based on the child's right to choose, yet in the context of assumptions which adults have made already. Goldstein and Freud, for instance, in discussions about children's needs and rights, have acknowledged that children whose parenting is interrupted for one reason or another have a paramount right to good parenting from the best available potential parent. But then it emerges that this right only operates within the constraint of the authors' own a priori assumption that, say, a child/foster parent relationship has little chance of being effective.[58] In such circumstances, it is difficult to understand how the rights of children to choose effective relationships may be maintained when their actual power to choose is taken away beforehand by the assumptions of experts. It may be possible to tackle this dilemma by distinguishing circumstances in which children's offences make them the net losers, when protection is thus the appropriate tactic, and circumstances in which someone else is the net loser, in which case control should be uppermost. But while this simple distinction may apply in most circumstances the complexities which arise in child care cases make it difficult to apply in all situations.

Proceduralism

The efforts of proceduralists tend to be concentrated upon the complex processes of juvenile justice. Lawyers and other professionals with an interest in legal reform are most likely to adopt a proceduralist stance. Procedural reform is a banner under which traditional and radical lawyers may fight side by side, and it intersects with the concerns of exemptionists and socialists.

In the USA the Juvenile Justice Standards Project some years ago set up ten juvenile justice principles: proportionality of sanctions to the class of offence, determinate sentences, the least restrictive alternative, the removal of non-criminal misbehaviour from the jurisdiction of the court, making decision-making visible and accountable, the right of the juvenile to counsel, the right of the juvenile to decide on actions affecting his or her life (such as whether to accept treatment), recognition of separate roles and representation for parents and children, the limitation on intervention prior to adjudication, and the waiver of juvenile court jurisdiction where the age of the young person and the seriousness of the offence warrant transfer to a higher court.

These standards seem to offer a clear way forward and have been used by some as a basis for a natural justice approach to young people's rights.[59] But they have been criticized for their ambivalent rejection of the idea of treatment while advocating voluntary treatment. They have been further criticized for not clarifying priorities in circumstances where a juvenile's interest may conflict with the community's interest. More important limitations emerge, however, in the implicit recognition of the lack of effectiveness of treatment. Further, 'the standards barely disguise the author's mistrust of the major decision makers in the juvenile justice system: the police, the probation service, the judiciary and the correctional authorities.'[60]

But how can substantive change take place in the system by mere technical improvement in its procedures, if fundamental reasons for mutual lack of faith in the effectiveness and activities of its components need tackling? Progress in juvenile justice is not synonymous with procedural or legal reforms and depends for its significance on the context and spirit in which they are operated.[61] Further, legalistic trends in juvenile justice may divert attention from the political nature of the problems that law claims to solve. But this argument deserves only qualified support. It is reminiscent of the criticism of community law centres, about which justifiable reservations have been expressed.[62]

So the legalization of children's rights in juvenile justice is a mixed blessing. The strength of law lies in its capacity to provide positive safeguards and restrictions on violations of personal space. Its weaknesses include the risks of distancing children from the means to exercise their own rights, through the mystification that tends to accompany the professionalization of activity.

Implicit in this last observation is the realisation that the conceptualization of children's and young people's rights only makes sense when juxtaposed to a notion of power as an imposition, as a superimposed force, against which some counter-force has to be posed.[63] Further, the limitation of jurido-legal attempts to conceptualize and grapple with power is that in these terms power is seen simply as negative, rather than as a process of emerging partly from below, that is from the young themselves, and therefore as capable of producing its own resistances. The problem is first to appreciate this, and then to do something constructive about it.

Exemptionism

The rationale for exemptionist activity is the principle that individual offenders have the right to no more involvement in the juvenile justice system than is absolutely necessary to meet the requirements of society, and within that system no more than is consistent with their own felt or expressed wishes. Thus, exemptionism is more concerned with the boundaries of juvenile justice than the content of its processes. It may be preoccupied with young people's possessing the right not to be involved more than is necessary, rather than with the quality of that involvement.

Contemporary exemptionists include criminologists and sociologists working to reduce the size and scope of the penal system, with particular reference to institutions. Their concern with the crime-inducing character of many aspects of the juvenile justice system — and custodial institutions in particular — leads them to prescribe the management of delinquency in local authorities on the basis of multi-agency strategies for minimizing the penetration of juveniles into the system, wherever possible. The general consensus among researchers is that the further young people get into the juvenile justice system the more harm it does them.[64] Evidence that the system actively sucks young people in[65] means that exemptionism cannot be achieved simply by turning our backs on its imperialist nature.

Clearly, exemptionism is not radical if used in the sense that the retreatist's escape from the world is a fundamental withdrawal. But it is unfair to belittle the concept in this way. The justice system in general, and the custodial sector especially, are peculiarly resistant to change, if change implies any contraction in power or resources.[66]

Within custodial establishments, exemptionism acquires a

particular force. There is a strong case for offenders having the right to opt out of treatment programmes, and more particularly to be exempted from procedures requiring them to submit to psychotropic and other drugs. This is linked with a longstanding controversy concerning whether offenders have the right to choose punishment rather than treatment, and this issue runs through many parts of the system.

Effectivism

Effectivists ask how the juvenile justice system as it stands can be made more effective. This implies that both the offender and society at large have rights to an effective system, but it does not indicate which of these rights is paramount. The choice is important, because effectiveness may be measured according to different criteria, some of which may be in conflict with each other. For instance, a definition in terms of cost-effectiveness is likely to compete with the attempt to develop an expensive, resource-intensive regime to reduce offenders' future delinquency.

Everyday conflicts may arise also between different parties to the juvenile justice system, and of these the issue of determinate sentences provides a striking example. Indeterminacy is a recurrent butt of critics of various aspects of criminal justice, from those who campaign for bail rights and maximum remand periods, or for remand time in custody to count towards the sentence, to the lobby for the abolition of indeterminate sentences.

Prisoners' rights groups, civil rights organizations and their legal and criminological allies have been in the vanguard of campaigns for determinate sentences. Admittedly, much of this concern has been concentrated on prisoners serving long sentences, but, since the late 1960s, under pressure the Borstal sentence has shifted towards determinacy. This pressure has come partly from the rights lobby and partly as a result of research into the effectiveness of custodial sentencing, which has shown that longer sentences are no more effective than short ones.[67]

Arguments from many diverse viewpoints have converged on indeterminacy. Rights groups claim it is physically and psychologically harmful. The advocates of law and order argue that the offender orientation of indeterminacy may underplay the seriousness of the offence. Judicial critics maintain that giving sentencers and penal staff discretion has increased disparities in sentence lengths.[68] At this point the argument runs parallel with the exemptionist line: the effectiveness of penal sentencing is not affected adversely by a shift towards determinacy. Therefore, offenders should be able to elect for straight determinate punishment sentences rather than rehabilitative sentences where discharge dates are linked with progress towards successful treatment.[69] However, while laudable in itself, the concern with improving the effectiveness of the juvenile justice system neither removes inherent failings of the custodial sector in particular, nor compensates for the failure of the system as a whole to reform individuals or to curb crime.

Liberation

The liberationist assumes that children and young people in trouble, whether with the law or not, possess essentially the same inalienable rights as all other people. Children's liberation challenges the dependent, subordinate status of childhood in society. Liberation movements for children are the converse of, and to an extent complementary with, protectionist campaigns. After all, the libertarian argument for merely achieving equivalent legal regulation for children and adults seems unexceptionable. But, paradoxically, the liberation argument for freeing the young from legal regulation, though consistent with natural justice, can be countered by the view that natural justice is best served by protecting the child's rights at all stages through the due process of law. The difficulties do not end there, since it is undeniable that in some ways children are different from adults. For instance, a child's sense of time differs from that of adults.[70] This raises problems for both libertarian themes just mentioned, but especially it makes much more problematic the task of working out the meaning of an equivalent form of regulation for both children and adults. Quite apart from anything else, there is the difficulty of determining whether the interests of children or adults should have priority, in any conflict of claims to rights.

A further complication is that in no way can the pure liberationist ensure the liberation of all delinquents because there will always be a proportion of young offenders who may need to be dealt with by controlling means. Of course, populism or democratization is one aspect of liberationism which argues for the viability of lay, not to say consumer, participation in the juvenile justice system. But in practical terms the involvement of young people directly as executives is not likely in the juvenile justice system as it stands. Neither, if the history of prisoners' rights movements is anything to go by, would such involvement be likely to succeed on its own in enhancing their rights.[71]

Reconstruction

This radical perspective starts from the recognition that the double ineffectiveness of the juvenile justice system – in curing individual delinquency or curbing juvenile crime – continually contradicts the claims of its professionals. The radical reconstruction of juvenile justice which this implies would necessitate enumerating general principles of children's and young people's rights as referred to above.[72] There is no single blueprint for this reconstruction. Within it, abolitionist,[73] constructivist[74] and social justice[75] stances can all contribute valid versions. Such validity is speculative, though, since the reconstruction of juvenile justice presumes a sympathetic social and political context, a long way from current day-to-day trends, particularly in England and Wales. In this light, it is very hard for radical prescriptions to avoid vacuous generalization and single-line solutions to complex problems on the one hand and tokenism on the other. But there is a case for trying to establish a number of principles in terms of which the rights of children and young people in any particular juvenile justice setting may be worked out, recognizing also the problematic nature of the concept of rights in the system and the contradictory character and consequences of many proposed improvements.[76]

Initially, we need to consider the implications for all parties to juvenile justice of restructuring and relocating professional powers in line with the eradication of inequality, unfairness and inhumaneness in the system. This paves the way for campaigns for the rights of children to be supplemented and even replaced by direct lay and community intervention in the politics of police, juvenile court, custodial and community alternative provision, including agencies such as probation and social services. Even presuming a substantial shift towards a socialized and democratized society, the practical implementation of these principles is likely to involve continual struggles on many fronts simultaneously, to move forward in settings of great complexity.[77] It is necessary to appreciate the ease with which tokenistic change cools out and replaces substantive changes in justice systems which are inherently so resistant to significant change.[78]

The interests of individual children, as well as of classes and groups of children, should be advanced, recognizing the difficulty of managing and reconciling these, where they conflict. Such circumstances provide the 'hard cases' Dworkin uses to clarify principles of rights as applied in practice. Further, children's rights should be viewed from the twin aspects of their parity with, yet difference from, adults. Thus, to fulfil the latter, the developmental needs of children may need to be guaranteed by means of positive protection of their situation. Radical change will not eradicate the awkward reality of negotiating the complexities of coincidence and conflict between the interests of children, professionals and other adults.

Children and young people as offenders need to have their rights as people guaranteed from curtailment by the juvenile justice process. If rights mean also the power to demand,[79] then recognition should be given to the legitimacy of outlawed groups such as offenders in custody to make collective protests as outsiders, making due allowance for their relative powerlessness as a transient or dispersed interest, in contrast with the relatively concentrated and stable power of staff and authorities.

Conclusion

This chapter has demonstrated the complexity of the question of rights and the variety of issues it raises in different parts of the juvenile justice system. Rights in juvenile justice emerge as at least as problematic as the status of children and young people in society as a whole.

Inevitably, such a brief review is incomplete. Each aspect of the juvenile justice process, each agency, deserves a chapter on its own. But enough evidence has been given to indicate that there is massive scope for the improvement of the circumstances of children and young people in a system which itself is failing so obviously either to reform individual delinquents or to reduce the incidence of recorded crime in society. This depressing observation has led to a consideration above of a number of ways in which the situation of children and young people may be improved. Clearly, given the present widespread weaknesses and injustices of the system, a sound reformist argument can be made to support the whole range of improvements represented by the first five perspectives on rights which are outlined. However, we cannot be confident that such moves would achieve any significant improvement. They share the defect that they tend to focus on the situation of the individual rather than upon shortcomings in the juvenile justice system itself. It is hard to escape the conclusion that what is needed is a radically reconstructed juvenile justice system in a fully socialized society. In that case, the reconstruction of the rights of children and young people would also need its own full statement.

In the meantime, perhaps the most paradoxical and penetrating observation on radical endeavour, in the face of the status quo in the criminal justice system, has come from Mathieson: namely, the perception that, in the absence of immediate and major societal change, attempts to make radical shifts, particularly in the rights of offenders, will only survive by remaining perpetually half stated, half spelled out and unfinished. This sobering comment on the tendency of the authorities always to try to outflank reformers and preserve existing structures and processes in the system implies that a manifesto for children's rights should not be spelt out beyond the sketch of general principles in the 'reconstruction' above.

This may be the most honest and realistic way to demonstrate the unfinished and essentially precarious character of rights in juvenile justice. It remains to be seen whether children and young people could do more for themselves than adult reformers have managed to do on their behalf. But there is little evidence that as a whole young offenders are collectively about to exercise their natural right to protest and radically reform the system. We would probably hit them pretty hard if they dared try.[80]

Notes

1   E. Schur, Radical Non-Intervention: rethinking the delinquency problem (Prentice-Hall, 1973).
2   G. Pearson, *Hooligan: a history of respectable fears* (Macmillan, 1983).
3   P. Morgan, *Delinquent Fantasies* (Temple Smith, 1978).
4   J. Cunningham, 'The outnumbered generation', *Guardian*, 29 May 1985, p. 11.
5   Pearson, *Hooligan*.
6   S. Brody, *The Effectiveness of Sentencing: Home Office research study no. 35* (HMSO, 1976).
7   S. Millham, *Locking up Children: secure provision within the child care system* (Saxon House, 1978).
8   S. Hall et al., *Policing the Crisis* (Macmillan, 1978).
9   P. Hall, 'Detention centres: the experiment which could not fail', in *Change, Choice and Conflict in Social Policy*, ed. P. Hall et al. (Heinemann, 1975), pp. 311–70.
10 A. E. Bottoms, 'On the decriminalization of English juvenile courts', in *Crime, Criminology and Public Policy: essays in honour of Sir Leon Radzinowicz*, ed. R. Hood (Heinemann, 1974), pp. 319–45.
11 J. Clarke, 'Critical sociology and radical social work: problems of theory and practice', in *Social Work, Welfare and the State*, ed. N. Parry (Edward Arnold, 1979), pp. 125–39.
12 C. Smart, *Women, Crime and Criminality: a feminist critique* (Routledge and Kegan Paul, 1976).

13 M. D. A. Freeman, *The Rights and the Wrongs of Children* (Frances Pinter, 1983).
14 L. Davies, *Pupil Power: deviance and gender in school* (Falmer Press, 1984).
15 E. Younghusband, *Social Work in Britain, 1950–1975: a follow-up study* (Allen and Unwin, 1978), vol. I.
16 L. Taylor et al., *In Whose Best Interests? the unjust treatment of children in courts and institutions* (Cobden Trust/Mind, 1979).
17 V. George and P. Wilding, *Ideology and Social Welfare* (Routledge and Kegan Paul, 1975).
18 A. M. Platt, *The Child Savers: the invention of delinquency* (University of Chicago Press, 1969).
19 P. Priestley et al., *Justice for Juveniles* (Routledge and Kegan Paul, 1977).
20 K. Woodroofe, *From Charity to Social Work in England and the United States* (Routledge and Kegan Paul, 1962).
21 R. Dworkin, *Taking Rights Seriously* (Duckworth, 1977).
22 G. Salaman, *Work Organizations: resistance and control* (Longman, 1979).
23 Priestley et al., *Justice for Juveniles*, p. 35.
24 *Young People and the Police Act: information sheet* (Children's Legal Centre, 1985).
25 *The Brixton Disorders, 10–12 April 1981: report of an inquiry by the Rt Hon. Lord Scarman, OBE* Cmnd 8427 (HMSO, 1982), p. 110.
26 D. Smith, *Young People and the Police: the written evidence of the National Youth Bureau to the Royal Commission on Criminal Procedure* (National Youth Bureau, 1979).
27 Ibid., p. 14.
28 H. Parker et al., *Receiving Juvenile Justice* (Blackwell, 1981).
29 Priestley et al., *Justice for Juveniles*, p. 36.
30 Smith, *Young People and the Police*, p. 15.
31 P. Parsloe, *Juvenile Justice in Britain and the United States: the balance of needs and rights* (Routledge and Kegan Paul, 1978).
32 M. King (ed.), *Childhood, Welfare and Justice* (Batsford, 1981), pp. 55–8.
33 Priestley, et al., *Justice for Juveniles*, p. 105.
34 R. Anderson, *Representation in the Juvenile Court* (Routledge and Kegan Paul, 1978).
35 Parker et al., *Receiving Juvenile Justice*, p. 247.
36 P. Carlen, *Magistrate's Justice* (Martin Robertson, 1976), p. 19.
37 R. Byrne et al., *Prisoners' Rights: a study in Irish prison law* (Co-op Books, 1981), p. 5.
38 Ibid., p. 4.
39 *Guardian*, 29 July 1985.
40 *Guardian*, 30 July 1985.
41 R. D. King and R. Morgan, *A Taste of Prison: custodial conditions for trial and remand prisoners* (Routledge and Kegan Paul, 1976), pp. 35–40.
42 S. Cohen and L. Taylor, *Prison Secrets* (NCCL and RAP, 1978), p. 95.

43 Byrne et al., *Prisoners' Rights*, p. 57.
44 Ibid., p. 61.
45 Hall et al., *Change, Choice and Conflict in Social Policy*.
46 *Tougher Regimes in Detention Centres: report of an evaluation by the Young Offender Psychology Unit* (HMSO, 1984), p. 243.
47 *Young People and the Police Act*, p. 15.
48 Scottish Home and Health Department, *Report of the Review of Suicide Precautions at HM Detention Centre and HM Young Offenders Institution, Glenochill* (HMSO, 1985), p. 40.
49 *Locked up in Care: a report on the use of secure accommodation for young people in care* (Children's Legal Centre, 1982).
50 *Restricting the Liberty of Children in Care: guidance on the new laws* (Children's Legal Centre, 1983).
51 P. Cawson and M. Martell, *Children Referred to Closed Units*, Research Report No. 5 (HMSO, 1979).
52 DHSS, *Inspection of Secure Accommodation for Children and Young People: DHSS guidance on inspections* (DHSS, 1979).
53 *Children in Care – The Need for Change: evidence submitted to the Inquiry into Children in Care by the Social Services Committee of the House of Commons* (Children's Legal Centre, 1983).
54 R. Adams, 'Contradictory face of I.T. practice', *Youth and Policy* (Autumn, 1984), pp. 9–15.
55 Byrne et al., *Prisoners' Rights*, p. 8.
56 P. Carlen, 'On rights and powers: some notes on penal politics', in *The Power to Punish: contemporary penality and social analysis*, ed. D. Garland and P. Young (Heinemann, 1983), pp. 202–16.
57 Platt, *The Child Savers*.
58 J. Goldstein and A. Freud, *Beyond the Best Interests of the Child* (Burnett, 1980), p. 25.
59 Taylor et al., *In Whose Best Interests?*
60 A.M. Morris, 'Revolution in the juvenile court: the Juvenile Justice Standards Project, *Criminal Law Review* (1978), pp. 529–39.
61 T. Prosser, 'Poverty, ideology and legality: supplementary benefit appeal tribunals and their predecessors', *British Journal of Law and Society*, 4 (1977), p. 177.
62 P. Alcock and P. Harris, *Welfare, Law and Order* (Macmillan, 1982).
63 D. Garland and P. Young (eds), *The Power to Punish: contemporary penality and social analysis* (Heinemann, 1983), p. 66.
64 Alcock and Harris, *Welfare, Law and Order*, p. 19.
65 D. H. Thorpe et al., *Out of Care: the community support of juvenile offenders* (Allen and Unwin, 1980).
66 T. Mathieson, *The Politics of Abolition* (Martin Robertson, 1974).
67 Brody, *The Effectiveness of Sentencing*.
68 Advisory Council on the Penal System, *Sentences of Imprisonment: a review of maximum penalties* (HMSO, 1978), pp. 168–9.
69 A. Hirsch, *Doing Justice: the choice of punishments* (Hill and Wang, 1979).

70 Goldstein and Freud, *Beyond the Best Interests of the Child*, pp. 40–9.
71 Mathieson, *The Politics of Abolition*; M. Fitzgerald, *Prisoners in Revolt* (Penguin, 1977).
72 Dworkin, *Taking Rights Seriously*.
73 Mathieson, *The Politics of Abolition*.
74 Carlen, 'On rights and powers'.
75 R. Adams et al., *A Measure of Diversion? case studies in intermediate treatment* (National Youth Bureau, 1981), ch. 15.
76 P. Hirst, 'Law, socialism and rights', in *Radical Issues in Criminology*, ed. P. Carlen and M. Collison (Martin Robertson, 1980), pp. 172–7.
77 Carlen, 'On rights and powers'.
78 Mathieson, *The Politics of Abolition*.
79 Freeman, *The Rights and the Wrongs of Children*, p. 33.
80 I should like to acknowledge the help given me with an earlier draft of this chapter by Derek Crothall and Malcolm Golightley.

Further reading

R. Dworkin, *Taking Rights Seriously* (Duckworth, 1977)
M. D. A. Freeman, *The Rights and the Wrongs of Children* (Francis Pinter, 1983).
M. King (ed.), *Childhood, Welfare and Justice* (Batsford, 1981).
H. Parker et al., *Receiving Juvenile Justice* (Blackwell, 1981).
P. Parsloe, *Juvenile Justice in Britain and the United States: the balance of needs and rights* (Routledge and Kegan Paul, 1978).
L. Taylor et al., *In Whose Best Interests? the unjust treatment of children in courts and institutions* (Cobden Trust/Mind, 1979).
Publications from Children's Legal Centre, London.

6

Children's Rights at Work

Emma MacLennan

We continue to do what we can ·within a free society and within the family framework of this country to ensure that young children who work are not exploited, that their safety is looked after, that they are well paid and that they are not made use of.

John Patten, MP, Under-Secretary of State for Health and Social Security[1]

Introduction

Legal restrictions on children's employment have arisen from a desire to prevent work from adversely affecting children, by damaging their moral and emotional wellbeing, their health, safety, educational performance or family life. But legislation has also been influenced by employers' desires − particularly those of the larger firms − to prevent unfair competition through the use of cheap labour; to prevent the situation where, in the words of Winston Churchill, 'the good employer is undercut by the bad, and the bad employer is undercut by the worst.'[2] A further, less apparent motivation behind legislation on the employment of children is in order to control the supply of labour. In past centuries, the concern has sometimes been to ensure an *adequate* supply. This was the intention of an Act of 1388 when the plagues of the fourteenth century left a shortage of agricultural labour. The aim might also be that of reducing the supply of 'cheap' labour which could undermine the competitive position of other workers; or, again, the current government preoccupation with 'deregulating' the employment of young workers is based on the argument that legislation, particularly minimum wage protections (and not the poor economic climate), has been mainly responsible for high levels of youth unemployment.

Not everyone is convinced of the value of protective legislation, and advocates of a 'free-market economy' consider such legislation an imperfection in the labour market. Thus, for example, Digby Anderson, writing in *The Times*, welcomed as 'excellent news' the publication of a Low Pay Unit/Open University survey which uncovered high levels of illegal employment among schoolchildren: 'This young economy is partly illegal and not covered by the mass of regulations which is now hardening the arteries of the formal adult economy.'[3] Apart from the arguments of free-market economists who regret any form of protective legislation, there has also been opposition to restrictions on children's employment on other grounds.

First, it has been suggested that the immediate effect of such legislation would be to reduce the incomes of poor families. When the Education Act (1920) raised the school-leaving age to fourteen, which then became the minimum age for full-time employment, one member of parliament, Sir J. D. Rees, asked the Prime Minister

> whether, in view of prevailing high prices, heavy taxation and general financial stress, the Government will postpone the operation of the Education Act, and more particularly of the clauses which will render it impossible for the poor to profit any longer by the help afforded by their own children?[4]

Second, part-time work is seen by some as a healthy, industrious and profitable pastime, by which children 'can learn the value of money'. To suggest that children should not work is to advocate a generation of hothouse plants or, worse, to let 'idle hands do the devil's work'. Thus one journalist claimed it was an 'undisputed fact' that

> if (juveniles) are not fully occupied in some harmless occupation, they will seek an outlet for their energy in one that is harmful ... all the hundred and one offences that bring juvenile delinquents to the Children's Court are due, in many cases, to the fact that healthy youngsters have, outside school hours, not enough to do.[5]

Third, it is argued that children benefit from the knowledge that they are contributing to the general economic good. *Daily Mirror* columnist Keith Waterhouse argued that part-time jobs for children are

> good news – good for the economy, good for the customer and above all, good for the pint-sized entrepreneurs themselves. . . . Of course children are a source of cheap labour. That is as it should be. What spoiled little brats they would be if they were a source of expensive labour.[6]

In contrast with these views, the *Daily Mirror* of 20 October 1982 condemned the widespread employment of children on low wages as 'Slave Labour'. Other headlines report the 'Scandal of Pin-Money Pupils',[7] the 'Child Labour "Scandal" in Hospitals'[8] and that 'Working Children Face Irreparable Damage'.[9] This alternative, 'Dickensian' view of child labour is most apparent when the accidental death of a child at work is reported, or when blatant cases of exploitation come to light. Three schoolboys were found to be employed in factory 'operating highly dangerous, defective, power presses' for 17 pence an hour.[10] A fourteen-year-old 'butcher's boy' died when a knife he was using severed the main artery in his leg.[11] In Glasgow one child had his arm wrenched off and another was crushed and killed by machinery. Because of the circumstances the children were uninsured, but the parents of the dead boy were offered an *ex gratia* payment of £50 as compensation. These sorts of incidents are always followed by a call for tighter enforcement of the legislation to protect children, and are often accompanied by a demand for an end to child labour altogether. As put by the coroner during the inquest on the death of the butcher's assistant, 'There are so many unemployed young people over the age of 16 that it is appalling that these youngsters should be employed.'[12]

This chapter will consider the extent and nature of children's employment today, beginning with a brief summary of the history of employment legislation and a description of protections currently in operation. This will be followed by an examination of the findings of a survey of schoolchildren carried out in 1982–3 by the Low Pay Unit and Open University.[13] The survey found evidence of the widespread neglect of legislation governing the employment of children, and the existence of a significant minority of children whose work conforms to the 'Dickensian' stereotype of child labour. In a final section some of the reasons for the poor enforcement of legislation are considered, both ideological and procedural.

The history of child labour law

From the earliest times children have played a role in the economic life of the family, working alongside their parents at whatever tasks they were capable of doing. In the late sixteenth century children who were orphaned through the death or poverty of their parents became the responsibility of the parish in which they lived and were apprenticed to local craftsmen or, alternatively, placed in special workshops where they would also learn a trade. With the coming of the industrial revolution, these parish workshops evolved into factories, and the use of children as 'slave labour' was common. As late as the 1840s, the Boards of Guardians in Staffordshire, Lancashire and Yorkshire were found to be 'still getting rid of pauper boys of six, seven and eight, by apprenticing them to colliers, with a guinea thrown in "for clothes"'.[14] Child labour was common, too, in the mines which fuelled British industrial growth, 'where the roadways were sometimes so narrow that children could most easily pass through them'.[15]

Some of the first pieces of legislation to limit the hours of children's employment were concerned with pauper apprentices. The Health and Morals of Apprentices Act of 1802 provided for the abolition of night work and limited the working hours of apprentices in cotton mills to twelve. A further Act in 1819, sponsored by Sir Robert Peel, forbade the employment of children under the age of nine in cotton mills, but as with its predecessor no independent inspectorate was established to police the Act, and both were equally ignored by mill-owners.

A more substantial reform, the Factory Act of 1833, was prompted by the findings of the Sadler Committee of 1832 and the Factory Commission of 1833. The Act outlawed employment in all textile factories before the age of nine but, because there was no civil registration of births until the 1830s, evasion was at first relatively easy. But, unlike previous legislation, the 1833 Act included provision for the appointment of four 'independent factory inspectors', although they had to monitor 3000 textile manufacturers.

Riding upon the same wave of public indignation which produced the Factory Act, a commission was set up in 1840 to investigate employment in the mines. It found conditions were worse, if possible, than in the relentless labour of the mills. Small children were used to operate ventilation traps, sometimes sitting in the dark for thirteen or fourteen hours. Other children 'hurried' the coal down the shafts, pushing the great loads for miles with their heads while bent almost double. Accidents were frequent. Soon after the commission published its report in 1842, the Mines Act was passed which prohibited the employment of children under ten and women underground and restricted the number of hours and types of work done by children.

A turning-point was reached in the control of child employment when the Elementary Education Acts of 1870 and 1880 made school attendance compulsory until the age of ten. Other laws enacted during the 1870s placed additional restrictions on child employment. The Factory and Workshops Act (1878) extended the previous Act of 1833 to all factories, raised the minimum age of employment to ten and limited the working hours of children under the age of fourteen to half the normal working day.

In this century the Employment of Women, Young Persons and Children Act of 1920 laid down that the minimum age for all full-time employment in factories should be fourteen, which at that time was the compulsory school-leaving age. Since then the minimum age has been raised to sixteen, but most provisions of the 1920 Act still apply. Modern law governing the employment of children is a hotchpotch of provisions which takes bits and pieces from statutes enacted over the last century.

The law today

In 1920, the International Labour Organization and the League of Nations met in Washington to draw up a convention relating to the employment of children which would be binding upon all member nations who chose to ratify it. In Britain, the convention was embodied in the Employment of Women, Young Persons and Children Act of 1920, which had the advantage of tying together past legislation and providing a list of types of employment which were prohibited to children. The Act basically states that no child under the age of fourteen years shall be employed in an industrial undertaking or on board any ship other than a family vessel or school or training ship. The Act also requires that every employer in an industrial undertaking must keep a register of all persons under the age of sixteen employed by him or her.

A second important piece of modern legislation, the Children and Young Persons Act, came on to the statute book in 1933 and restricted the number of hours which may legally be worked by children under the age of sixteen. No child may work more than two hours on any school day or begin work before 7 a.m. or continue beyond 7 p.m.

Together these two pieces of legislation form the basis of modern child labour law, the most important aspects of which are the prohibition of child employment in industrial undertakings, the minimum age of thirteen for part-time employment and restrictions on the hours and times of work done by children. Two final provisions of the 1933 Act prohibit street trading by children and young persons under the age of seventeen, and set penalties for those employers who contravene any of the provisions of the Act at a maximum of £20 for the first offence and £50 for the second.

These national regulations limit the employment of children under sixteen, but, in addition, local authorities have wide-ranging powers under the Children and Young Persons Act of 1933 to improve upon the statutory restrictions on child labour in virtually any way they see fit. There is wide variation between local authorities concerning both the restrictiveness of by-laws and the ways in which they are enforced. Some local authorities have made no use of their statutory powers, while others have developed a set of regulations which go beyond the model by-laws circulated by the Department of Health and Social Security in 1976.

The by-laws set by the Inner London Education Authority (ILEA), for example, surpass the minimum recommendations of the DHSS. No children may work in the mornings before school except in newspaper or milk deliveries. Sunday employment is limited to two hours between 7 and 10 a.m., and the maximum weekly hours set by the ILEA are five hours shorter than the government recommendations. In addition the ILEA has detailed provisions for the registration of all children in employment. No child may be employed without an employment card issued by the local authority, which must be returned at the end of employment or when the child reaches the age of sixteen. Moreover, within fourteen days of the commencement of employment as well as once every twelve months, the child must obtain a medical certificate from the local specialist in community medicine.[16]

Local authorities clearly have a vital role to play in regulating child employment. However, the variation between local authorities and the gap between local by-laws and national legislation make it difficult to publicize the regulations except on a very local basis. Employers understandably complain that such regulations appear arbitrary. For these reasons, in 1973 the Employment of Children Act provided a uniform set of regulations which were intended to apply equally to all local authorites, end the prevailing confusion and ensure that children everywhere were subject to the same employment protection. The provisions of this Act will be discussed later.

Enforcement

Responsibility for the enforcement of the different statutory rules and by-laws which relate to the employment of children is divided among three main agencies, the Health and Safety Inspectorate, local authority environmental health officers, and the education and welfare service. In addition, other government inspectors, such as the Wages Inspectorate, the police and national insurance or tax inspectors, bear some responsibility and may come across evidence of the illegal employment of children in the course of their work. This diffusion of duty among various authorities has not produced any greater vigilance.

Under the Health and Safety Inspectorate, factory inspectors are employed to perform routine inspections of industrial premises, which should include the discovery of any illegally employed children. There are an estimated 750 general factory inspectors in Great Britain to police over 730,000 manufacturing establishments. Their responsibilities are obviously much wider than simply hunting out child workers, and, not surprisingly, the number of yearly convictions is low. Table 1 gives the number of cases and convictions of illegal child employment from 1972 to 1981 (the most recently published figures).

Table 1   Health and Safety Inspectorate: cases and convictions of illegal child employment, 1972–81

	Employers	No. of cases	Convictions	Penalties (in £s)
1972	7	29	29	1160
1974	26	86	79	1496
1976	10	11	10	595
1978	11	26	25	2055
1980	8	18	18	975
1981	4	5	5	350

Source: Hansard, 18 May 1977, 9 December 1982

Environmental health officers' concern is primarily with the types of establishments not pursued by the factory inspectors – offices, shops, takeaway restaurants – but like the factory inspectorate they have wider duties than just chasing child labour. The police have responsibilities for some types of illegal employment, mainly employment in licensed premises and street peddling. While both they and the health inspectors may inform local education welfare officers where any employer is suspected of breaking the law, in practice information tends to flow in the opposite direction. It is the EWOs who know the children, whereas an inspector looking for health hazards may tend to assume any young workers they come across are of a legal working age. However, unlike the police and health inspectors, EWOs cannot actively inspect employers' premises.

Nevertheless the brunt of inspection duties falls upon the local education welfare officers, but they too have other responsibilities which demand their attention, and have difficulty in discovering the more serious instances of infringement. Consequently much of the education and welfare surveillance work on child labour is done by EWOs working voluntary overtime, patrolling the streets either before or after normal office hours. Apart from newspaper deliveries or milk rounds, few children are likely to be spotted at work by these means. Low prosecution rates, together with the small number of national inspectors and employees' ignorance of the law, all contribute to the ease and frequency of infringements. Despite the legal protection available to working children, the exploitation of child labour still occurs.

Estimates of employment

There is no official source of information on the employment of workers under the age of sixteen. The Census of Employment is limited to adult workers, and even the General Household Survey draws the line at sixteen. Where estimates are necessary, they involve a certain amount of guesswork and extrapolation. According to ILO estimates, only 1000 children under the age of fifteen were working in the United Kingdom in 1978.[17]

A more convincing estimate was made by the DHSS during a correspondence with local authority organizations in 1975 concerning the possible effects of compulsory registration of all child workers. The DHSS then estimated the number of registrations which would be necessary on a national level to be 750,000 in England and Wales during the first year of operation, with 'subsequent annual numbers of at least 200,000'.[18] In June 1975 there were 2,296,300 children aged thirteen, fourteen and fifteen in England and Wales.[19] Total estimated registrations, expressed as a proportion of this figure, were nearly 33 per cent of this population. Yearly additions imply that at least one in four children have some sort of part-time employment other than informal jobs such as babysitting and running errands.

In 1972 the DHSS commissioned a research project, 'Work out of School', by Emrys Davies. Davies conducted his survey in forty secondary schools distributed over the Department of Education and Science regions in England and Wales. Random samples of third- and fourth-year pupils were selected, totalling 1413 boys and 1361 girls. This sample was analysed for its range of ages and abilities and the socio-economic status of the children's families, as well as the occupations of the fathers, to ensure that the sample was adequately representative of all children between the ages of thirteen and sixteen.[20]

The purposes of the enquiry were: first, to reach an estimate of the extent of part-time employment among children; second, to gain some indication of the effectiveness of local by-laws and statute in regulating employment; third, to assess the effects of part-time employment on the educational development of children. The data revealed that 23 per cent of girls and 42 per cent of boys had part-time jobs which came under the scope of by-laws and statute. Children were also working in jobs that were not subject to legal regulation, which involved mostly domestic work, child care and manual jobs such as car washing and gardening – tasks normally performed for parents or other relatives. When both categories of work were considered, nearly half of all schoolchildren between the ages of thirteen and sixteen were found to be in paid employment, whether formally covered by statute or not.

Davies's study uncovered a number of disturbing connections between children's part-time employment and their behaviour at school. Independently of such factors as socio-economic status, the survey found that

> pupils who spend more of their out-of-school time in employment tend to be less able, less industrious and less well-behaved; they attend less regularly, play truant more frequently, are less punctual and wish to leave school at an earlier age than those who work for fewer hours or not at all.[21]

Moreover, the researchers found that, in general, by-laws were simply ignored. Many children in the sample first began employment before the statutory minimum age of thirteen, and those by-laws which require notification of employment to local authorities were rarely complied with, although employers who did so were significantly less likely to contravene other regulations.

Davies summarized the factors which account for the ineffectiveness of by-laws as follows:

> the inadequate staffing of education welfare departments, variations in the regulations made by LEAs, especially where variations occur in the regulations of neighbouring authorities; the unwillingness of many employers to apply regulations which limit or hinder their work; the not uncommon assumption among administrators, educators and others that part-time employment develops desirable qualities in the young; and the reluctance of authorities to prosecute employers, except in serious cases.[22]

He concluded that in light of the detrimental effects of heavy involvement in part-time employment upon educational performance, steps should be taken to standardize provisions over all local authorities and ensure adequate staffing levels within the education welfare service for supervision and enforcement; it is worth noting that Davies never explored the possibility that work might be more beneficial to the children than schooling. The report, published in 1972, effectively shattered popular myths concerning child labour. The survey found that a large majority of employers were guilty of some type of infringement, and that some children were working longer hours each week, when time spent in school was taken into consideration, than most full-time adults. The result, as with earlier enquiries into the nature and extent of child labour, was new legislation to limit the problem.

The Employment of Children Act, 1973

The publication of Emrys Davies's report in 1972 sparked off a public debate on the statutory regulation of child labour, which resulted in the Employment of Children Act of 1973. However, although this piece of legislation is currently on the statute books, it is not actually part of the law of the land. Section 3(4) of this Act provides that the Act shall only come into force 'on such a day as the Secretary of State may appoint by order made by statutory instrument',[23] and that different provisions under the Act may be brought into force at different times. To date, none of the provisions has been called into force.

The major purposes of the Act were to standardize the existing local authority by-laws and to strengthen the local education officers' power of enforcement in two ways: first, local authorities would be able to demand particulars of employment from prospective employers; and, second, a two-tier system of fines would be created. The member of parliament who originally introduced the Bill, Jeffrey Archer, summarized the thoughts of the entire standing committee when he said: 'There has been a demand for it in the constituencies, and it is wanted by all parties. We shall be glad to see it passed into law and on the statute book.'[24]

In practice, however, there were certain obstacles yet to be overcome. Immediately after the passage of the Act, the DHSS wrote to the various local education authorities soliciting their views of what should constitute the details of the national provisions to supersede all local authority by-laws. On the basis of their responses, the DHSS in 1975 circulated LEAs with a consultative document containing a provisional draft of the new uniform regulations, requesting comments. At that time the majority of local authority organizations developed cold feet. Their reasons, however, were practical: the immediate implementation of the new regulations, particularly regarding notification and registration, would involve additional adminstrative time and effort and a financial strain upon local authority resources. In December 1977 the DHSS again began writing to local authorities. This time the response was more varied but, given the DHSS insistence that no extra funding would be forthcoming, the issue was ultimately dropped.

Today, the local education authorities have even fewer resources at their disposal. Rate-capping and growing pressures on other services will allow little scope for additional spending on the education and welfare service, while even the factory inspectorate have suffered cuts. The government has recently reiterated its rejection of the 1973 Act:

> Consultations with local authority associations took place in 1975 and 1977. Because of the resource implications for local authorities, it was decided that the introduction of the provisions of the Act would not be justified. It remains inappropriate to impose these further responsibilities on local authorities.[25]

The National Association of Social Workers in Education disagrees:

> The first step should be to implement the Employment of Children Act 1973 in a positive way NOW and then to consider what further can be done to eradicate illegal and harmful employment of children for good.[26]

Since NASWE members carry the burden of enforcing the existing regulations, the government would perhaps be wise to heed their words.

Child labour: survey results

This section reports the results of a questionnaire survey, conducted in 1982–3, among 1700 schoolchildren in London, Luton and Bedfordshire, along with information collected in interviews with a sub-sample of 145 children from all of the survey schools. Preliminary results for London were compiled by December 1982, at a time when the survey was still in progress in Luton and Bedfordshire. The results for Luton and Bedfordshire, rather than establishing child labour as a metropolitan phenomenon, showed a remarkably similar pattern of work for children of all ages. Findings also lend support to the early DES study of 'Work out of School'. It is clear that a large proportion of schoolchildren do work on a part-time, and even full-time basis. As we shall see, there are costs as well as benefits associated with this.

The survey was conducted in eleven schools – six in London, three in Luton and two in mid-Bedfordshire. Four of the schools were single-sex schools, and all were comprehensive in the state sector. A total of 1712 children between eleven and sixteen years old were surveyed, and completed questionnaires were obtained for 1055 boys and 643 girls. The bias towards boys in the sample can be partly explained by the three single-sex boys' schools included in the survey, although there were also more boys than girls present in the mixed schools. As boys are slightly more likely to be employed than girls, this feature would have a marginal effect on the total proportions of those working. A breakdown by sex and age of the children in the survey is shown in table 2.

Table 2   Children in the survey, London and Luton/Bedfordshire

Age	No. boys	No. girls	Total	%
11	54	40	94	6
12	178	136	314	18
13	261	156	417	25
14	289	171	460	27
15	246	127	373	22
16	27	13	40	2
All	1055	643	1698	100

Employment

Forty per cent of all the children in the survey were working during term time in jobs *other than babysitting, running errands, or other unregulated employment*. As can be seen in table 3, eleven- and twelve-year-old children were almost as likely to be working as the older age groups. Boys were generally more likely to be employed than girls, with the notable exception of the eleven year old age group where 53 per cent of girls were working compared to 35 per cent of boys.

Close to one in ten children surveyed had more than one job, and half of these had more than two, so that even the high proportion of

Table 3   Distributon of employment[a] by age and sex

Age	Boys working No.	%	Girls working No.	%
11	19	35	21	53
12	59	33	45	33
13	113	43	52	33
14	126	44	60	35
15	106	43	58	46
16	13	48	6	46
All	436	41	242	38

[a] Defined as employment in a trade or occupation carried on for profit.

children working underestimates the extent to which child labour is used. Children were employed in a wide range of jobs, though predominantly in services such as retailing, catering, cleaning and, of course, newspaper deliveries. The largest category of employment for all children was, in fact, newspaper deliveries, employing nearly one-third of all children working. Shop work was second in popularity, accounting for one in five of all children employed, followed by farm work (13 per cent) and cleaning (8 per cent). In addition, a variety of other jobs were commonly reported, including hotel and catering employment, painting and decorating, sewing-machining, modelling, clerical work and work in street markets. Overall, more than one in five children worked in the manual jobs of cleaning, furniture removals, construction labour and garage work.

When preliminary results for London were published in 1982, there was some speculation that child labour might be a peculiar feature of London life. In fact a breakdown by region shows that children were considerably more likely to be working in rural Bedfordshire or Luton (table 4). Some differences were found, not unexpectedly, in the types of jobs done with more children employed in farm work or gardening in Luton and Bedfordshire than in London (18.2 per cent compared to 7.8 per cent). But these figures relate to jobs performed by the children during the week of the survey and tend to understate the extent of child labour. Table 5 shows that, when asked about all employment, including recent jobs outside the survey week, the proportions of children working rose significantly.

Two-thirds of all children in Luton and Bedfordshire, 70 per cent of boys and 60 per cent of girls, were found to be working.

Table 4 Employment by area

	Boys	% working Girls	All
London	37	29	35
Luton/Bedfordshire	51	45	48
All	41	38	40

Table 5 Children's employment, Luton/Bedfordshire, survey week, holiday jobs and jobs normally done

	Boys	Girls	All
Total number	448	325	773
Number working	314	196	510
% working	70	60	66

Another feature of the survey tended to underestimate the numbers of working children. A 10 per cent rate of absenteeism is normal in most secondary schools, and may be exceeded in some areas. It is estimated that something like one-third of all absenteeism is caused by truancy, or unjustified absence, often related to work commitments.[27] School-based surveys thus miss a proportion of children, some of whom are likely to be working.

The extent of children's employment, the types of jobs done by children and the age distribution of children's work do not support the view that child labour is purely marginal. In some industries – certainly in newspaper deliveries – children may be as important a source of labour as part-time adults or school-leavers. The possible substitution of child labour for these groups must therefore be a serious concern.

Hours and earnings

The majority of children in our survey worked ten hours or less a week (see table 6). This was true for both sexes, and for all areas surveyed.

On average, boys in London worked longer than other children – over a third worked more than ten hours a week during school term and one in five worked sixteen hours or more. Some children, though a small number, worked very long hours indeed. A boy in London, for example, worked forty-seven hours a week in the family takeaway restaurant.

Table 6   Hours of work

| | London (%) | | Luton/Beds (%) | |
	Girls	Boys	Girls	Boys
3 hours or less	47.5	28.7	41.4	47.3
6–10 hours	32.5	43.0	37.4	32.9
11–15 hours	11.3	14.3	10.2	9.7
16–20 hours	8.7	12.9	5.4	6.1
Over 20 hours	1.3	6.7	5.4	3.9

Yet wages for child labour are low (see table 7). Most earned £1 an hour or less, and even in London an average of 15 per cent earned less than 50p an hour. Some children had very poor earnings, such as the boy given the equivalent of 2p an hour for helping his mother clean offices.

Table 7   Hourly earnings

| | London (%) | | Luton/Beds (%) | |
	Girls	Boys	Girls	Boys
Less than 50p	11.7	19.8	30.2	20.0
51p–£1	38.3	44.6	35.4	42.8
£1.01–£1.50	28.3	26.0	27.1	22.8
£1.51–£2	13.3	7.9	4.2	9.3
More than £2	8.3	5.6	3.1	5.1
Average hourly earnings	£1.23	£1.08	£0.82	£0.93

Moreover, the majority of children appeared to be working illegally on one count or another. Analysis of the London data found that over four out of five children working were illegally employed, either because they were underaged, working illegal hours or working in jobs they should not have been doing. Information on other infringements, such as underpayments of wages council rates or breaches under the Shops Act (which require minimum rest periods, etc., for young workers) might add to this pattern. Perhaps more disturbing is evidence that the considerable health and safety regulations which apply to the employment of children were ignored. A large minority of children in our survey reported having accidents while working in their current jobs. Nearly one-third of all boys and 29 per cent of girls reported some accident or injury. The main causes included lifting heavy weights – specifically prohibited under the Children and Young Persons Act (1933) – broken glass, slipping or falling, and injuries caused by materials or machinery. In addition, animal bites were reported by children employed in agriculture, stables or kennels, and milk or newspaper deliveries.

Child labour and family income

The interviews with schoolchildren found that 65 of the 145 children interviewed received pocket money from their parents – usually between £1 and £2 a week. Of the 67 children who were working, however, only 13 received any pocket money. Evidently earnings can be a replacement for pocket money, possibly because parents see no need to give extra money to a child who is already earning. It may also be that, in families which cannot afford any extra expenses, children work to cover their own expenses rather than make demands on their parents.

Using the Office of Population Censuses and Surveys classific ation for social class, we were able to examine the proportion of children working according to the socio-economic and employment status of their parents. As can be seen in table 8, though the numbers are small and must be treated with caution, there appears to be a relationship between parents' unemployment and the likelihood of children to be working. Thus, where parents are unemployed or on a low income, there may be added incentive for their children to work.

The relationship between children's income and family income, however, may be indirect. Only 2 children out of the 67 who were working actually admitted to helping out with the bills. Children

Table 8   Child labour and social class

Social class	Total	% working	No. in family business
I	0	–	–
II	13	38	4
III (Non-manual)	8	25	1
III (Manual)	43	51	8
IV	28	36	–
V	5	20	–
Unemployed	21	52	–

are more likely to subsidize family incomes indirectly by paying for the things which parents would otherwise be asked to fund. The main items of expenditure mentioned by children working – clothing and entertainment – would tend to support this view.

Children may also subsidize family income by working in the family business. However, in the sample as a whole, only a minority of children were employed within the family – 19 per cent of boys and 18 per cent of girls – and this employment is mainly concentrated among middle- and lower-middle-class children. The same rules and regulations apply to children working in a family business as to other children in employment and, as we have seen, there are strong arguments to support this. Where children work forty hours and more per week in the family shop, the effects on their health and education may be equally severe, whether or not they are employed by a parent.

Conclusions and proposals

As we have seen, legal restrictions on children's employment have arisen from a desire to prevent work from adversely affecting their future lives, either by taking time away from education or by causing physical or emotional damage to the child. Some of these regulations also have an explicitly moral aim. But, whatever one's view of the morality of child labour, there is evidence that employment does have a serious effect on children.

Enforcement of the law relating to child labour is a central problem which derives from the complexity of the rules and the absence of any

authority with both overall responsibility and adequate powers. The
variations caused by local by-laws exacerbate this by confounding
any attempts to publicize widely employers' responsibilities. But there
are other factors which may explain the reluctance of the enforcement
agencies actively to police the law. The short-term financial interests
of both employers and families may stand in the way of any serious
attempts to eradicate the problem.

Researchers for a BBC 'Brasstacks' documentary on child labour
found some collusion between employers and families in the employment of children for agricultural labour in East Anglia:

> Local parents favour the system. They know where their
> children are, it keeps them out of mischief, and even if the child's
> wages do not go straight into the family kitty it takes financial
> pressure off the family. For a family where the dole or carrot-
> topping wages are the only income, a child's £8 is a significant
> amount of money.[28]

Child labour is, of course, extremely attractive to employers who may
use children as a 'casual', easily disposable workforce. Children are
invariably paid cash in hand, and may not appear on an employer's
records. They are not subject to national insurance contributions, nor
do they tend to be members of a trade union, even in union-organized
firms. They have none of the employment rights of adult workers,
such as the right to claim unfair dismissal, the right to an itemized
pay slip or, because they pay no national insurance, the right to
receive sick pay. They are not even classified as 'employees' under the
Health and Safety at Work Act, so that if they are accidentally
injured at work they have no right to claim any compensation unless
their parents can prove in court that their employer was 'negligent' in
some respect. If the child is employed illegally, as most children are,
then his or her parents may also be considered parties to this
negligence.

Thus, because children are not technically 'employees', they have
none of the protections afforded to adults, yet their employment is
regulated by a wide variety of rules and restrictions which do not
work. As one MP commented during the debate on the Employment
of Children Bill, 'it is a curious anomaly that, on the one hand, the
normal protections cannot be set up against exploitation in
employment because it does not occur, but, on the other, it is
legislatively implied that it can occur.'[29] So long as existing
regulations are so poorly enforced and complied with, this situation
will continue.

Part of the problem may, in fact, be employers' ignorance of their responsibilities rather than outright flaunting of the law. The Employment of Children Act (1973), by standardizing the law, would make it possible to publicize employers' responsibilities nationally. It would also make it a requirement of all local education authorities to establish a system of licensing. Other requirements could then be built into the licensing procedure, such as the provision of compulsory employers' insurance cover for children working under licence. Moreover, if licensing itself were more widespread, those firms would then be more visible to public health inspectors and could be included in their priority list of firms.

Legislation, of course, is not the only answer. Other factors, such as 'consumer rejection' of the type of education provided in schools, certainly have a role to play. It might be, too, that ideas of what children should or should not do are changing, and that the lack of compliance with the law partly relects a lack of consensus that the law is correct. But there are real risks associated with children's work, and these risks will continue so long as children effectively fall outside the law.

A serious discussion of what the law should be, and how children's interests might be best served, is long overdue. There is a need, also, for policies which strike at the factors that 'push' children into employment. Employers' search for cheap and casual labour, combined with widespread family poverty, forces the problem. Most people would not wish to see the return of 'pauper apprentices' to Britain. The current preoccupation with deregulation and free-market neglect, if not checked, may eventually lead to this.

Notes

1 Hansard, 2 April 1985, col. 1198.
2 Hansard, 28 April 1909, vol. 4, col. 388.
3 *The Times*, 23 January 1985.
4 Hansard, March 1920, col. 2369–90.
5 *Birmingham Mail*, 16 February 1949.
6 *Daily Mirror*, 21 January 1985.
7 *Daily Express*, 12 December 1977.
8 *The Times*, 18 January 1985.
9 *The Teacher*, 22 February 1985.
10 *The Times*, 4 December 1973.
11 *Guardian*, 29 October 1982. For a study of the hazardous conditions which working children may face, see R. Belfield, 'Out of school activities', *New Statesman*, 1 February 1985.
12 *Guardian*, 29 October 1982.

13 The results of this survey are also reported in E. MacLennan et al., *Working Children*, Low Pay Pamphlet No. 34 (Low Pay Unit, 1985).
14 E. P. Thompson, *The Making of the English Working Class* (Pelican, 1968), p. 369.
15 Ibid., p. 366.
16 By-laws made by the Inner London Education Authority, 9 September 1968.
17 J. Challis and D. Elliman, *Child Workers Today* (Quartermaine House, 1979), p. 13.
18 Association of Metropolitan Authorities Education Committee, Minutes of meeting, 6 April 1978.
19 Office of Population Censuses and Surveys Monitor, ref. PP1 77/3.
20 E. Davies, *Work out of School* (DHSS, 1972).
21 Ibid., p. iv.
22 Ibid.
23 The Employment of Children Act (1973), section 3(4).
24 *House of Commons Official Report Standing Committee C*, 14 March 1973, col. 6.
25 Tony Newton, MP, Hansard, 17 January 1983.
26 Norman Oakden, NASWE press release, 16 January 1985.
27 Hansard, 1 June 1982, col. 116.
28 'Clocking on', BBC2, 16 January 1985.
29 *House of Commons Official Report Standing Committee C*, 14 March 1973, col. 9.

Further reading

R. Belfield, 'Out of school activities', *New Statesman*, 1 February 1985.
J. Challis and D. Elliman, *Child Workers Today* (Quartermaine House, 1979).
E. Davies, *Out of Work* (DHSS, 1972).
H. Hendrick, *Kept from History: aspects of the status of children, part 2, 1800–1914* (Justice for Children, n.d.).
E. MacLennan, *Child Labour in London* (Low Pay Unit, 1982).
E. MacLennan et al., *Working Children* (Low Pay Unit, 1985).

7

Children's Sexual Rights

Richard Ives

Introduction

My interest in sexuality (apart from the 'natural' interest in such matters that most people have) arises from my belief that a study of sexuality helps us to understand people's values and their attitudes to a wide range of issues. Nowhere is this clearer than in the relation between childhood and sexuality. A study of this topic, and of adult reactions to it, helps us to understand the nature of the oppression of children and the limited rights which they possess. The power relations between adults and children are nowhere made more explicit than in adults' responses to children's bodies. Children may be patted on the head or chucked under the chin; they can be examined against their will or even beaten. Children are frequently displayed as sex objects in art, literature and in advertising, but paradoxically their own self-directed sexuality is denied and punished by adults.

In the chapter I wish to suggest that children possess at least three sexual rights: the right to freedom from sexual exploitation, the right to express their sexuality, and the right to sex education (and I mean education, not mere teaching). I shall discuss each in turn, although I consider the last to be of central significance. However, this assertion of rights must be placed in the context of two preceding discussions. The first considers some difficulties involved in the definition of sex, illustrates the diversity of sexual behaviour with anthropological and historical examples, and concludes with a review of research into childhood sexuality. The second examines arguments in favour of societal and parental restriction of children's sexual rights.

The social construction of sex

We first need to clarify what we mean by sex, since if this is left undefined it will generally be taken to mean heterosexual intercourse with penetration, but for young people who are at the stage of exploring sex it is a particularly narrow and confining definition. So what counts as sex? Suppose it was defined as anything involving the genitals. That would include masturbation, but what about two teenagers engaged in heavy petting above the waist? This would fall outside the definition so far, but it is none the less sexual activity in the generally understood sense of the phrase. We might then take a less restrictive definition such as anything involving touching. But this is obviously unsatisfactory, since there are many ways of touching each other which are non-sexual: comforting grieving people, shaking hands or restraining someone. If the definition of sex was limited to 'touching with arousal', this initially appears more satisfactory but prompts questions about what constitutes arousal which are not easy to answer.

A discussion of children's sexuality raises particular difficulties, since activity which would count as 'sexual' if performed by adults should not necessarily be seen as such when enacted by children. Games like playing 'doctors and nurses' or 'mothers and fathers' are good examples. These games frequently contain overtly sexual elements, which are sanctioned by custom and practice and by their familiarity to adults. They are allowed, albeit generally covertly, without the sexual elements appearing problematic. For children, such sexual play is exploratory and sensual but not imbued with the meaning it would have if it was a game played by adults. This is important, because the mistake that is made equally by proponents of children's sexual liberation and by those who seek to protect children's innocence is to assume that children are sexual. In fact, children are only potentially sexual, and childhood and adolescence are processes of becoming sexual, of learning a sexuality, of developing sexual desires and acquiring sexual behaviour. For some children and young people, because of their make-up and their experiences, this will happen earlier than for others. It is this which makes age-related criteria of sexual maturity so difficult to justify, and it is the different rate of this developmental process in different children which can confuse adults. The world of the child is nowhere more different from the world of the adult than in sexual behaviour; consequently adults' confusion abounds. Like bad anthropologists, we will look at a piece of children's behaviour (a little girl pulling up her skirt, a boy dreamily masturbating) and interpret it in the light of our own understanding of sexuality. Instead we must try to get inside the child's world before we can make any meaningful interpretations of children's behaviour. As Jackson points out, anyone who can remember masturbating to orgasm as a child without knowing quite what they were doing will realise that the physical sensations they felt then are just the same as those they feel as adults. But it is doubtful if the act meant the same in childhood. As adults we can relate masturbation to other aspects of sexuality. . . . But this ability to make sense of masturbation in sexual terms is likely to be beyond the reach of the child. She or he knows that the activity is pleasurable and gratifying, but so are many other things. Masturbation may feel unique because of its climaxes and its ability to release tension, but it is still not prompted by the sexual arousal that an adult might feel.[1]

Such possibilities for misinterpretation of children's behaviour make definitions of sex problematic. However, there is a second difficulty. Sexuality, despite its undoubted biological basis, is to a large extent culturally determined and socially learned behaviour, and the evidence of anthropological writings illustrates a variety of sexual practice and experience. Exploring the extent to which sex in other cultures is different from our own helps to illuminate the often hidden cultural norms which underpin our sexual conduct, and enables us to envisage different kinds of sexual behaviour. Unfortunately, not a great deal of anthropological evidence relating to children's sexuality is readily available to the non-specialist, and what is accessible is often of doubtful reliability. For example, Margaret Mead's pioneering work[2] is now seen as suspect in its observations and conclusions. So evidence must be approached with caution.

In some societies, paedophilic acts are a normal part of cultural life. The Kiwai of New Guinea, for example, require young males to be sodomized during puberty rites. One of the most interesting pieces of anthropological evidence which hints at the possibilities of a different kind of approach to young people's sexuality is contained in the writings of Elwin.[3] He spent many years studying the Muria, a group of hill tribes in India, who operated a Ghotul, or children's house system. Such village dormitories for the young were common in a variety of Indian tribes, but among the Muria they were for both sexes and were run on permissive lines. Children went to live in them from the age of about ten or eleven and stayed there until their marriage at around the age of seventeen. The members of the Ghotul had work to do in the fields, and important ceremonial tasks, especially when visitors came and at weddings and funerals. They were self-governing and elected leaders, both male and female (although strictly sex-segregated), for a variety of tasks. What happened inside the confines of the Ghotul was seen as privileged, and it included heterosexual relations between its members. Although officially discouraged, sexual liaisons between boys and girls of the Ghotul were an inevitable and welcomed part of the system. A Muria saying (which must lose something in the translation) ran: 'the mouth that desires its fill and the genitalia that are excited never listen to advice.' Elwin comments that the sexual openness and experience gained in the Ghotul ensured that subsequent marriages were more likely to be successful and happy than those of neighbouring tribes that did not have a Ghotul system. What can be learned from the anthropological evidence is that there is no 'natural' sexuality. Sexuality is not determined by biology or by anything else, but by individual choices made within the more or less constraining framework of the culture in which one lives: it is learned. The childhood years are thus extremely important, since it is during childhood that much of our sexual learning takes place.

Another source of information outside our culture concerning childhood sexuality is historical writings. But these suffer from even greater problems, in that the record of historical events is secondhand, and most frequently focuses on the habits of the ruling classes. Philippe Ariès's book *Centuries of Childhood*[4] ignores these points, since he constructs a theory of children's sexuality in the Middle Ages based largely on the account by the Dauphin's physician, Heroard, of the young Louis XIII's life, including his active sexuality which was encouraged by adults. But, as Linda Pollock points out,[5] the Dauphin was the last in the line of male heirs, and an excessive concern with his sexuality was connected with the expectation of his producing offspring. He was married at the age of fourteen (to a girl of thirteen), which by that time was young for a male (although thirteen was not for a girl). Life was very different for the peasantry. Here the poverty and lack of private space must have meant that children were aware of the facts of life from an early age. One of the things that exercised the Victorian reformers was a concern that the innocence of children would be corrupted by this proximity.

In Britain before the nineteenth century there was less difference between the treatment of children and adults in matters sexual than there is today. However, at the time of the Reformation the state began to take over from the church jurisdiction for certain laws, including some rules of personal morality. Condemnation of and, in certain circumstances, punishment for sex acts outside marriage was one of these. By a slow process of legal change, accelerated in the nineteenth century (when the age of consent for females was raised twice, initially from twelve to thirteen and later from thirteen to sixteen, and the 1885 Criminal Law Amendment Act effectively banned all male homosexual activity), the laws of the state began to invade areas of personal sexual morality.

The situation in other western European countries was (and is) different. In France, the Napoleonic Code loosened previous connections between laws and morals. In Holland all kinds of childhood sexual relations (except where an adult used violence against the child, or where the child did not consent) were legal until 1886, when the age of consent was raised to sixteen. Since the 1960s, some western European countries have lowered their age of consent, and total abolition of age-related laws has been suggested in some.

What the historical and anthropological evidence shows, despite the problems of interpretation, is that in Western industrial societies there has been an increasing differentiation of childhood and adulthood, with an expanded intervening period of adolescence. Only a relatively rich society can afford to treat increasingly older 'young people' as 'children', and only a complicated society needs to do so in order to enable youth to undergo a complex learning process; as Musgrove pointed out, adolescence is an invention that came with the steam engine. But if young people are to be made to stay 'young', and subservient to their teachers, they must be subject to a different set of rules from those applying to adults, and in this way age-related laws become established. The control of young people's sexuality is one of the most important areas in which young people are maintained as 'children', and consequently restrictive, but often confused, legislation abounds. Since the prevailing ideology is that girls are 'innocent' and not sexually active, it must be the male who is to blame for any sexual activity by the young female, and British law punishes the male who has intercourse with a girl under sixteen, and not the female herself. Sexual relations between young men under the age of twenty-one are illegal in Britain, whereas no equivalent legislation is considered necessary for young women. More recently the Gillick challenge to the ability of doctors to prescribe contraceptives to girls under sixteen expressed the continued desire to control the sexuality of young women.[6]

The irony of this legislation is that we know very little about children's sexual behaviour and research is scarce. Sexuality is a very difficult area to research because people may consider their sexual life to be a very private affair. In this, humans are unique among social animals, all of which copulate in view of others of their species. It is particularly difficult to study the sexual behaviour of young people, since many are reluctant to admit to sexual encounters. This is especially true of girls, whereas boys generate a different problem, since they may be inclined to exaggerate their sexual experience. Schofield[7] found that, in his sample of single young people aged fifteen to seventeen years, 11 per cent of the boys and 6 per cent of the girls had experienced sexual intercourse. Among a slightly older age group (young people aged seventeen to nineteen) 30 per cent of the boys claimed to have had sexual intercourse, compared to 16 per cent of the girls. Schofield's book was originally published in 1965, and it is interesting that almost half the youngsters of both sexes had taken part in sexual fondling which did not necessarily lead to intercourse. A later survey by Farrel, published in 1978,[8] found a far higher incidence of sexual intercourse, and more equality between boys and girls: 55 per cent of the males and 46 per cent of the girls in her sixteen- to nineteen-year-old sample had had intercourse, and (according to their own reports, of course) 12 per cent of the girls and 31 per cent of the boys had been fully sexually experienced before their sixteenth birthday. Neither of these studies appears to take into account the possibilities of homosexual experiences. It seems likely that such experiences form a substantial, if hidden, aspect of young people's sexual experience. Homosexual organizations have estimated that the gay or lesbian population is about one in ten, and a figure of one in twenty seems a conservative estimate; many of these homosexuals will be active in childhood and adolescence. Although homosexuality in young people is fairly hidden, it is not uncommon.

There has been very little research (but much speculation) on the sexuality of young children. Kinsey, Pomeroy and Martin[9] found that, in their sample of pre-adolescent boys, 70 per cent reported taking part in sex play, and the figure is probably higher, since it is likely that they had forgotten or suppressed memories of some experiences. The most common pre-adolescent sexual activity was genital exhibition and genital contact with other children. Most of this play occurred between eight and thirteen, and Kinsey et al. state that the fact that there is a break in this activity before a more adult sexuality replaces it is 'clearly a product of cultural restraints, for pre-adolescent sexplay in other anthropoids is abundant and continues into adult performance.'[10] Three-fifths of the pre-adolescent boys in Kinsey's sample reported homosexual contact, while two-fifths reported heterosexual contact. Among his female sample, three-tenths recalled pre-adolescent heterosexual play and slightly more, a third, recalled homosexual play.

What is the child's understanding of these activities? R. and J. Goldman[11] made a cross-cultural study of children's sexual thinking in North America, Britain, Australia and Sweden, finding that children's understanding of sex develops as a continuous unbroken sequence of increasing sophistication; there was no evidence of a latency period, during which children's sexual thinking became moribund. But they did find that Swedish children were considerably more sophisticated in their sexual thinking at a younger age than children from the other countries studied, a finding which they attribute to the enlightened sex education provided from an early age in Swedish schools.

Societal and parental restriction of children's sexual rights

Is there a case for the protection of children from sexual relationships until they reach a certain age or maturity? The problem, however, is how to define maturity. We could do so in terms of physical maturity. We would not want children to be physically harmed by engaging in sexual relationships. Pregnancy is an obvious possible result of heterosexual intercourse once the girl has reached (or is near to) puberty. An unterminated pregnancy will have far-reaching effects on a girl, if she has to bear and raise a child for which she is not prepared. If the pregnancy is terminated by an abortion, there may still be physical, psychological, social and emotional repercussions. Neither would we want children to suffer psychological or emotional damage through engaging in sexual relationships, but it is harder to quantify these effects.

Possible injury to oneself is not, however, necessarily sufficient grounds for placing restrictions on an activity. Children, and indeed adults, may justifiably be restricted from doing something, it has been argued, if it can be shown that a particular activity is especially harmful to (1) a certain section of society or (2) the individual actor concerned or (3) society as a whole. These three qualifications are major ones, and crucial when looking at children's sexual rights.

An approach that seeks to restrict rights where their exercise could prove damaging to a sector of society can be seen in present-day Britain, where, for example (some) pornography is restricted on the grounds that it might prove harmful to certain groups seen as susceptible to its 'influence'. Included in this group are children and young people, on the grounds that their developing sexuality may be harmed.

The second qualification, prevention of harm to the individual, is seen by J. S. Mill as insufficient justification for the restriction of a person's freedom. 'The only purpose for which power can rightly be exercised over any member of a civilized community against his will', Mill claims, 'is to prevent harm to others. His own good, either physical or moral, is not sufficient warrant.'[12] This approach was followed by the Wolfenden Committee[13] when looking at the law in relation to homosexual offences. The committee took the view that the law should not interfere with people's lives or sexual behaviour except where there were special reasons. One of the special reasons they gave was the need to safeguard the young or inexperienced from exploitation or corruption. Along the same lines, certain campaigners argue that, since under-age sex can be harmful for young girls (because of the dangers of pregnancy, cervical cancer, and so on), their freedom to take part in sexual activities should be restricted; in other words, it would be 'for their own good'. Perhaps a more powerful concern is the fear that young girls may, through their exploration of sexuality, come to reject the role of mother and home-maker which society needs them to take on. 'Protection' can very easily become 'control'. Therefore, the problem for a strategy based on 'prevention of harm to the individual' is that anything can be construed as harmful – too much food is bad for you – and if a society chooses to ban something then it can generally come up with evidence, some of which may be called 'scientific', to justify the prohibition. Recently renewed attempts are being made to convince people of the apparent dangers of promiscuity – particularly homosexuals, via the AIDS scare. Thus conditions are created for a clampdown on 'non-normal', non-heterosexual sex, and, because it is when people are young that much experimentation takes place, strictures against 'non-standard' sex are especially applied to them.

The third area where the restriction of rights is justified is where damage might be caused to society as a whole. Attacks on fundamental institutions of British society are viewed in this way. When paedophiles attempted to support each other via the now-defunct Paedophile Information Exchange (PIE), they were seen as such a threat to society itself, and to society's perception of what it is to be sexual and what it is to be a child, that they were hounded by MPs, the police and the press until their organization crumbled. By virtue of the threat they posed to commonly held values about the sexuality of children, they have been denied the fundamental right of association, and prevented from producing a newsletter.[14]

However, the question of young people's sexual rights is more complex than suggested by a consideration of these three cases for their restriction. It is one thing to assert that certain rights should be available to particular groups of people, and quite another thing to visualize how they could be made available to these groups in practice, given the kind of societies in which we live. An example of what I mean by this concerns the 'dual standard' operating in the treatment of young women and young men. Most people of a 'liberal' persuasion would agree that any restrictions placed on the freedom of girls and young women should be no more burdensome than those placed on the freedom of boys and young men. However, given the different ways in which men and women are treated in our society, it may well be expedient to provide more 'protection' for girls than for boys – for example, since girls are more likley to encounter attempts to exploit their sexuality. Other, more appropriate ways of dealing with this probelm – by tackling adult male sexuality and providing young women with the methods of resisting unwanted advances – are seldom considered. Unfortunately, this may mean that girls are subject to more burdensome restrictions than boys, over such things as staying out late at night.

Those who have 'care and control' of children – in general, their parent or parents – have particular power over them, and there will at times be conflicts of interest between parents and children about sexual matters as about all others. Indeed, for girls in the adolescent years, disputes about sexual conduct may be the major point of conflict. It seems reasonable that parents should have certain rights in the development of their offspring's sexual conduct – young people need a certain amount of protection from exploitative adults – but how and how much? And since, if a young girl gets pregnant and has a baby, it will often be her mother who will spend a great deal of time looking after it, surely there should be some degree of parental control over childhood and adolescent sexuality? What are the rights of parents in relation to the sexual rights of the child? Dingwall, Eekelaar and Murray, arguing, perhaps unfashionably, for the importance of state intervention in protecting the rights of individuals, point out that parents' rights are not like rights in the commonly accepted sense:

> Parental rights are different from, say, a property-owner's rights to enjoy his or her own property, in that they must be exercised for the child's benefit. In this respect the rights of parents also have the characteristics of duties . . . they are 'duty-rights' which parents are not free to abandon, extinguish or waive, so long as the child is in their care.[15]

Although parents have 'care and control' of their children, the nature of their responsibility is viewed differently in different societies.

Perhaps the most celebrated example is Sweden, where there is a children's ombudsman and even anti-spanking legislation. Sweden is the only country in the world to introduce a law giving every child the right not to be subject to any form of physical or psychological punishment. Within this context of the acceptance of children's rights, and the limitation of parental rights, it becomes easier to investigate and take action against adults involved in sexual abuse of children. But Sweden is a very special case. Seventy per cent of Swedish women go out to work, and many children are in state day-care provision.[16] This makes it possible for early identification of problems, and engenders a greater acceptance by parents of professionals' roles. However, the ethos of the legislation and its implementation is one of protection – by the state rather than by parents – rather than one of the liberation of the child.

Children's sexual rights

The International Children's Rights Monitor sets out three rights in relation to adolescent sexuality:

> ensuring that children and young people have the right to express their sexuality;

> ensuring their access to knowledge and conditions of life that enable them to cope with the consequences of their sexuality;

> ensuring that they are protected from exploitation of their sexuality.[17]

These three rights are rather a mixture: the first is the most controversial, because it is concerned with the expression of sexuality, the right of young people to *be* something. The second is about the right of access to knowledge, an area which will be taken up at the end of this chapter. The last one is relatively uncontroversial, being about the protection of the child. I turn first to this, looking at the issues surrounding the sexual exploitation of children.

Freedom from sexual exploitation

Childhood sexual experiences with adults may be more widespread than commonly thought. Gagnon, in a retrospective study of 1200 American college-age females, found that a quarter had had sexual experiences with an adult before the age of thirteen. Many of these were relatively minor incidents of exposure or voyeurism, but many were not, and only 6 per cent of all cases had been reported to the authorities.[18] West, in a recent study of 223 women in England, found that 42 per cent had been subject to some kind of sexual abuse or harassment in childhood.[19] What are the harmful effects of such experiences? R. and C. Kempe, who studied both sexual and physical abuse of children for many years, found that no harm appeared to come from a single sexual 'molestation' of a child if she/he were secure in a stable situation and the carers were ressuring, but they report a great deal of harm from incest.[20] But actual sexual abuse by an adult family member is only a part (often major, sometimes only relatively minor) of the problems for a child living in that family. Although the abuser himself must take the major responsibility for the offence, sexual abuse in the family is arguably a symptom of disordered relationships, rather than a cause, and, although it is important to look carefully at this particular symptom, it is equally important to address the other issues in that family.

Although no one would wish to minimize the harmful effects of sexual contact with adults, especially when violent, or when involving a previous trusted family member (or both), we can agree with Fraser that 'The opinion of most experienced professionals is that children are much more emotionally traumatized by the uproar and questioning which follows discovery than by the sexual encounter itself.'[21] The harm that is done to the child by an early sexual experience with an adult will depend crucially on the nature of the experience, whether it is violent and sudden or (apparently) loving and gradual. But the extent of harm will also depend on the sexual awareness of the child, the stability of her/his relationships and, perhaps most importantly, on the reaction of adults when they find out about the abuse. In a review of thirty studies of the effects of early sexual experiences with adults, Constantine found that the worst outcome of an experience of sexual abuse occurred for the sexually naïve child who was forced into sexual compliance over a long period of time, and who was aware of the taboos on sexual relationships.[22] West found that, of the fairly small proportion in his sample who told of their abuse, many were simply disbelieved.[23] But if their accounts were accepted they faced questioning by the police, a court case and the prospect of being taken into care.

Against this background, children's own role in asserting their right to freedom from sexual exploitation becomes apparent. As Chris Bagley puts it:

Existing helping and protection services for children have failed dismally in the past to offer a comprehensive service which children could safely or easily turn to. Instead, a different movement has given advice to children, in the context of the children's rights movement, that children have the right to say 'no' to the sexual advances of adults, and have the right to expect other adults to help them in resistance. The children's resistance movement still has ground to cover but is a potentially powerful counter to the emotionally, physically, structurally and indeed politically abusive and exploitive things which the adult world lays on childhood.[24]

The Child Assault Prevention Programme seeks to provide children and young people, from an early age, with the knowledge that they can say no to adults, and, even more controversially, the programme provides children with the skills to resist unwanted advances.[25]

But can children consent to sexual relations? Finkelhor, in a much-quoted paper, states baldly that because children are children

they cannot consent; they can never consent. . . . For the consent to occur two conditions must prevail. A person must know what it is that he or she is consenting to, and a person must be free to say yes or no.[26]

Finkelhor does not believe that children can understand what they are consenting to, since children are not only ignorant about the mechanics of sex but are also unaware of the 'rules and regulations surrounding sexual intimacy'. But many children, if they have had enlightened sex education, are arguably better informed than many adults about the mechanics of sex. Anyway, people have managed for a long while without this knowledge. Leaving this point aside, Finkelhor's is still an extraordinary argument. On his reasoning you can't consent until you know what it is all about, and you can't know what it is about until you have experienced it. How does anyone ever get started! Finkelhor's other point makes more sense. He argues that in both a legal and a psychological sense children are not free to say 'no' to demands from (certain) adults. While children are under the control of adults to the extent to which they are today, it is questionable whether they are really freely able to give consent.

People who favour the liberalization of laws relating to sexuality tend to play down the significance of sexual experiences, because, if sexuality is seen as unimportant, then social regulation of sexuality may become less of an issue for society, which will leave those with statistically unusual sexual preferences (e.g. for children) to their own devices. Thus, Tom O'Carroll in his book *Paedophilia: The Radical Case* says: 'there is no need whatever for a child to know "the consequences" of engaging in harmless sex play, simply because it is exactly that: harmless.'[27] Most parents would agree that sexual play between young children of roughly similar ages is generally harmless, or even beneficial if it encourages knowledge of others and an openness about touching. But almost all parents would have doubts about the harmlessness of young children's being involved in sexual play with adults. This is not only because of the important role which our society ascribes to sexual matters; we would probably be similarly disturbed if a child was spending too much time in the company of adult gamblers. (We might not mind if the child played pontoon with his (*sic*) mates behind the bike sheds most lunchtimes.) This is not because we necessarily see gambling or sex as bad in themselves. But we may feel that an excessive preoccupation with gambling or sex is a bad thing for someone of any age, and also that children may be drawn into something which they are too immature fully to understand or deal with. But how far and at what age are preferences or predilections for certain sorts of behaviour formed by certain sorts of experiences? This debate is central to the arguments about the lowering of the age of consent to homosexual relationships and was a major issue with which the Wolfenden Committee wrestled. In a significant passsge, their report states that the function of the law is:

> To preserve public order and decency, to protect the citizen from what is offensive or injurious, and to provide sufficient safeguards against exploitation and corruption of others, particularly those who are specially vulnerable because they are young, weak in body or mind, inexperienced, or in a state of special physical, official or economic dependence.[28]

In 1975 the Policy Advisory Committee on Sexual Offences were asked to report on the age of consent for hetero- and homosexual acts. Their report was not published until 1981, suggesting that the committee found the problem difficult. A majority of the committee were in favour of lowering the male age of consent for homosexual acts from twenty-one to eighteen, but a minority of five (from a fifteen-person committee) were in favour of a further reduction to sixteen years. They believed that other parts of the criminal law gave sufficient protection to young people, and that the law should not discriminate between male and female unless there were very strong reasons to do so. Since the heterosexual age of consent was sixteen, and the committee had recommended that it should stay so, there were strong arguments for reducing the homosexual age of consent to sixteen. The main argument of the majority of the committee was that psychosexual development was not complete in boys by the age of sixteen (they were impressed by submissions to the committee that boys at sixteen were less mature than girls at that age), and therefore: 'an immature young man could be disturbed by a homosexual relationship'. They felt that heterosexual relationships could be better coped with, despite this apparent immaturity, because of society's more positive and accepting attitude to hetero-sexuality.[29]

A joint working party of pregnant schoolgirls and schoolgirl mothers, publishing its report in 1979, expressed the view that 'there would be more advantages than disadvantages in repealing the law relating to the age of consent',[30] because they considered that the law set an arbitrary standard which failed to protect 'those persons who, while above the fixed age of consent, are unable (due to immaturity) to appreciate what is involved in the act consented to'.[31] They go on to recommend

> there should be no single age under which consent cannot be found in law. The law should simply prescribe that consent will be presumed to be absent if the subject of the alleged sexual assault, irrespective of his or her age, is, for reasons of physical or psychological immaturity or because he/she is suffering from a mental disability, incapable of giving real consent.[32]

But there are problems with such an approach, not least in the woolly notion of 'real consent'. Furthermore, in the moral climate of 1980s Britain, serious political consideration of this proposal seems unlikely.

The right to express sexuality

Turning to the first right mentioned above, what arguments are there for greater sexual freedom for children? I suggest the following: when restrictions on the liberties of certain groups are seen as especially onerous by those groups, then it is time to look at whether the restrictions are fair and just. Young people feel particularly restricted by attitudes to their sexuality. Plenty of evidence is given for this in relation to gay and lesbian young people in the publications of the London Gay Teenage Group.[33] For heterosexuals, there is widespread flouting of the law in relation to the age of consent. When restrictions that have some legal force are regularly broken, such as this law, which is supposed to prevent young women under sixteen engaging in heterosexual intercourse, then it is time to look at the workings of the legislation. As discussed earlier, sex is not just about intercourse, and is mostly a harm-free activity. Grounds for restricting it must be rather strong, therefore. Why is sexual activity subject to particular restrictions in a way that breakdancing is not, although the latter is probably just as dangerous? Given proper sex education and readily available contraceptive advice and facilities, plus adequate provision of abortion facilities as a 'back-stop' measure against unwanted pregnancy, conception would not be a significant problem for those engaged in heterosexual activities. The main change would come about if a different attitude could be developed, which sought to remove the embarrassment involved in seeking contraceptive advice.

The problem of venereal disease could similarly be vastly decreased by fuller provision of facilities. I have no evidence, but I suspect that those 'guardians of our morality' have been grateful for the herpes scare and the worries about AIDS. Venereal disease serves a useful purpose for such people because it provides a palpable curse which can descend on the heads of 'wrongdoers'. It gives them not only a *raison d'être* but also a means of discouraging indulgence in sexual activities: 'Sex can damage your health so don't do it.'

What is needed is less emphasis on the *protection* of children. Protection is very often translated and transformed by 'carers' and 'caring agencies' from meaning protection against others to protection from the child's own ideas and behaviour which are categorized as wayward or deviant. More emphasis is needed on the rights of children and young people to live their own lives as far as possible within the same boundaries which society sets for everyone else. For this to be realistic, two things must happen: the power of certain groups, in particular adult males and those who care for children (parents, teachers, social workers, etc.), will have to be curtailed; and children must be enabled, by education and training as much as anything, to cope with the greater complexities of their 'liberated' life. Sweden demonstrates how the former can be put into practice, and the Child Assault Prevention Programme is demonstrating one way in which this latter aim can be actualized. As Roger Moody puts it:

'protection' of young people without a guarantee of their rights to autonomy, privacy, sexual expression and non-ageist rela-tionships is not just meaningless. It is bound to lead to assault upon their minds and emotions, if not their bodies. Such assaults

will be considered cost-effective, where they deter other youngsters from entering 'illicit' relationships, or where they discourage
libertarian parents from permitting freedom to their kids.[34]

It is precisely because human behaviour is so little natural, so little
innate and so much learned behaviour that childhood has to be a
lengthy process, a process of learning the mores of society. Although
it may follow from this that we need to treat children differently from
adults, this does not imply that their treatment should be sub- or
inhuman. Similarly, although sexuality may require a different
protocol of human behaviour than other forms of social intercourse,
this does not mean that we have to treat it as something dirty or
shameful. But because many people do see things in this way –
children as innocents, sexuality as corrupting – 'never the twain shall
meet', and when the twain do meet (as in paedophilia) outrage knows
no bounds.

The denial of children's sexuality makes the transition from
childhood to adulthood via adolescence all the more difficult. And
since adult sex is almost always thought of as penetrative, genital sex,
the effects of society's attitudes on boys and girls are very different.
Girls are expected the retain the outward innocence of children but
combine it with the secret passive acceptance of sexual overtures from
'her' man; women are supposed to be attractive, not active. Women's
socialization into adult sexuality is linked to the culture of romance,
appropriate reading material for young women consisting of romantic
magazines and articles about male pop stars emphasizing their
homeliness and personality, rather than their music. On the other
hand, men's sexuality is supposed to be externalized and outwardly
directed. Approved reading material for adolescent boys can include
heterosexual pornographic material which presents passive images of
femininity on which male sexuality acts. This role differentiation
makes things easier for young men, since from early adolescence their
sexuality is recognized as a part of their growing adulthood. Girls are
unable to find sexual expression except within the ideology of
romance. But young men suffer, and as adults continue to suffer, from
the fragmentation of experience which is brought about by their being
trained to see sex as a more separate part of life, related to prowess and
performance rather than a part of a relationship with another person.

The right to sex education

The most important right which children have in relation to sexuality
is the right to know. If sexuality is an inbuilt drive, which everyone

possesses, then it is reasonable to argue that children could be sexual. Or if sexuality is only a physical phenomenon, involving the juxtaposition of bodies and the release of tension, then children could experience sexuality. But if (as I have argued) sexuality is a socially constructed activity, a set of learned behaviours, a young child can best be described as potentially sexual. That is not to say that a young child could not be sexual, only that in our society children are not given the necessary information to become sexual until they are older.

Children are kept in ignorance of sex, and much of what passes as sex education is either too biological, focusing on rabbits and pollination, or too twee. An international seminar on adolescent sexuality was united in believing that urgent priority needed to be given to sex education and, in particular, to contraception education.[35] A working party of the World Health Organization on young people aged fourteen to eighteen years said this:

> While induced abortion may be better than an unwanted child, contraception is better than an unwanted pregnancy and the best path to improved contraception is education for responsible behaviour. Increasing sexual activity among teenagers is a fact and, rather than ignoring its existence or trying to stamp it out, it would seem more expedient to educate young people so that such an activity becomes a positive and constructive experience in the developmental process leading to responsible adulthood.[36]

It is possible to lay down some general principles which should apply to the sex education of children and young people, and in this I draw on Kirkendale.[37] Sex education should be appropriate to children's developmental level, it should not be over children's heads by being unnecessarily technical, but, equally important, it should not be patronizing or conceal from young people salient facts about sexuality. There should be an awareness of the particular needs of special groups and individuals; opportunities should be provided for individual help and guidance. Sex education should be taught by people who feel happy about their own sexuality. Sex educators should be able to integrate an increasing freedom and openness in sexual attitudes and behaviour into a responsible context. The best methods for doing this will involve not a didactic process, but a free discussion of issues raised. Educators should be aware that their teaching is not given in isolation; they should acknowledge other sources of learning and help the learner to evaluate these.

Children have a right to have a sex education which is wide-ranging and integrates the emotional, physical, intellectual, political and social aspects of sex. This should avoid the establishment of dichotomies (e.g. hetero/homo) in sexual description, and should respect sexual preferences, encouraging the development of a value system which stands against the mistreatment of sexually defined groups in society. While emphasizing a satisfying sexual identity, sex should be firmly placed in the context of its socio-political aspects. Children should be made aware of the impact of the commercialization of sex, of changing gender roles, and of the relations between the sexes in a broader perspective to include the impact of sex roles on employment practices and parenting. Young people should be helped to evaluate their own possible potentialities as parents.

Sex education may be more appropriately taught to younger children in the first instance, since they are able to accept what they are taught without the complications of the inevitable emotional involvement of the older child. But the Goldmans found that few children in their cross-national sample received any sex education; less than two-fifths of their English sample said they received sex education at primary school.[38]

There is a lack of good sex education programmes in schools and elsewhere, although this is not only the fault of educators. It is hard to see how adequate programmes could be mounted in the current climate of opinion. Schools can only lead (if at all) a little way ahead of public opinion on particular issues, and the tide is running in the wrong direction for enlightened sex education. In 1983 the Health Education Council in Britain, under pressure from the government, withdrew Jane Cousins's excellent book[39] from its recommended list; neither is it stocked by the British Family Planning Association. The danger for the educator of attracting adverse criticism of their sex education programmes has led to watered-down versions, focusing mainly, or exclusively, on biological aspects – and the biological aspects of reproduction at that, rather than those of sexuality. This emphasis on reproduction reinforces the view of sexuality being between men and women in permanent relationships, and helps to solidify the view that sex is penetrative and goal-directed, centring on procreation. So a revised sexual education might be one step towards a new sexual order for children and for adults. However, although we may agree on the need for greater sexual freedom for children and young people, we also find it hard to envisage sexual freedom within the present structure of society.

Notes

1 S. Jackson, *Childhood and Sexuality* (Blackwell, 1982), pp. 69–70.
2 M. Mead, *Growing up in New Guinea* (Penguin, 1970) and *Coming of Age in Samoa* (Penguin, 1971).

3   V. Elwin, *The Kingdom of the Young* (Oxford University Press, 1968).
4   P. Ariès, *Centuries of Childhood* (Penguin, 1979).
5   L. Pollock, *Forgotten Children: parent–child relations from 1500–1900* (Cambridge University Press, 1984).
6   For a fuller discussion of this, see chapter 8 on girls' rights.
7   M. Schofield, *The Sexual Behaviour of Young People* (Penguin, 1968).
8   C. Farrel, *My Mother Said . . . the way young people learned about sex and birth control* (Routledge and Kegan Paul, 1978).
9   A. Kinsey, W. Pomeroy and C. Martin, *Sexual Behaviour in the Human Male* (Saunders, 1948).
10 Ibid., p. 167
11 R. Goldman and J. Goldman, *Children's Sexual Thinking* (Routledge and Kegan Paul, 1982).
12 J. S. Mill, *On Liberty* (Watts and Co., 1941), p. 11.
13 Wolfenden Committee, *Homosexual Offences and Prostitution* (HMSO, 1957).
14 CAPM, *Paedophilia and Public Morals* (Campaign against Public Morals, 1980).
15 R. Dingwall, J. Eekelaar and T. Murray, *The Protection of Children: state intervention and family life* (Blackwell, 1983), p. 224.
16 B. Carlsson, 'Children are fellow citizens', *Community Care*, 459, 5 May 1985, pp. 20–1.
17 International Children's Rights Monitor, 'An international focus on adolescent sexuality', *International Children's Rights Monitor*, 1, 2 (1983), pp. 7–11.
18 Gagnon, quoted by Fraser, in B. Taylor (ed.), *Perspective on Paedophilia* (Batsford, 1981), p. 50.
19 D. West, 'Paper to the International Association of Forensic Sciences meeting', reported in the *Guardian*, 21 September 1984.
20 R. Kempe and C. Kempe, *Child Abuse* (Fontana/Open Books, 1978).
21 Fraser, in Taylor (ed.), *Perspective on Paedophilia*, p. 57.
22 L. Constantine, in L. Constantine and F. Martinson (eds), *Children and Sex: new findings, new perspectives* (Little, Brown, 1981).
23 West, 'Paper to the International Association of Forensic Sciences meeting'.
24 C. Bagley, 'Childhood sexuality and the sexual abuse of children', *Journal of Child Care*, 1, 3 (1983), pp. 105–27.
25 M. Elliott, *Preventing Child Sexual Assault: a practical guide to talking with children* (Bedford Square Press/NCVO, 1985).
26 D. Finkelhor, 'What's wrong with sex between adults and children? Ethics and the problem of sexual abuse', *American Journal of Orthopsychiatry*, 49, 4 (1979), pp. 692–7.
27 T. O'Carroll, *Paedophilia: the radical case* (Peter Owen, 1980), p. 10.
28 Wolfenden, quoted in Policy Advisory Committee on Sexual Offences, *Report on the Age of Consent in Relation to Sexual Offences* (HMSO, 1981), para 35.
29 Ibid., para. 43.

30 Joint Working Party on Pregnant Schoolgirls and Schoolgirl Mothers, *Pregnant at School* (National Council for One-Parent Families/ Community Development Trust, 1979), para. 314.
31 Ibid., para. 309.
32 Ibid., para 310.
33 L. Trenchard and H. Warren, *Talking about Youth Work* (LGTG, 1985); L. Trenchard, *Talking about Young Lesbians* (LGTG, 1984); H. Warren, *Talking about School* (LGTG, 1984).
34 R. Moody, *Indecent Assault* (Peace News/Word is Out, 1981), p. 8.
35 International Children's Rights Monitor, 'An international focus on adolescent sexuality'.
36 *Problems of Children of School Age (14–18 years)*, Report of a Working Group, Regional Office for Europe, World Health Organization (Copenhagen, 1978); quoted in L. Davis, *Sex and the Social Worker* (Heinemann Educational, 1983).
37 L. Kirkendale, 'The sexual rights of children and youth', *AEP Journal*, 5, 4 (1980), pp. 38–9.
38 Goldman and Goldman, *Children's Sexual Thinking*.
39 J. Cousins, *Make it Happy* (Virago, 1978).

Further reading

J. Cousins, *Make it Happy* (Virago, 1978).
M. Elliott, *Preventing Child Sexual Assault: a practical guide to talking with children* (Bedford Square Press/NCVO, 1985).
C. Farrell, *My Mother Said . . . the way young people learned about sex and birth control* (Routledge and Kegan Paul, 1978).
S. Forward and C. Buck, *Betrayal of Innocence: incest and its devastation* (Penguin, 1979).
R. Goldman and J. Goldman, *Children's Sexual Thinking* (Routledge and Kegan Paul, 1982).
S. Jackson, *Childhood and Sexuality* (Blackwell, 1982).
R. Moody, *Indecent Assault* (Peace News-Word is Out, 1981).
I. Pinchbeck and M. Hewitt, *Children in English Society*, vol. 1: *From Tudor Times to the Eighteenth Century*; vol. 2: *From the Eighteenth Century to the Children Act 1948* (Routledge and Kegan Paul, 1969).
B. Taylor (ed.), *Perspective on Paedophilia* (Batsford, 1981).
L. Trenchard and H. Warren, *Talking about Youth Work* (London Gay Teenage Group, 1985).

8

Girls' Rights

Sue Lees and *Jenny Mellor*

Introduction

In liberal democracies the exercise of rights is regarded as a major component of adult citizenship. The acquisition of rights in the public and political spheres, together with the attendant duties and responsibilities, marks, if by somewhat blurred boundaries – since not all rights and responsibilities are acquired at the same moment – the symbolic transition to adult status. That this conception of rights – citizen and taxpayer – is a predominantly male one has been argued widely by feminists.[1]

What are these rights? Post-war British liberal thought has been influenced by T. H. Marshall's distinction of civil, political and social rights:[2] the rights of free speech and property ownership, which constitute the individual in liberal legal theory; the political rights of franchise and public organization which constitute what S. M. Lipset appropriately defined as liberal 'political man';[3] and lastly – what for Marshall himself was the outcome of the previous two, in a process of historical progress – welfare rights, including basic income, personal security and education.

Marshall's classification serves to illustrate one of the central ambiguities in liberal conceptions of rights and justice – that of the distinction between formal and substantive. It is clear, for example, that the formal equalities of 'free speech' or franchise or to own property (themselves relatively recent acquisitions for women) are very different from the substantive 'rights' of 'sufficient income' and other forms of welfare. No formal principle can establish the welfare needs of particular groups; they have to be investigated concretely and substantively. For this reason, recent liberal discussions of justice and rights, such as Rawls's, have been concerned with the conceptions of substantive equality.[4]

Similarly, discussions of 'positive discrimination' have illustrated the role played by substantive inequalities, suffered by women and blacks, in undermining the effective exercise of rights *formally* ascribed equally to all citizens. By showing how massive changes in the distribution of substantive resources and in the structure of institutions is necessary, to allow women to exercise rights which they possess formally as citizens, Eisenstein sees feminism as having 'played a leading role in uncovering the contradictory aspects of liberalism: that equality of opportunity is an unequal system that privileges men by their ascribed status of male.'[5] What are the main forms of substantive inequalities faced by women, and how do they relate specifically to the lives of girls?

1 First, the liberal theory of rights presumes a division between the public and private sphere and therefore condemns attempts to 'invade' the private realm of family life. However there are important pressures on girls which stem from the nature of the family – women's role in domestic labour, for example, and the tendency for daughters to be pressured to take on such responsibilities while still at school – which affect their capacities to participate in public educational institutions formally devoted to equal treatment. In this way, even where substantive welfare rights have intervened in the family, they have reinforced rather than undermined the subordinate status of married women.

2 The inferior position of women in public life is not simply a consequence of subordination in the private sphere. Sexism at work and in political life impedes the ability of women to exercise political rights by means of direct and indirect discrimination. Women face direct discrimination in trade unions and political parties but also, because they are often confined to employment in sectors of the economy where labour organization is politically at its weakest, they must confront indirect discrimination. Equal access to formally equal structures is thereby obstructed and constitutes one of the strongest arguments for positive discrimination in such areas.

3 The obstacles faced by women in the full exercise of rights extend beyond male behaviour in particular institutional contexts such as family, work or political organizations. The power of discourse and language in constraining the sexuality and autonomy of women is pervasive in all areas of social life. The exercise of rights – particularly those of a civil and political nature (to use Marshall's classification again) – requires a 'non-gendered subjectivity'[6] in which individuals' self-perception is defined by goal-oriented behaviour and attributes and skills acquired in public life. Participating in politics requires a self-definition as a political animal, and such an animal will

remain male as long as women's self-definition is constrained to the area of sexuality. This is not to *deny* that there is a politics involved in sexuality, but rather to identify one aspect of it: the role of prevailing conceptions of sexuality in denying women a public and political existence. By focusing on these forms of substantive inequality which impede access to areas of established formal equality, feminism can turn the concept of rights from a positivist concept enshrined in much legal theory (a statement of what is) into a critical transformative concept – as Eisenstein suggests – capable of showing what *changes* need to occur in order for substantive sexual equality to be achieved.

Girls' rights

From the perspective outlined above, we can now turn to approach the question of girls' rights. We immediately face a paradox: historically, liberal theory has identified progress with the separation and exclusion of children from rights and the responsibilities that accompany them. A critical feminism involves a a reversal of such a perspective. Instead of shielding 'minors' from the legal process through an assertion of their 'pre-rational' state, the question is turned on its head and reformulated as what rights need to be *acquired* by girls in order for the substantive inequalities mentioned above to be removed in their transition to adulthood.

Until recently the question of children's rights did not address itself to the way in which gender specifically impinges on girls or ask how the experiences of growing up as girls contribute to their oppression both as children and later when they are women. Youth culture studies have focused on boys and often neglected sex–gender relations. The savage chauvinism of male youth culture, rather than being examined, has been embraced as a 'celebration of masculinity'. Such studies have accepted sexism uncritically and, by depicting rock bands, skinheads and other groups romantically, have implicitly extolled it. The reason why the day-to-day experience of sexism has been rarely questioned is because of the commonsense view of sexuality and gender as 'natural' and biological and therefore unchangeable. This transforms the experience of very unfair relations between the sexes into the acceptance of these relations as natural.

But what is meant by girls' rights? In an equal society everyone should have the right to equal opportunities in education, the right to receive a living wage as adults, to decide when and whether to have children and to develop their potentiality to the full. What needs to be explained is why it is that so few girls develop to their full potential, why and how they are subject to discrimination in the home and outside, and why they are subject to sexual abuse and harassment, and as women why many lead constricted lives and are subject to domestic violence.

Questions about rights are questions about fundamental freedoms to do certain things that others are able to do, or freedom from interference by other people in aspects of life normally left to personal choice. These freedoms are present or absent not in theory, but in concrete social contexts. We shall therefore start with an examination of the rights of girls in a family context, and then move on to a study of girls in education and in the peer-group subculture.

The family

Families influence the rights of girls on two levels. First, there is an informal level. Girls are socialized in the family to accept what is virtually second-class citizenship as a 'different but equal' place in the sun. Furthermore, they learn to regard it as natural that they should relate to the world primarily as sexual rather than cognitive beings. But girls' rights are also affected at a formal level, when the family is unable to manage its affairs in private. Once the outside world becomes involved, a girls' sexuality may become a problem which is treated in a different way from the sexuality of her brothers. We begin with a discussion of socialization.

When a new baby is born, the first question everybody asks is 'Is it a boy or a girl?' Immediately, appropriate cards and presents are bought which already assume that the two genders have developed distinct personalities. 'Pink for a little girl, blue for a boy' implies far more than merely different-coloured baby clothes. It suggests a whole set of ideal characteristics which are looked for and subsequently 'discovered' in the new baby on the basis of supposed biological and psychological differences.[7] Girls *are* 'gentle, demure, sensitive, submissive, non-competitive, sweet-natured and dependent' – in other words, passive. Boys are 'aggressive, dominant, ambitious, strong and independent' – in other words, active. Boys have the characteristics required to succeed in an economy based on individualism and competition, whereas girls 'naturally' provide a nurturing, caring background for them. In spite of the anthropological and historical evidence which demonstrates that biological differences contribute very little to gender differentiation,[8] the belief that boys and girls are different 'by nature' persists as part of common sense. Moreover, as Sue Sharp argues, in 'a society in which obvious discrimination is condemned, "natural" sex differences help to preserve the separation of roles and thus the inequalities upon which the economic system still depends.'[9]

Considerable attention has been paid to the way that family socialization influences girls' development,[10] and more recently feminist writers have turned their attention to the role played by toys, books and comics in reproducing the feminine subject. It is impossible to do justice to this literature here, but there are some points worth noting, since they are particularly relevant to the issue. For example, Sara Delamont notes that, whereas boys' toys are essentially active, promising adventure and fun, girls' toys are essentially passive, often reproducing aspects of domestic life within the household. Toys encourage girls to cook, sew, nurse, wash and care for 'the baby', whereas boys' toys encourage the recipient to fight, to build and construct and plan long-term battle strategies; these activities all occur in the world outside.[11] Home-centredness for girls is also encouraged in early reading schemes and children's books. For example, as Rosemary Stones remarks, reporting a review of forty-six stories featuring girls out of a list of 200 picture books:

> The only time that girls show any spirit is when they help mother dust, sweep or polish. . . . Boys' career books emphasize the need for every human being (in an all male world) to live life as fully as possible; girls' career books either describe the world of daydream or encourage her to accept second best as normal, by the choice of career which they put in front of her, the way in which it is treated and by how they portray her final goal.[12]

If books for small children present girls with a limited vision of their everyday lives in the future, comics and popular magazines, while superficially liberating, work to control and condition the inner psyche. In a penetrating analysis of pre-teen comic stories, Valerie Walkerdine shows how real and difficult situations are presented in a world of fantasy and are overcome through the selfless and patient responses of the heroines. The girls in the stories suffer from many of the problems which affect the readers in real life. These, however, are transposed into a dramatic world in which the situation can be resolved. This occurs by projecting negative, undesirable traits on to distant and evil characters in the story, in contrast to the 'beautiful' character of the heroine herself. As Walkerdine says:

> The heroines all suffer in silence; they display values of patience and forbearance and are rewarded for silence, for selflessness,

for helpfulness. Any thought of self, any wanting, longing desire or anger is in this way produced within the texts as bad ... girls are not presented with heroines who ever get angry ... it is never justified nor is rebellion ever sanctioned ... it is in this way that girls become 'victims' – for example angry and hostile feelings are projected on to the other and are suppressed in the self – passivity is thus *actively* produced as the result of an internal struggle.[13]

Although *Bunty* and *Mandy* readers are still too young for romantic stories, they are nevertheless learning to identify with the typical traits of the heroines of romantic fiction. By the time they move on to *Jackie* they are prepared 'to value themselves only insofar as they are valued by boys'. As Angela McRobbie says of the commercial media, although

Apparently devoted to leisure and fun their idea of fun ... especially Jackie's is almost wholly restricted to the neurotic search for 'a fella'. It is in these limited self images and the narrow possibilities they present that the brunt of my critique lies.[14]

However, even if one may be critical of the sexist bias in books, toys and comics, it may seem rather far-fetched to suggest that they contribute to undermining the rights of girls. After all, not all parents buy girls' toys for their daughters, nor attempt to subdue their personalities or overburden them with domestic pursuits. In fact parents are far more worried if their sons can't stand up for themselves or don't act in a masculine and aggressive way, than if their daughters show an undue amount of spirit. It is far worse for a boy to be a sissy than it is for a girl to be a tomboy, because that is considered to be something 'she'll grow out of' once she becomes interested in boys. Here, perhaps, is the crux of the matter: once a girl has learned to measure her worth in terms of her ability to attract men through her sexuality, and accept that if she is unsuccessful in this she has failed as a woman, she is unable to make the most of her potential in other areas of her life. she tends to concentrate exclusively on the emotional aspects of her 'self' and to undervalue her cognitive ability. This not only has disastrous consequences for the future, but tends to make her very unhappy. In magazines, sexuality is legitimated through the ideology of romantic love. Girls learn to expect that relationships will last and become the focal point to which they will dedicate their lives. Boys, on the other hand, are encouraged to repress their sensitivity to other people's feelings and to despise and reject the 'feminine' aspects of their natures.[15] Sexuality is to be regarded as an adjunct to the masculine ego.[16] Girls are often no more than a series of conquests, while lasting friendships are reserved for their 'mates'.

Girls do report[17] being treated differently from their brothers by their parents, who are more concerned about the hours girls keep and expect more help at home from them. In some families their freedom may be unnecessarily restricted and, therefore, their rights curtailed. However, the most effective and universal limitation on a girl's capacity to act as an autonomous individual is the one she imposes on herself by accepting her unequal relation to men as both 'natural' and inevitable. The socialization of girls, with the emphasis it places on the definition of self in terms of a sexuality defined by men, limits their capacity to exercise formally guaranteed rights in the public sphere.

So far, we have examined the informal mechanisms whereby girls are persuaded to depend on men for their self-esteem. However, there are particular circumstances in which sexuality affects the rights of girls and boys formally in a different way, particularly in the case of family breakdown or even poor family relationships, which may expose a girl to outside intervention. Here we shall discuss schoolgirl pregnancy, contraception, and sexuality and social control.

In their report *Pregnant at School*[18] the National Council for One-Parent Families stated that, in 1977, 3625 girls under sixteen became pregnant, as did 8424 single girls aged sixteen. Pregnancies to single sixteen-year-olds increased by 19 per cent between 1971 and 1973 but have decreased by 11 per cent since then.

There are several disturbing aspects of this report which suggest that a girl's rights may be threatened if she becomes pregnant while she is still at school. The first issue concerns a girl's right to adequate information and effective contraception without having to suffer disapproval or embarrassment. The report argues that girls who became pregnant were not more sexually experienced, nor were their family circumstances unusual. Pregnancy was not a form of psychological response to social or family deprivation,[19] but usually happened inadvertently because of faulty or inadequate knowledge about birth control. Girls under sixteen, especially, were afraid that help would be refused; that their boyfriend would be prosecuted for under-age sex or that their parents would be notified. In certain schools, the report noted, there was an unenthusiastic response to offers of help in improving the teaching of sex education, because they didn't consider it an important item on their curriculum. Some schools were even opposed to it altogther. More significantly, boys' schools often do not see the need to include health education in the curriculum at all. This makes nonsense of the idea that pregnancy should be a shared responsibility. In fact, as the Association of Headmistresses claim in *Unplanned Pregnancy*,[20] 'Improved contraceptive techniques for women may have reduced male responsibility even more.'[21] The authors of the report recommend that advice about contraception should be made available to both boys and girls, who should be encouraged to seek it together, through the youth advisory service which is not connected either with authority figures or with the medical profession. If a girl felt she could ask for advice in a supportive and non-disapproving atmosphere, unwanted pregnancy might be prevented.

The second important issue that the report raises is that girls who do become pregnant and have the baby seem to lose their last years of schooling. Few girls returned to school after the baby was born, and 'too many LEAs are using their powers to excuse girls from school on medical grounds and are failing to use their powers to provide adequate alternative education.'[22] In some instances the school felt that if pregnancy was accepted as normal the moral standards of the whole school would be undermined. A girl who has failed to complete her education has a low earning capacity, poor job prospects and, as a single parent, is likely to be permanently dependent on supplementary benefit – a depressing future for both the mother and the baby.

Finally, as might be expected, the report makes it clear that schoolgirl pregnancy has the most negative effect on girls who are already disadvantaged in some way. For example, girls who are in care and become pregnant while living in a children's home may find that they are asked to leave. Equally, a girl from a low-income family, even if they want to help her, may find that relations become strained because she is imposing an added financial burden on the household. Schoolgirl mothers are not entitled to maternity allowance because it is contributory, or to supplementary benefit or family income supplement in their own right. However, as the report notes,

> If she leaves school when she is 16 she is immediately entitled to apply for Supplementary Benefit without registering for employment; if she gets a job which is low paid she may be entitled to Family Income Supplement. There is therefore a strong incentive for her to leave school.[23]

When the damage that can be done too a girl's future by unintended early pregnancy is considered, it would seem that access to efficient contraception should be available as a right to any young girl, and this important principle was supported by the DHSS in their circulars of 1974 and 1980. Although both circulars advised doctors or counsellors to do their best to persuade a patient under sixteen to discuss the matter with her parents, they nevertheless recognized the importance of confidentiality between doctor and patient, and that the decision whether or not to prescribe contraception should finally be a matter for the doctor's clinical judgement.

In 1981 Victoria Gillick sought an assurance from her local health authority that they would in no circumstances 'give any contraceptive or abortion advice or treatment whatsoever to my four daughters while they are under 16 years without my consent.'[24] On failing to receive the required assurance, Mrs Gillick commenced proceedings against both her local health authority and the DHSS in relation to the 1980 circular. In July 1983 her claims against the local health authority were dismissed by Mr Justice Woolf in the High Court. However, his judgement was reversed in the Court of Appeal on 20 December 1984 by Lord Justice Parker, who ruled

> that any doctor who advises a girl under 16 as to contraceptive steps to be taken or affords contraceptive or abortion treatment to such a girl without the knowledge and consent of the parent save in an emergency . . . infringes on the legal rights of the parent or guardian.

The DHSS circular of 1980 was declared 'contrary to the law'. The Childrens' Legal Centre (CLC) claimed that the implications of the Court of Appeal judgement were that

> under 16s have no independent or confidential rights to medical treatment or choice or self determination on important matters affecting their bodies or their lives: parents have the right completely to control the bodies of their children until they reach 16 unless a court intervenes. Thus a parent can, for instant, insist on an abortion or contraception for a 15 year old against her wishes.[25]

The CLC was specifically critical of the Appeal Court decision on two counts. First, accepting a different age of discretion for boys (fourteen) and girls (sixteen), as the Parker judgement did, offended section 29(1) of the Sex Discrimination Act (1975) and article 14 of the European Convention on Human Rights, which prohibits discrimination on the grounds of sex. Second, they argued that the right to consent to medical treatment should not be based on some arbitrary and fixed age but rather on the maturity and understanding of the individual concerned.

It is ironic that the Appeal Court judgement would have had the most harmful effect on the same population of girls who are most adversely affected by schoolgirl pregnancy. Where family relations are supportive and girls get on well with their parents, the Gillick judgement was unlikely to make any difference. But where a girl has poor relations with her parents or disagrees profoundly with their attitudes it would be more difficult for her to find someone to turn to for help.

However, the right of a girl to control her own sexuality was clearly recognized by the law lords who over-turned the Appeal Court's decision on October 18 1985. The legal rights of young girls to avoid the interruption and pressure of unwanted pregnancy have now been conceded, (even if the vote was not unanimous). Nevertheless, the court's decision does not alter the fact that a girl's freedom to develop in her own way still depends very much on her family.

In some families the mere fact of female sexuality leads to trouble, with parents imposing stricter rules on daughters than on sons. As one group of girls, writing to *Spare Rib*, put it ruefully,

> We ... feel that boys have far fewer restrictions put on them. ... They are allowed to stay out until anytime they like and go where they like but we're cross questioned about where we're going and told either that we can't go, or that we must come back at a certain time.[26]

Once rules are imposed, they are also easily broken, and this can lead to rows and arguments. If a girl stays out late too often, and either outside help is called in or she is picked up by the police and returned home several times, then the family loses the greatest protection it can afford its members – its anonymity. Once it comes 'to the attention of the local authority', a girl's sexual behaviour may come under scrutiny and further restrictions may be imposed on her as 'beyond the control of her parents' or 'in moral danger', particularly if she is suspected of under-age sex. This process is well described by a young woman writing to *Spare Rib*.

> I'm fifteen and have just been threatened with being taken into care. I went to court last Thursday for shoplifting, and I've also been suspended from school for having two colour hair. However throughout my case sex and boys came up all the time.

The police made me see a psychiatrist, would you believe, and when they brought my whole file into court about 75% of their case was in fact to do with having under age sex. Often when I've stayed out at night my Mother has got worried and sent the pigs after me. The police did manage to pick me up a couple of times and threatened to give me a medical to see if I'd been having USI – Unlawful Sexual Intercourse – I didn't even know what they meant at first.[27]

Research in two girls' Borstals in the early 1970s showed that a girl could be sentenced to Borstal training without having committed an indictable offence, but simply by having been taken into care at an early age and having 'absconded' from a series of increasingly secure institutions.[28] The 1982 Criminal Justice Act, which requires the court to give reasons for rejecting a non-custodial sentense, should make such an event less likely today. However, a report, 'Children Still in Trouble',[29] suggests that the use of custodial sentences for young people is still rising faster than the rise in crime and that there is a 25 per cent rise in the use of custodial sentences for females.[30] As Gillick's attempt to undermine the confidential relationship between a young girl and her doctor shows, girls are particularly vulnerable to the kind of legal intervention which prevents them from managing their own sexuality in a responsible manner, and that vulnerability will remain until a girl's right to control her own sexuality is enshrined in law.

It is difficult to argue conclusively that families in general either protect or undermine girls' rights, for a number of reasons. First, it is true that girls' socialization usually occurs in a family setting, and they learn how to become women from their mothers. But, even though most girls still accept the feminine role as 'natural', recent research suggests that a substantial minority of girls are beginning to recognize the unfair strain imposed on their mothers by the work they are expected to do, both inside and outside the household, and these girls at least plan a very different future for themselves.[31] Second, the family undermines girls' rights to the extent that it is a vehicle for passing on to its members the unequal opportunities doled out by the British class structure; but that is true for all children, not only for girls. Finally, in a society which encourages individual freedom as one of its most important political priorities, the private sphere is the natural habitat for children. Public provision is consequently second rate both ideologically and financially. A family protects its members as long as it has the capacity to remain free from outside interference. However, that same privacy also allows various forms of child abuse, neglect or domestic violence to remain undetected for long periods of time. Girls specifically tend to suffer from domestic oppression in the household and more seriously from incest, which, of course, violates girls' rights on a formal level as well. Parents are regarded as the natural guardians of their children's rights. If they abuse them instead of protecting them, the children suffer twice over – first, because they are afraid they won't be believed or that they'll be punished if they talk about it and, second, because they are afraid of the effect on the family if anything should come to light. It might be split up and they might lose its protection. Any form of family breakdown increases children's vulnerability, and, to the extent that battles over the control of female sexuality impose an added strain on family relations, girls are more vulnerable than boys.

Education

Education is a vital preparation for the effective exercise of civil and political rights, and therefore inequalities in the educational experience of girls and boys necessarily affect their respective abilities to exercise such rights in adulthood.

Schools, at least since the Sex Discrimination Act (1975) have a formal policy of equality of opportunity, and cannot legally discriminate against any pupil on the grounds of race, sex or class. However, as Michelle Stanworth argues, our education system 'favours those who are already privileged and puts further obstacles in the path of those who are disadvantaged.'[32] It is therefore not surprising that feminist writers found that gender was a source of educational inequality. But the issue is not simply a straightforward case of relative failure. As Jennifer Shaw points out, the question is:

How is it that girls who began their school career with what appears to be a flying start over boys, being as much as two years ahead in reading and in physical and psychological maturity, come to leave school with far fewer qualifications?

She goes on to comment:

the other side of all selective educational systems is systematic discouragement, but the paradox of the British model is that by its own criteria of success its most promising pupils persistently underachieve.[33]

It is not that girls fail to achieve altogether; in fact, they are now doing relatively better than they have done in the past. It is rather that, in areas crucial to future career or job prospects, boys appear to have the advantage at every level. For example, in 1981, 58 per cent of girls left school with at least one GCE O level grade A–C compared with 52 per cent of boys. But, whereas 44 per cent of girls leaving school passed O-level English compared with 33 per cent of boys, 31 per cent of boys passed O-level maths compared to only 26 per cent of girls.[34] As Stanworth points out,

> Mathematics at 'O' level or its CSE equivalent is a necessary prerequisite for careers in computer programming, textile technology, dentistry, architecture, horticulture, engineering, the police force, market research, printing, radiography, chemistry, economics, surveying, town planning, advertising, banking and astronomy to name but a few.[35]

Although more girls than boys obtain two A levels, more boys pass three A levels, with the good grades necessary for a place at university. In 1981–2, 9.1 per cent of male school-leavers were taking degree courses as against only 6.9 per cent of females.[36] However, the changes between 1970 and 1981 were greater for girls than for boys. The percentage of girls on degree courses rose from 5.3 to 6.9 per cent whereas the percentage of boys taking degrees only rose from 9.0 to 9.1 per cent over the same period.[37] Women still predominate in the humanities and education, whereas there are noticeably more men in the physical sciences, engineering and technology.

It is, however, those with the least advantage that are most affected by these differences. In 1977, 49 per cent of men but 60 per cent of women at work possessed no educational qualifications at all.[38] Moreover, there is a substantial difference between men and women concerning the availability of 'on the job' training, with 3.3 per cent of all male employees in manufacturing receiving some sort of training, compared to 1.4 per cent of female employees.[39] However, the recession and high youth unemployment may bring some advantages for women. As Ann Wickham points out, Youth Training Schemes cannot so easily exclude girls, and since life skills are included in the programme the old equation of skill with apprenticeship may be forced to change.[40] However, at present women remain financially disadvantaged in the labour market. In spite of equal pay, the average weekly wage for men in full-time employment was £167.5 per week in April 1983 whereas for women it was £108.[41]

Empirically, women are at a disadvantage in the labour market, and this is true not only for manual workers. There are relatively few women in senior positions in the professions, management, administration or higher education. The education system is the main agent for allocating young people into a hierarchy of differently valued and differently rewarded social roles and therefore plays an important part in reproducing class and gender relations for each new generation. We cannot here do justice to the wide variety of research which has investigated the way in which schools perform this task[42] and so will confine discussion to two questions. First, why do girls underachieve? Second, why do schools allow them to do it?

First, there is the simple argument that girls underachieve because as they grow older it becomes more important to them to get married than to do well at school.[43] Yet, as Jenny Shaw asks,

> Do girls really believe that marriage and a family are going to provide a life long activity, when even as long ago as 1950 the average age of first marriage was 22 and women's age at the time of the birth of their last child was 26? With 42% of all married women working and more in the working class is it likely that girls are totally unaware of this; especially if they take their mothers as models?[44]

She goes on to suggest that the idea of marriage interrupts girls' view of the future and therefore discourages long-term planning. It may well be true that many girls do put marriage first, but why do women subordinate their career aspirations to their family role? There are, of course, arguments that men resent female encroachment on their preserves and therefore ensure that female jobs remain poorly paid, low in status and unattractive goals for which to strive. Even where structural change encourages the creation of well-paid senior posts in a traditionally female occupation, the top positions are often occupied by men; this has certainly occurred in nursing.[45] The important point to note is that, although there has been an enormous increase in numbers of women working, neither their relative economic position nor their status has improved. Additionally, the attempts to make education more responsive to the needs of industry may effectively discourage girls from wanting to work for qua-lifications at all. The latest government Green Paper on Education[46] (May 1985) proposes to divert resources away from the humanities and social sciences, which are traditionally 'girls' subjects', and to encourage the development of technological courses in applied sci-ence, usually taken by boys. It also proposes to move the humanities

and social sciences out of the public sector and, even so, to offer a
reduced number of places in these subjects in universities. These
proposals would affect girls' opportunities in two ways: first, because
polytechnics offer places to candidates with only two A levels and,
second, because the scarcity of places in these subjects will increase
demand in the university sector, making it harder for women to get
accepted. Moreover, in traditional areas where girls have made
successful careers, such as teaching, nursing and social work, the
number of training places have been cut or qualification levels raised.
Girls have been increasingly successful in medicine, but fierce
competition ensures there are never enough medical-school places for
everyone who wants to be a doctor. However, there are encouraging
signs that the need for new directions in women's career patterns,
particularly in science and technology, is now being recognized. The
Equal Opportunities Unit has been established centrally to promote
and monitor policy, and the Sex Equality Education Fund set up to
aid small school based projects. In 1984 the 'Women in Science and
Engineering' group held a conference to discuss new initiatives to
attract girls into technological careers. The WISE '84 Report
describes imaginative schemes and projects designed to make careers
in science more attractive and relevant to women, and to prevent girls
from giving up science and mathematics early in their school careers.

   To understand why many girls don't at present fulfill their potential
or obtain good qualifications in mathematics and science during their
schooldays, we now turn to the process of schooling itself. At primary
school, boys are taught to avoid girls' toys, are discouraged from
playing girls' games and seem aware that if they do they are
demeaning their sex. Katherine Clarricoates, who has examined sex
role typing in primary schools, tells a story of two little boys who were
playing at housekeeping in the Wendy House. When the teacher asked
them what they were playing they looked shamefaced and replied
'Batman and Robin'.[47] Early school readers reinforce the picture
presented in children's books read at home: there is mummy at home
in her apron helped by her daughter, while daddy and his son go out
on an exiciting adventure. Later the English curriculum concentrates
on male authors, and history is mainly about men. Clarricoates argues
that teachers' perceptions of the same actions vary according to their
expectations of appropriate behaviour for each sex. If a girl was eager
to answer a question the teacher interpreted it as showing off, whereas
if a boy showed the same keenness it was regarded as a sign of
intelligence. She considers that the girls were continually being sent
hidden messages that they were the inferior and undervalued sex, who
only did better because they were attentive, neat and conforming.

In secondary schools, although theoretically all subjects are equally available to everyone, girls tend to make a mixture of subjects including biology as their one science, rather than physics, chemistry and mathematics or biology as boys do. In some schools, researchers found girls were channelled into domestic vocational subjects and discouraged from attending classes in metalwork or technical drawing. As we have seen, girls are less successful at mathematics. Since relative failure in this subject has been blamed on poorer teaching, the general trend towards coeducation, which accompanied comprehensivization, should have improved both girls' standards in maths and the facilities available for science and technology. However, Jennifer Shaw argues that, although coeducation has improved academic results for boys, the performance of girls has tended to deteriorate specifically in maths and science, where girls are least confident. The relations between the two sexes in the classroom goes some way to providing an explanation. In areas where there is a degree of choice, boys refuse to discuss topics that might interest girls; if a girl does resolutely decide to take up a 'boys' subject', she is made the butt of sexist jokes; and in general boys demand and teachers give more attention to them. Dale Spender reports that when she taped classes she was teaching, although she felt she was giving equal attention to both boys and girls, she found that

> the maximum time I spent interacting with the girls was 42% ... and the maximum with the boys was 58%. It was nothing short of a substantial shock to appreciate the discrepancy between what I *thought* I was doing and what I actually *was* doing.[50]

This is important in a subject like mathematics where individual attention may be necessary to progress to the next stage. Stuart Smith describes an experiment undertaken in his school which provided segregated maths teaching for girls. Over a two-year period the girls became much more confident in class and their results improved.[51]

Writers are by no means agreed on the relative merits of coeducation and single-sex schooling. Those in favour of coeducation put forward the 'social' argument that it is better for boys and girls to grow up together naturally. This would be all very well if 'natural' in our culture did not mean that it is natural for boys to regard themselves as automatically superior, thus distorting the idea of equal relations between the sexes. There is evidence that boys in mixed schools frustrate the ability of girls to hold their own in competition with boys. We get glimpses of the extent of boys' disruption of the classroom; their noisiness, their sexual harrassment of girls, their demands for attention, their need of disciplining and their attitudes to girls as the silent or 'the faceless bunch'.[52] Furthermore there is the academic argument that the pioneering tradition developed by women like Frances Mary Buss, who demanded both excellence and equality from girls' education, will be lost. In this tradition, subsequently followed in many girls' grammar schools, pupils were expected to take education seriously, to do well in public examinations and to go on to higher education.[53] Tensions still arose for working-class girls in relation to their peers outside schools,[54] and for middle-class girls later in life if they attempted to combine motherhood with a career, but nevertheless there was present in these schools an academic tradition for girls which is found neither in many upper-class boarding schools[55] nor in the contemporary comprehensive.

The direction that educational initiatives will take in the future is, of course, ultimately a political issue. If girls' rights are to be defended and improved, it is essential that new proposals are carefully scrutinized in the light of their effect on equality of opportunity for both sexes. At the level of the school, the work that feminists are now doing is of critical importance in helping teachers to become aware of sexist practices and to find ways of overcoming them.

Language and discourse

The third area of substantive inequality concerns the construction of female sexuality through language and discourse. How male and female sexuality is talked about and conceptualized is a crucial determinant of boys' and girls' experience.

It would be a mistake to assume that children are only influenced by parents and teachers. Increasingly, as they grow older, it is the opinions of 'other kids' that also matter. The independent life that develops in the interstices between home and school, at football, on the street, at the disco, has been interpreted as a form of resistance by working-class children to the unfair deal they have received at the hands of 'respectable' society.[56] Girls have been neglected by these studies, partly because most of the sociologists working in this area have been men. However, recently girls' social life has been given more attention. Drawing on her research among a group of girls attending a Birmingham youth club, Angela McRobbie argues that, like the boys in Paul Willis's studies, girls develop an anti-school culture. It takes the form of an exaggerated feminity, particularly in class, and a great deal of time spent at home in the bedroom with a best friend listening to records and talking about boys and pop stars. It leads to leaving school early with no qualifications, and therefore a boring job. The only way out is early marriage which may, at the time, appear to be the end of a romantic story, but which in reality is more likely to be the beginning of a life of drudgery. The resistance effectively locates the girls in a subordinate position, both economically and in regard to men.

Sue Lees, whose work is based on interviews and group discussions with about a hundred London schoolgirls aged between fifteen and seventeen, also accepts that the lowering of girls' aspirations is a reconciliation to a life centred on love and marriage and subordination to men, but suggests that this happens in a rather different way.[57] Contra McRobbie, she argues that the bedroom culture, rather than being a resistance or anti-school culture, is a way of conforming to the dominant ideology of inferiority and confinement to domestic life. She began her study intending to investigate girls' attitudes towards school, friendship and marriage, but was immediately struck by the girls' concern with their sexual reputation and the double standard of morality that oppressed them. She therefore turned her attention to the way in which sexual relations are socially structured.

Girls, she suggests, are controlled because their sexual reputation is so precarious and crucial to them in a way that it is not to boys. First, for boys, respectability is not a master status as it is for girls. A boy's reputation depends on many other things, like being tough, witty, smart or good at sports. Second, a boy's reputation is enhanced with sexual experience, so he boasts about it, whereas the same experience can destroy a girl's reputation, so she is desperate to keep it quiet. Third, sexism is an imporant component in male bonding. Making sexist jokes and generally denigrating women is crucial to male camaraderie. This asymmetry between boys and girls is illustrated by the term 'slag', which an be used by both boys and other girls in a wide range of circumstances. It implies that a girl sleeps around, but this may in fact have nothing to do with the case in point. A girl can be referred to as a slag if her clothes are too tight, too short, too smart or in any way sexually provocative, if she hangs about with boys, if she talks to another girl's boyfriend, if she talks too loud or too much. It is an ever-present threat; a mechanism whereby boys can control girls' sexual behaviour, although no equivalent term exists for boys. Any girl is potentially in danger from the 'slag' label at any time, and the girls agreed that the one way to redeem yourself was to get a steady boyfriend.

In point of fact the term 'slag', rather than referring to actual sexual behaviour, appears to act as a censure against being unattached. There is no legitimate place for female sexuality except in the context of an exclusive relationship. Nice girls cannot have sexual desire without love; therefore the only protection a girl has is to restrict herself to one boyfriend, and if she does she is even more vulnerable, the moment he drops her. Some of the girls in the study had been 'in love loads of times'. This might well be a rationalization after the event, but it was the only approved context within which a girl might have sex without losing her reputation. Love steers sex into a safe place – marriage. What was interesting, however, was that the girls were realistic about marriage. They knew from their mothers' experience that it was a poor deal for women, since it made them never free of domestic responsibilities, whether or not they worked outside the home. Moreover, the girls were not in a hurry to get married. They knew how tied, poor and hard-worked they'd be once they'd had children, so they wanted a good time first when they could go out and buy 'loads of clothes' and even perhaps work abroad. But in the long run they saw no alternative to marriage. In fact *failure* to get married was an awesome threat which haunted them even as schoolgirls.

From the girls' conversation it would appear that the status of an unattached woman today is as stigmatized as the governess or maiden aunt in the nineteenth-century novel. Even if she is successful in a career, her social life is restricted and lonely. If she goes out alone at night she's in danger of being physically harmed or regarded as a tart. She imposes an unwelcome embarrassment at a social gathering in a way that the 'eligible bachelor' certainly does not. The girls regarded being 'left on the shelf' as a distant but awful possibility, but they did not challenge the asymmetry of the relations between boys and girls which allowed them to think in these terms. They made excuses for boys' behaviour when they treated girls badly. Even if a girl was sexually assaulted, other girls suspected that she'd 'asked for it' or was at least partly to blame, by being out late at night or 'leading a boy on'.

Girls who failed to comply with the norms were considered by both boys and other girls to be at fault. But a girl faces a situation in which she cannot win. If she says 'yes' she risks being labelled as a slag, but if she says 'no' she may be thought of as a 'tight bitch' and not worth bothering about. Boys and girls conspire together to ensure that female sexuality is kept strictly under control while male sexuality is given a free rein. As McRobbie and Garber note,

Boys who had, sexually and socially, 'sown their wild oats' could 'turn over a new leaf' and 'settle down'; for girls the consequences of getting known in the neighbourhood as one of the 'wild oats' to be 'sown' was drastic and irreversible.[58]

Moreover, although it takes different forms, this unequal relation between the sexes is essentially the same, regardless of social class. For girls the experience of class is always mediated through gender in the sense that, first, as children growing up, girls are subject to different constraints and expectations from boys in the same social group. Second, in adolescence, a girl's self-esteem is crucially affected by her relations with boys, whereas a boy derives his status from a wider set of social relations and many different activities. These differences seem to hold in all social classes. Furthermore, in later life a girl's social class is nearly always determined by her relation to men. Whatever a woman's status and income at marriage (and over 90 per cent of women marry at some time in their lives), divorce invariably leads to rapid downward social mobility. The increase in divorce has led, as Hilda Scott points out, to the 'feminisation of poverty'.[59] This occurs because a woman's economic position is generally inferior to her male partner, as it is assumed that naturally she will be the one to interrupt her paid employment to undertake the necessary caring and domestic duties which are both undervalued and unpaid.

It is clear that such forms of behaviour as interpersonal relations and language are less amenable to precise formulation as *rights* than are more formal institutions like schools and even families. A process of language change and educational reform is required. Nevertheless the ultimate impulse for such change can be seen as the rejection of the doctrine of natural differences and the upholding of the right to equal treatment.

Conclusions

There are broadly two different ways in which girls' rights have been threatened or undermined. First, at the level of public policy:

1 Where policies are designed to promote formal equality of opportunities are implemented in a way that discriminates against girls (for example, choices available on a curriculum, sex-biased vocational subjects, even coeducation without adequate consideration of girls' problems in maths or science).
2 Where biological factors make girls vulnerable to legislative battles over issues like contraception and abortion, so that sexual

relations, which after all are *relations*, have a different outcome for each sex.
3 Where parents or adults in a position of responsibility violate the trust that this position implies. This is applicable to all children, but girls are specifically at risk from (a) an overload of domestic chores which hamper their education, (b) unnecessary restriction on their freedom in some cases and (c) sexual abuse.

Second, there is the private or internal sphere where girls' rights are restricted by the attitudes towards them which they encounter from adults, boys and other girls, and the resulting attitudes they develop towards themselves. It is this evaluation of their own worth, or lack or it, that is specifically relevant to the relation between boys and girls, which reflects the imbalance of power between men and women in public life, in the economy, and perhaps most of all in the family. Although the two-parent couple with two children and mum at home may no longer represent the statistical norm in Britain today, it nevertheless remains the standard against which all other forms of social arrangement are measured. But, unless the unequal relation implicit in its structure and in the structure of society more generally is continually challenged, each new generation will construct for themselves the kind of social relations which re-create this imbalance of power anew.

Notes

1   Z. Eisenstein, *'Feminism and sexual equality'*, Monthly Review Press (1984).
2   T. H. Marshall, *Sociology at the Crossroads* (Heinemann, 1963).
3   S. M. Lipset, *Political Man* (Mercury Books, 1963).
4   J. Rawls, *A Theory of Justice* (Clarendon Press, 1972).
5   Eisenstein, *Feminism and sexual equality*, p. 13.
6   M. Black and R. Coward, 'Linguistic, social and sexual relations', *Screen Education*, 39 (1981).
7   S. Delamont, *The Sociology of Women* (Allen and Unwin, 1980), p. 19.
8   A. Oakley, *Sex, Gender and Society* (Temple Smith, 1972), ch. 2.
9   S. Sharpe, *Just Like a Girl* (Penguin, 1978), p. 62.
10 For example, J. and E. Newsom, *Seven Years Old in the Home Environment* (Allen and Unwin, 1976), pp. 144–8.
11 Delamont, *The Sociology of Women*, pp. 37–41.
12 R. Stones, *'Pour out the Cocoa Janet': sexism in children's books*, Schools Council Programme, 3 (Longman for Schools Council, 1983), p. 12.
13 V. Walkerdine, 'Someday my prince will come', in *Gender and Generation*, ed. A. McRobbie and M. Nava (Macmillan, 1984), p. 173.

14 A. McRobbie, 'Just like a Jackie story', in *Feminism for Girls*, ed. A. McRobbie and T. McCabe (Routledge and Kegan Paul, 1981), p. 116.
15 M. Arnot, 'How shall we educate our sons?', in *Coeducation Reconsidered*, ed. R. Deem (Open University Press, 1984), pp. 45–6.
16 P. Willis, *Learning to Labour* (Saxon House, 1978), pp. 43–6.
17 S. Hemmings (ed.), *Girls are Powerful* (Sheba Feminist Publishers, 1983), pp. 62–6.
18 National Council for One-Parent Families, *Pregnant at School* (Community Development Trust, 1979).
19 As argued by A. Pettigrew, S. Wolkind and E. Zadijec, 'Psychiatric aspects of pregnancy in schoolgirls: a review', *Psychological Medicine*, 8 (19   ), pp. 119–30.
20 Royal College of Obstetricians and Gynaecologists, *Unplanned Pregnancy*, Report of the Working Part (1972).
21 National Council for One-Parent Families, *Pregnant at School*, p. 14.
22 Ibid., p. 21.
23 Ibid., p. 36.
24 Quoted in *Young People's Rights and the Gillick Case*, Children's Legal Centre Briefing (Universal Pictorial Press, 1985), p. 3.
25 Ibid., p. 1.
26 Quoted in Hemmings (ed.), *Girls are Powerful*, p. 64.
27 Ibid., pp. 104–5.
28 J. Mellor, 'The route to Borstal *Youth and Policy*, 2, 2 (Autumn 1983), p. 3.
29 Association of Directors of Social Services, 'Children still in trouble', a report of the ADSS Study Group chaired by John Jillings, presented to the Association, 21 March 1985.
30 Ibid., p. 14.
31 For example, Hemmings (ed.), *Girls are Powerful*, p. 109.
32 M. Stanworth, *Gender and Schooling* (Hutchinson, 1983), p. 9.
33 J. Shaw, 'Finishing school', in *Sexual Divisions and Society: process and change*, ed. D. L. Barker and S. Allen (Tavistock, 1979), p. 134.
34 Central Statistical Office, *Social Trends*, 14 (HMSO, 1984), pp. 46–9.
35 Stanworth, *Gender and Schooling*, p. 11.
36 *The Fact about Women Is* (Statistics Unit, Equal Opportunities Commission, 1984), p. 2.
37 Central Statistical Office, *Social Trends*, 14 (1984).
38 *General Household Survey 1977*, quoted in Stanworth, *Gender and Schooling*, p. 10.
39 *The Fact about Women Is*, p. 3.
40 A. Wickham, 'Gender, schooling and work', *Journal of Education*, 165, 3 (Summer 1983), pp. 279–81.
41 *The Fact about Woman Is*, p. 3.
42 Two particularly useful collections of essays on this topic are D. Spender and E. Sarah (eds), *Learning to Lose* (The Women's Press, 1980), and R. Deem (ed.), *Schooling for Women's Work* (Routledge and Kegan Paul, 1980).

43   For example, this argument is put forward by J. B. W. Douglas in *The Home and the School* (Panther, 1964), p. 99.

44   Shaw, 'Finishing school', p. 139.

45   L. Doyal, G. Hunt and J. Mellor, 'Migrant workers in the National Health Service', *Report for ESRC*, vol. 2 (April 1984).

46   *The Development of Higher Education into the 1990s* (HMSO, May 1985), p. 9.

47   K. Clarricoates, 'The importance of being Ernest . . . Emma . . . Tom . . . Jane – the perception and catagorization of gender conformity and gender deviation in primary schools', in *Schooling for Women's Work*, ed. Deem, pp. 26–41.

48   For example, M. Scott, 'Teach her a lesson: sexist curriculum in patriarchal education', in *Learning to Lose*, ed. Spender and Sarah, p. 106.

49   J. Shaw, 'The politics of single sex schools', in *Schooling for Women's Work*, ed. Deem, pp. 21–36.

50   D. Spender, *Invisible Women* (Writers and Readers Publishers Co-op, 1982).

51   S. Smith, 'Single sex setting', in *Schooling for Women's Work*, ed. Deem, pp. 75–88.

52   M. Arnot, 'How shall we educate our sons?', in *Schooling for Women's Work*, ed. Deem, p. 38.

53   J. Lavigueur, 'Coeducation and the tradition of separate needs', in *Learning to Lose*, ed. Spender and Sarah, pp. 180–90.

54   For example, I. Payne, 'A working class girl in grammar school', in *Learning to Lose*, ed. Spender and Sarah, pp. 12–21.

55   J. Oakley, 'Privileged, schooled and finished: boarding education for girls', in *Defining Females*, ed. S. Ardener (Croom Helm, 1977), pp. 109–39.

56   S. Hall and T. Jefferson (eds), *Resistance through Rituals* (University of Birmingham/Hutchinson, 1976).

57   S. Lees, *Learning to Love* (Hutchinson, 1985).

58   A. McRobbie and J. Garber, 'Girls and subcultures', in *Resistance through Rituals*, ed. Hall and Jefferson, p. 213.

59   H. Scott, *Working Your Way Up To The Bottom* (Pandora, 1984).

Further reading

R. Deem (ed.), *Schooling for Women's Work* (Routledge and Kegan Paul, 1980).

Z. Eisenstein, 'Feminism and sexual equality', *Monthly Review Press* (1984).

S. Hemmings (eds), *Girls are Powerful* (Sheba Feminist Publishers, 1983).

S. Lees, *Learning to Love* (Hutchinson, 1985).

A. McRobbie and M. Nava (eds), *Gender and Generation* (Macmillan, 1984).

A. McRobbie and T. McCabe (eds), *Feminism for Girls* (Routledge and Kegan Paul, 1981).

D. Spender, *Invisible Women* (Writers and Readers Publishers Co-op, 1982).

D. Spender and E. Sarah (eds), *Learning to Lose* (The Women's Press, 1980).

M. Stanworth, *Gender and Schooling* (Hutchinson, 1983).

9

Black Children's Rights

Keith and Shahin Popple

Introduction

The rights of black immigrants' children were systematically ignored or marginalized when they arrived in Britain soon after the Second World War. Since then the overall position of second and third generations has not improved, although there are certain aspects of black children's rights which could be interpreted as having been extended.

There are two main strands to our assessment that black children's rights are constantly withheld. One is that as *black children they are treated unequally in comparison with white* children. Children's skin colour is a strong determinant of their life chances, and so black children fair worse on a whole range of social and economic indicators in comparison to whites. Class and gender add further dimensions to a black child's status, as do particular handicaps.

The other strand to our argument is that black children find that the culture and language of their parents' homeland are negated and the rights to societal respect for these are ignored. The majority of black children living in the United Kingdom were born here and are therefore black British. They are, though, first-generation black British, and their families have languages and cultures predating British culture. Welfare and educational services appear to have no real understanding of Asian and Afro-Caribbean cultural processes and expect black children to adopt a 'white mask'. The irony is that, when black children do become honorary whites, they continue to face discrimination and racism. They therefore miss out on their own cultural processes and solidarity and also fail to achieve in the white world. This explains why black people often use a designation such as 'black British' or 'British Asian', indicating that they are not entirely comfortable with the term 'British', just as white society does not fully accept them as United Kingdom citizens.

This chapter is dedicated to Daniel Popple.

This chapter examines three of the dominant concerns in black children's lives – school, work, and the police and courts. There are several other areas of black children's lives where their rights are constantly threatened, for instance, while in care, and in the workings of the juvenile justice system; some of the points we make here are equally applicable to those areas.

Throughout this work we have used the term 'black', which is a shorthand term for Afro-Caribbean, Asian, Chinese, Cypriot, Vietnamese and any other group which is often labelled as an ethnic minority. These groups have many obvious and specific differences in their cultural process, but they share many similarities in the way that white British society has received and treated them; in particular, they all suffer structural and racial disadvantage and discrimination. The term 'Afro-Caribbean' is used rather than the more popular 'West Indian' because the former describes more accurately the links with Africa, whereas the latter has its roots in Britain's colonial past and is a label coined by white colonizers.

Readers will also find the word 'racism' employed throughout this chapter. Racism is a shorthand term for the theory that the world's population is divisible into unequal and hierarchical categories based on physical differences, particularly skin colour. The dominant groups, which are largely white, impose their understanding on the rest of society. This theory can be interpreted as 'prejudice plus power equals racism'.

Racism, colonialism and post-war immigration

Racism has its roots in Britain's colonial tradition. The British exploration of the previously unknown world of Africa and Asia was inspired by the search for trade, new markets, minerals and cheap labour, which were vital to Britain's economic and industrial development. The consequences of contact with the British, for the countries concerned, were horrific. In Africa the massive transfer of slaves to the Caribbean plantations lead to the break-up of an untold number of families, the deaths of millions of people, and the near destruction of thousands of years of black people's customs, culture, language and religion. In India, too, imperialism demanded the subordination of indigenous cultural tradition, and any developed industry which might compete successfully with its British counterpart, such as cotton, was destroyed. Africa and the Indian subcontinent were systematically underdeveloped.[1] White people needed to justify this appalling treatment of black people as mere objects and began to develop the racism theory mentioned earlier. The myth of white superiority over black skin became incorporated in the majority of European philosophical, religious and scientific literature.

Today the myths continue, as schools proudly display maps of the world with one-third of the land mass printed in pink to mark Britain's extensive domination. Geography books continue the imagery with pictures portraying black people as peasants and therefore 'inferior', whereas the missionaries or developers are seen as educated, 'superior' and, of course, white. Comics and story books, as well as schoolchild 'humour', maintain the stereotyping of black people as inferior, less able and figures of fun. Rejecting such nonsense is difficult for many people, since it has an insidious grip on their subconscious: to challenge it is to challenge themselves and their beliefs.

One particular feature of colonization, the underdevelopment of the local economy and the creation of a labour force willing to travel almost anywhere for employment, is important for current concerns. After the Second World War Britain was enjoying an economic boom but suffering a chronic labour shortage. Like many Western countries, Britain encouraged labour migration from its Empire, primarily from the Afro-Caribbean islands and the Asian subcontinent of India and Pakistan (including East Pakistan, which in 1972 became the independent state of Bangladesh). Economically these countries were heavily dependent on Britain and consequently had become underdeveloped, with a large percentage of their peoples unemployed. Migration was, therefore a realistic solution to a materially impoverished life.

The areas in which black people live currently is related to where these early immigrants of the 1950s and 1960s settled. They moved generally to large conurbations, such as London, the South-East, the West Midlands and the North-West, where there was a demand for unskilled and semiskilled labour. They established homes and began raising families.

The Office of Population Censuses and Surveys (OPCS) estimates for 1980 show that people of Asian, Afro-Caribbean and African origin at present number, 1,774,000, which is just over 3 per cent of the British population. Moreover, figures from the 1981 Census indicate that the adult black population is much younger than the adult white population. A comparison of age profiles of the entire population, including children, shows that more than half of the black population, compared with 25 per cent of the general population, are under twenty-five years of age. The main reasons for the greater proportion of children in the black population are that more black adults are in the child-rearing age groups and because black children tend to come from larger families.

Two important points emerge from these data. First, black children are a numerically significant proportion of the overall black population. Second, the statistics indicate that nearly half of Britain's black population were born in these islands and are therefore black British who are entitled to the same rights as white British.[2] The fact that this clearly does not happen has led some young blacks to believe they are *in* Britain but not *of* it. How this will be overcome demands a major reappraisal of black children and widespread changes in how white people view them, as well as major reforms and changes in the British economic, social and legal systems.

Schooling and black children's rights

Schools, as Tony Jeffs has argued,[3] consistently reflect prevalent social norms and values and thereby neglect the needs and rights of black children. Black children are discriminated against on at least two levels – as blacks and as children – and consequently their rights are doubly denied. Society, through schools, has considerable power over children by making and enforcing the written and unwritten rules which control and regulate children's behaviour, attitudes and learning. When black children rebel against this, consciously or unconsciously, either through truanting or resisting by not participating in lessons, they tend to be the losers. Such children leave school without the skills of numeracy and literacy and are therefore less likely to be considered for employment, which is difficult enough to find, given the state of recession and the acts of discrimination that they face. Schools fail black children in terms of educational skills but also by offering a curriculum that is with few exceptions Eurocentric, and consequently negates the cultural processes, self-images and identities of black children. Exactly how much of this gross neglect is internalized by black pupils is unrecorded.

Fortunately, although schools may explicitly or implicitly indicate that blacks are inferior, not all blacks agree with that judgement. This resistance to white values is an example of black children's asserting their rights to their own positive self-image. Distrust of the white educational system has led many black pupils in the Birmingham LEA to be disruptive and consequently suspended. A recent report showed that, of 626 boys suspended between 1974 and 1980, 241 were black and, of 287 girls, 113 were black.[4] On the other hand, there are also

cases of children who have internalized this racism and wish to wash
their skins white, literally and symbolically.

We wish here to concentrate on schools' delivery of certain servies
and messages, and their treatment of the curriculum, leaving aside the
positive resistance of pupils.

There is a considerable amount of evidence, from Bernard Coard[5]
to the Swann Report,[6] that the Afro-Caribbean child underachieves
within the British system. The National Foundation for Educational
Research (NFER) stated: 'there is an overwhelming consensus that
research evidence shows a strong trend to underachievement of pupils
of West Indian [sic] origin on the main indicators of academic
performance.'[7] Fuller discovered in her research that Afro-Caribbean
girls achieve better than Afro-Caribbean boys.[8] However, research is
often contentious, and some critics maintain that, in comparing
groups of Afro-Caribbean, Asian and white children, researchers
have sometimes taken middle-class groups and compared them with
working-class groups, thus not taking into account class differences
that affect the performance of any one group. None the less, Coard,
the NFER, the Swann Committee and many others cannot be entirely
wrong in their evidence of Afro-Caribbean underachievement. They
underachieve at CSE, at GCE O level and at GCE A level (groups of
white and Asians performed better at these examinations), and only 1
per cent of West Indians (sic) go on to university or full-time degree
courses. This evidence was collected from six local education
authorities with high concentrations of black children which
constitute approximately half the black school-leavers in this
country.[9]

Why do Afro-Caribbean pupils underachieve? One possible cause
is the racism that operates in schools. Racism may lead teachers to
hold low academic expectations of black pupils, which the pupils in
turn play out, and thereby they academically underachieve; this
becomes a self-fulfilling prophesy. One example, cited in the tape–
slide programme produced by Birmingham LEA called 'Recognizing
Racism', is that of an Afro-Caribbean girl who had written an
excellent essay for her homework. The teacher refused to believe that
the girl had written it herself and accused her of copying. From then
on the girl made sure that her essays were not her best, in order that
the teacher would believe that she had written them. Similarly,
Afro-Caribbean pupils are often perceived to be good only at sports
and not at academic subjects. Young blacks do achieve well at sport
but often because they are prevented from academic fulfilment.[10] One
of us has worked in primary schools where this has happened and
witnessed the practice in many others. This is gravely detrimental to

the children's education, since they leave for secondary schools barely literate and numerate and with their central life chances severely limited.

Another possible cause of underachievement is the neglect of language provision. Asian children have generally received 'English as a second language' (ESL) assistance in schools and specially provided units. Teachers too were alerted to Asians' need for help with learning English. Afro-Caribbean children have not received this help. Although Creole has a totally different grammatical and syntactical structure from English, it was underestimated as a factor in the process of educational achievement. Creole developed during the period of slavery in the Afro-Caribbean islands as a means of communicating between planters and slaves and in many cases between slaves who frequently came with different languages. Although the vocabulary is mainly English the sound system and syntax are not. It is now accepted that the Afro-Caribbean children of today may face particular difficulties in understanding and producing standard English. The reality is that they have needed ESL help as much as any other group. We are aware of situations where Afro-Caribbean children who needed help were either ignored or given 'unofficial' support by a minority of sympathetic teachers.

Some evidence to the Swann Committee located the home background of Afro-Caribbean children as a cause of their underachievement.[11] It is true that many Afro-Caribbean children come from materially deprived homes, precisely because parents are often unable to obtain good employment or are trapped in poorly paid jobs with all the attendant deprivations, such as poor housing, inadequate study facilities for children and poor leisure facilities. So the reality for black pupils is an interactive one, where racism within schools, intentional or unintentional, ensures that they underachieve, and because of racism in society their parents are engaged in poorly paid employment. Therefore, jobs that black pupils are likely to get on leaving school will be of the same type as their parents', and a cycle of deprivation is established.

Evidence suggests that Asian children achieve well within the educational system – equally well as their white peers in examination subjects except English language. Like Afro-Caribbean children, Asian children suffer from racism, so it might be their high motivation that helps them to achieve good standards. Bengalis from Bangladesh are the only group of Asians who do not do well within the educational system, but they are also the latest arrivals in Britain, and their parents undertake the lowest-paid jobs of all those done by blacks, and live in some of the worst housing in the country. One reason for the motivation of Asian children is the supportive and extensive family networks which encourage and foster educational achievement as a vehicle for upward social and economic mobility. Our work inside education has revealed to us, however, that few white teachers respond positively to what the Asian child brings to the classroom, and therefore achievement by Asian children must be seen as happening often in spite of the education system and not because of it.

Where black communities have felt their children were academically underachieving within the state system, and not learning about their own languages, religion and cultural processes, they have established weekend and after-school supplementary education. There are some separate schools for blacks – for example, the Moslem school in Bradford – and some black people are demanding further separate schools for their children. Our belief is that if all blacks were to be educated separately this would remove the responsibility from white schools to implement any anti-racist curriculum or policies. White children could continue to imbibe and be brought up in a totally racist educational atmosphere. The best solution is to make anti-racist teaching obligatory in all schools, so that all whites grow up to be non-racist. Everyone would then be citizens of a truly multi-racial society. The spirit of this is reflected in the Swann Report, especially in its title *Education for All*.

Anti-racist teaching (ART) developed from multicultural education (MCE), which in turn grew out of 'immigrant teaching'. The continuing debate about the relative merits of anti-racist and multicultural perspectives on education is at times confused, because there is no clear and logical definition of either ART or MCE. It is important, however, to examine some of the issues that are being raised.

During the late 1960s and early 1970s, MCE developed an emphasis on an openness to all cultures and a will to promote pluralism within schools. ART, which developed in the late 1970s, is summed up in its main tenet, which regards teaching only about cultures as insufficient and misleading because it builds up stereotypes, and instead advocates the need to tackle the underlying white racism. Educationists need to focus on the location of race within the structures of society, to examine the power relations between whites and blacks, and to discuss notions of inequality, discrimination and disadvantage that are suffered by groups of blacks. ART requires schools to formulate and display anti-racist policies and calls upon teachers to declare individually and as members of a school team their perspectives on race and related educational issues. Teachers are required to 'unlearn' their racism, examine their social and educational roles within society, and consider whether by anti-racist teaching they can change society or whether they are simply agents that perpetuate the status quo. ART maintains that there are no neutral teachers, and states that if people are committed to eradicating racism they have to struggle against it and cannot be objective, simply by virtue of their roles as teachers and white citizens. Teachers must tackle issues of racism openly and fairly. Our experience has shown us countless examples where teachers have ignored issues of racism in the classroom and playground. One involved some Bengali children who were openly racially abused by white children in front of teachers, who ignored the whole matter and, to make the situation worse, later visited the homes of the same Bengali children over some petty misdemeanour that they had committed.

ART claims that groups are not equal in terms of social and economic power. It identifies the problem as racism within the white community, and demands that white people tackle the issues themselves. ART insists that the whole school curriculum must be reviewed and revised to fit the needs of a multiracial Britain. The open and hidden curricula have to date been Eurocentric, all subjects being treated in a manner that favours whites. In history, for example, the Moslems who fought Richard I and his crusaders are seen as infidels. The Moslems would not label themselves thus, and they would certainly have another interpretation of that particular chapter of history. Nearly all books reflect a culture that is white, and where blacks appear they are characterized as stupid, immoral and uncivilised. ART would remove all biased books and replace them with others which portray blacks in a fair way. The hidden curriculum – including teachers' attitudes and expectations, and the school ethos – should aid the process of ART by ensuring that any form of racism expressed by children and teachers is dealt with swiftly and handled openly. The organization of anti-racist schools would require the advertising for and employment of black teachers, who were not treated as tokens. The whole school, not simply black teachers, is responsible for tackling issues of race.

ART does connect racism with other forms of inequality, such as sexism, and relates them to the structures of society in general and schools in particular, where the dominant group tries to impose its hegemony. Chris Mullard argues that the parameters for discussion of ART must be set and controlled by blacks (alongside likeminded whites), that ART is an attempt at collective change for groups of people, and that it should relate issues in schools to the wider society.

ART would also ensure that mother-tongue teaching provision is made in schools and that the languages of black children gain equal respect compared with European languages.[12]

Until recently, central government policy on MCE has been uncoordinated, if present at all. There is now more pressure of an advisory nature from the Department of Education and Science on LEAs to take up issues of ART/MCE. Within Britain there is no central government control of the curriculum and practice, and therefore different LEAs have taken up the issues with varying levels of commitment. Some schools have made a co-ordinated effort to implement ART, but generally the debate has not reached most schools, where the majority of teachers remain unaware of the in-depth concerns of ART and how it could enhance the rights of black children.

Job opportunities and young blacks

We have suggested that black children are failed in a number of ways by the educational system. We are critical of this state of affairs but acknowledge a slow realization by some local auithorities that black children have particular needs and rights which demand more systematic attention. This is not the case, however, in the labour market where the brutality of competition places white and black youngsters against each other. Evidence shows that, as a group, black young people are more likely to be unemployed than their white counterparts; if employed they will be engaged in unskilled or semiskilled work and will be earning less than white young people. All these factors continue to limit their life chances.

In this section, we want to examine how black children on Youth Training Schemes (YTS) and black school-leavers fare in the labour market. The Commission for Racial Equality (CRE) published a disturbing report (1982) which indicated that 59 per cent of young people of Afro-Caribbean origin were unemployed, compared with 41 per cent of their white peers.[13] This is supported by the 1981 Labour force survey which found unemployment rates were in general appreciably higher among young blacks than young whites. In the sixteen to twenty-four years of age male category, white unemployment was around 18 per cent, while for Afro-Caribbeans it was double this rate at 37 per cent, and for Asian young men the figure was 25 per cent. In the same age group for females, white unemployment was 16 per cent, for Afro-Caribbeans 28 per cent and for Asians 30 per cent.

In Birmingham the unemployment rate among young blacks has risen at twice the rate of white youths as a whole in the city.[14] A report in *The Guardian*, 11 September 1985, reveals that in the summer of 1985 only 9 per cent of all Birmingham school-leavers were expected to secure employment and only 4 per cent of all black leavers were likely to get a job. The same report shows that unemployment among sixteen- to nineteen-year-olds in the Birmingham area of Handsworth was 659 of which 71 per cent or 469 were black.

Research in Bradford, which has a large Indian Pakistani and Bangladeshi community, reported that 72 per cent of Asian youngsters in the city were without real jobs 12 months after leaving school and when the next cohort of school-leavers were entering the job market. This is compared with a figure of 31 per cent for all school-leavers in the city.[15] According to *The Sunday Times*, the number of registered unemployed young blacks aged between nineteen and twenty-four years in Brixton, South London, rose by 71 per cent between April 1981 and April 1982.[16]

Youth Training Schemes are not immune to discrimination against young blacks. *The Guardian* reported in February 1985 that the CRE had found in an informal enquiry that further education colleges in Birmingham had been complying with instructions from employers to send only white applicants for YTS vacancies.[17] The report warranted sufficient concern by the local city council, which is responsible for the YTS college courses, to justify a formal investigation. The CRE explained that 'for many black youngsters, the Youth Training Scheme is the only lifeline.'

The House of Commons Home Affairs Select Committee on Racial Disadvantage supports this position by pointing to studies of school-leavers and YOP trainees that showed that in some cases Afro-Caribbean school-leavers were significantly better qualified than white young people. None the less, the white youngsters were more likely to be taken on by employers. As the committee conclude, 'Taken together these developments may cause many young West Indians to reject with some bitterness the way of thinking and way of life both of the mainstream society and their parents, and to find that this leaves them with nowhere to go.'[18]

In summary, first-generation blacks travelled to Britain with hopes of a better future for themselves and their children, but too often these hopes were dashed. However, many decided that staying here and working was preferable to returning to an island or country ransacked by imperialism. Young blacks' presence in Britain is therefore due to their parents' decision to work here. Second- and third-generation blacks' inability to secure employment is a devastating and degrading blow that must make them question Britain's request for migrant labour in the 1950s and 1960s. It would be surprising, therefore, to find young blacks were happy and content with their place in society. They will have progressed through an educational system which does not encourage themselves or white young people to look outside a Eurocentred world and, when it does consider other cultures, patronizes them. Their rights to their own culture will be dismissed or incorporated as part of an assimilation process, making black children consider themselves inferior. On leaving school they will face appalling job prospects. To say that black children are treated equally in our society is to ignore their experiences in school and their first encounters with the labour market.

Police, courts and young black people's rights

The relationship between the police and black people has always been problematic. In 1974 Louise Chase commented: 'The history of relations between the police and West Indians in Britain has led to mutual suspicion, distrust and a polarization of relationships.'[19] A number of commentators believe that the main reason for this lies in the history of colonial domination found in Afro-Caribbean islands, which has been continued in another form and in another time in history on British streets.

> It is precisely because the role of the police in the colonies was that of any occupying force – and not of the 'friendly bobby' – that the traditional 'immigrant' view of the police is one of distrust. The reasons are historical rather than social or cultural. The first experience of a police force – and it is that force's colonial tradition which still persists among their indigenous police even after independence.[20]

In early post-war Britain, the police were held in high regard by a society untroubled by widespread crime and large-scale unemployment. It was a period when most people knew their place in a society where consensus politics played a major part in uniting a war-weary country.

By the 1960s and 1970s Britain had experienced a rapid growth in urban crime which some writers, including Hall et al.,[21] attribute to the economic and social disintegration that was and still is taking place in the country's major cities. The presence of black families in urban areas led to the accusation that black people equal crime. Such accusations are not new: in the 1950s black people were accused of living off immoral earnings; in the 1960s they were thought to be pushing drugs; and in the 1970s they were supposed to be engaged in mugging. The underlying and unproven message has been that the black crime rate is disproportionately higher than the white crime rate. There is no evidence that black people commit crimes more than whites, and there is no evidence whatsoever that the more blacks who live in an area, the higher the indictable crime level. Facts have a way of being quickly forgotten in this emotive issue, so that we now witness fact giving way to fiction, with many whites demanding that forceful policing needs to be exercised in relation to black, particularly Afro-Caribbean, young people.

The present economic recession has raised the issue of the police's role in relation to young black people as political rather than professional, and Hall et al. argue that the police are one of the state's institutions of control, which respond to the booms and slumps of the economy by focusing on those that are most likely to reflect and react against the inequality in our society:

> Policing the blacks threatened to mesh with the problem of policing the poor and policing the unemployed. . . . The ongoing problem of policing the blacks had become, for all practical purposes, synonymous with the wider problem of policing the crisis.[22]

The analysis challenges the position of police officers as neutral and impartial arbitrators of a relatively equalitarian society. The Institute of Race Relations (IRR) have argued that Britain is moving towards 'two societies, one black, one white – separate and unequal', and that the police will have had no small part to play in that polarization.[23] The evidence to support this view is persuasive, for there is considerable conclusive material from a number of organizations – including the West Indian Standing Conference, the IRR, the Runnymede Trust, the National Council for Civil Liberties, as well as youth workers, lawyers and local community relations councils – to show clearly that young black people's rights are continually denied in a whole range of contacts with the police and legal system.

One of the most notable examples has been in the contemporary workings of section 4 of 1824 Vagrancy Act, or 'sus' as it became widely known. The Act allowed police to arrest a person on suspicion of loitering with intent to commit an arrestable offence, without there having to be any evidence that another crime had been committed; or that there was a victim; or that there were any witnesses except two police officers. A 'sus' charge could only be tried in a magistrate's court, with no right to trial by jury. The operation of 'sus' came to be used indiscriminately by the police as a way of checking on the movements of young blacks in their own communities. It was, in effect, a version of South Africa's pass laws. Afro-Caribbean young people were particularly vulnerable to a denial of their rights to walk the streets freely. Arrests of blacks accounted for 44 per cent of London's 'sus' arrests in 1978 and 40 per cent in 1979, and in the Borough of Lambeth 77 per cent of those arrested on 'sus' charges were black. The operation of 'sus' did widespread damage to the relationship between the police and the black community, and this led to the repeal of the law in the 1981 Criminal Attempts Act. Euphoria over the repeal of the powers has quickly subsided, since the 1981 Act makes it an offence to interfere with a motor vehicle in a public place.[24] Although the operation of this Act has yet to be fully analysed, many in the legal profession believe it is open to the same form of abuse as the 'sus' law. This is not entirely unexpected if, as much of the evidence suggests, the 1824 Act was used in a discriminatory manner to harass and deny young blacks their rights to walk the city streets unstopped; its mere removal will not end police behaviour of this kind. The police will find alternative means, and certainly the new Police and Criminal Evidence Act (1984) will not hinder them in restricting young black people's rights. The latest estimates of stop-and-searches in London are more than 1,500,000 in 1982, of which only 5 per cent led to arrests.[25] There are no figures on how many of those arrested were subsequently charged or convicted. These stops uncover or generate a large amount of information on crime, but it has to be said that it is a very expensive form of policing for a poor rate of return. It is not too expensive, though, if the police are intent on containing the activities of young black people – which looks suspiciously to be the case.

Another significant area where black juveniles are discriminated against is in the courts. Landau highlights a 1978 study of the decisions made by the police in relation to young black people in five areas of London which found that black youths are more likely than whites to be treated more severely and to be charged rather than referred to a juvenile bureau. The study suggests that the main reason for this situation was that the police perceived black young people as being more antagonistic and therefore were more inclined to make criminal charges.[26]

The discrimination against young and adult blacks has led the black community to make formal complaints about the hostile treatment at the hands of the police. A Home Office Research Unit study[27] reflects the adverse conditions that result in black people complaining about police behaviour. Black people making complaints against the police are more likely to be alleging assault by police, to be under arrest, to be charged with an offence or to have previous convictions. The report indicates that because of the nature of such complaints the expectation must be that there will be a low rate of substantiation. It further suggests that allegations of assault against black people were not always as rigorously investigated as less serious crimes.

But black grievances relate not simply to what the police do, but also to what they fail to do – mainly, failure to protect black people from racist assaults. Attacks against racial minorities have been a frequent feature of English urban life, from the violence directed against Jews in London's East End in the 1930s, to the attacks on Asians living in the same area in the 1970s and 1980s. 'Paki-bashing' is one of the most frightening elements of white working-class racism, and one which continues to send ripples of fear across the black community. Klug indicates that the extent of racist violence has grown during the last decade.[28] At least twenty-six black people were murdered in racist attacks between 1976 and 1981, excluding the thirteen young people who died in a fire at a party in New Cross in January 1981, which many believe was a racially motivated attack. Figures from the Metropolitan Police area increased from 277 attacks in 1977 to over 700 in 1980. In the period from May to December 1982, the figure nearly doubled to 1293 incidents involving 1749 victims.[29] According to a report in The Guardian,[30] 96 racial incidents were reported in 1983 and 144 in 1984 in Newham, London, where 40 per cent of the population are black. In the first six months of 1985, 86 incidents were reported.

Part of this recorded increase is explained by the police force's widening definition of a racial motive, but none the less racial violence is growing. A report from a Home Office study into right-wing groups and racist attacks found that there could be as many as 7000 racially motivated attacks per year, Asians being fifty times more likely to be victims than whites, and other black people over thirty-six times more likely.[31] The majority of the black community believe that the police's response to these attacks has been lamentable. In its evidence to the Royal Commission on Criminal Procedure published in 1981, the IRR presented cases where the police had commented that attacks had no racial motive, although all the facts suggested the opposite, and where there was a delay by the police and an unwillingness to investigate incidents or prosecute alleged offenders. The IRR's evidence shows that in some cases the police were hostile to black people who complained, and in others it was the complainer who was arrested.

This failure by the police to protect black people is in stark contrast to the protection given to the facist and racist organizations that march and demonstrate in areas of black settlement. Many young blacks feel that white racists are given rights to demonstrate their vile propaganda while they continue to walk the streets in fear of racial attack. The number of racists involved may be small, but their impact on young blacks is considerable. Racist propaganda is an impingement on their lives that is not always recognized as serious by the white community. There is need here for urgent amendments to the law governing incitement to racial hatred, to enable young blacks to reclaim their rights to walk unimpeded in British streets.

There is little doubt that there is a considerable antagonism between the police and young blacks, and it is a major concern for the black community when they see their children's rights being negated and abused. The issue of police and black youth relations has not escaped the notice of the press and public and, together with the discussions on black immigration, is a major focus of attention in the debate surrounding black–white relations. The rights of young blacks are never really considered, because society appears to condone the police attitude towards what it considers to be a troublesome element in its cities. The recommendations of the Scarman Report relating to checking and changing police attitudes have had no noticeable effect, and it is still possible for a London police officer to scawl 'Fight racialism – smash a nigger in the gob today' on a station lavatory wall and remain in post.[32] The Police Studies Report found that racialist language and racial prejudice in the London police force was not only prominent and pervasive but actually fashionable. Senior officers apparently do nothing to discourage these attitudes. In the mind of the black community, individual officers and the police as a force are acting as a political agent of the state – a view that is a far cry from the post-war image of the bicycling bobby as an impartial and neutral arbitrator of day-to-day problems.

As the economic and social conditions for young blacks continue to deteriorate, their street life will become an important arena for resistance, bringing them into regular contact with the police. The outcome seems inevitable: the curtailment of their rights. Some senior police officers acknowledge, at least implicitly, their political role in relation to the black community. Sir Kenneth Newman believes

there are two particular problems in the Western societies which have a potential to affect the balance between order and freedom. The first is concerned with the growth of multi-ethnic communities. The second is related to indigenous terrorist movements.[33]

Conclusion

This chapter has shown how black children's rights are abused or ignored in three major areas affecting their lives. A combination of discrimination and racism has caused black children to be viewed and treated as unequal. They are frequently seen as either problematic when demonstrating resistance, or unproblematic and therefore to be incorporated and assimilated, in so far as they can be, into white society. Thus they lose certain rights and full acceptance of their identity, and the wider society fails to gain the richness of other cultures and languages.

It is our belief that the state of race relations in Britain will not improve unless there is a dramatic revisal and reversal of practice within the institutions of society. Whether black children themselves are the protagonists that will bring about change or whether the institutions themselves will change is yet to be seen. Perhaps changes of both kinds are required. Fortunately, black children are not the passive victims of racism and resist successfully, asserting their rights in schools, in the streets, in the dole office and workplace. What remains to be seen is whether our white society can meet the challenge and help create a more just one, where black and white children enjoy equal rights.

Notes

1 For a fuller account, see W. Rodney, *How Europe Underdeveloped Africa* (Tanzania Publishing House, 1976), and K. M. Pannikar, *Asia and Western Dominance* (Unwin University Press, 1974).
2 C. Brown, *Black and White Britain: the third PSI survey* (Heinemann Educational, 1984), ch. 2.
3 See chapter 3, 'Children's rights at school'.
4 *Arena* (The Magazine of the National Anti-Racist Movement in Education), 4 (1985).
5 B. Coard, *How the West Indian Child is Made Educationally Subnormal in the British School System* (New Beacon Books, 1971).
6 Swann Report, *Education for All: The Report of the Committee of Inquiry into the Education of Children from Ethnic Minority Groups*, Cmnd 9453 (HMSO, 1985).
7 Ibid., p. 59.

8   M. Fuller, *Schooling for Women's Work* (Routledge and Kegan Paul, 1980).
9   Swann Report, p. 62.
10 E. Cashmore, *Black Sportsmen* (Routledge and Kegan Paul, 1982), ch. 6.
11 Swann Report, p. 68.
12 C. Mullard, 'A theoretical basis for anti-racist teaching', paper at the NAME annual conference (Bath, 1984).
13 Commission for Racial Equality, *Young People and the Jobs Market* (Commission for Racial Equality, 1982).
14 M. Cross, J. Edward and R. Sargent, *Special Problems and Special Measures: ethnic minorities and the experience of YOP* (Research Unit on Ethnic Relations, University of Aston, 1982).
15 M. Campbell and D. Jones, *Asian Youths in the Labour Market: a study of Bradford* (EEC/DES Transition to Work Project, Bradford College, 1982).
16 *Sunday Times*, 4 April 1982.
17 *Guardian*, 1 February 1985.
18 House of Commons Home Affairs Select Committee on Racial Disadvantage, 1980–81, HC 424, p. lxxii.
19 L. Chase, 'West Indians and the police', *New Community*, III, 3 (Commission for Racial Equality, 1974), p. 205.
20 Institute of Race Relations, *Police against Black People: Evidence Submitted to the Royal Commission on Criminal Procedure: Race and Class Pamphlet 6* (Institute of Race Relations, 1979).
21 S. Hall, C. Critcher, T. Jefferson, J. Clarke and B. Roberts, *Policing the Crisis: mugging, the state, and law and order* (Macmillan, 1982).
22 Ibid., p. 332.
23 Institute of Race Relations, *Police against Black People*, p. 1.
24 See A. Brogden, '"Sus" is dead: but what about "Sas"?', *New Community* (Spring/Summer 1981).
25 Policy Studies Institute, *Police and People in London*, vols I–IV (Policy Studies Institute, 1983).
26 S. Landau, 'Juveniles and the police', *British Journal of Criminology* (January 1981).
27 P. Stephens and C. Willis, *Ethnic Minorities and Complaints against the Police* (Home Office Research Unit, 1982).
28 F. Klug, *Racist Attacks* (Runnymead Trust, 1982).
29 Greater London Council Police Committee, *Racial Harassment in London* (Greater London Council Police Committee, 1984), p. 4.
30 *Guardian*, 11 July 1985.
31 Home Office, *Racial Attacks: report of a study* (Home Office, November 1981).
32 Greater London Council Police Committee Support Unit, *Policing London* (Greater London Council, 1984), p. 8.
33 Ibid.

Further reading

E. Cashmore and B. Troyna (eds), *Black Youth in Crisis* (Allen and Unwin, 1982).

E. Cashmore and B. Troyna, *Introduction to Race Relations* (Routledge and Kegan Paul, 1983).

A. Haynes, *The State of Black Britain* (Root Publishing, 1983).

C. Husband (ed.), *Race in Britain: continuity and change* (Hutchinson, 1982).

Institute of Race Relations, *Roots of Racism (Book 1), Patterns of Racism (Book 2)* (Institute of Race Relations, 1982).

Open University, *Ethnic Minorities and Community Relations, E. 1983, Block 1–4* (Open University Press, 1982).

A. Pilkington, *Race Relations in Britain* (University Tutorial Press, 1984).

Runnymede Research Group, *Education for All: a summary of the Swann Report on the education of ethnic minority children* (Runnymede Trust, 1985).

M. Stone, *The Education of the Black Child in Britain: the myth of multiracial education* (Fontana, 1981).

10

Children's Rights:
A Scottish Perspective

Ruth Adler and Alan Dearling

The main justification for the inclusion of a separate chapter on
Scotland in this volume must surely lie in the existence of the unique
form of juvenile justice in operation since 1971 and known as the
Scottish children's hearing system. However, it seems misleading to
us to confine a discussion of the rights of children in Scotland entirely
to this system. The chapter will therefore be divided into five parts as
follows:

1   An introduction to the theoretical framework
2   An overview of the Scottish system of juvenile justice
3   A summary of the rights of children within the system
4   A brief guide to some services for young people in Scotland
    and rights within them
5   The way forward.

The theoretical framework

It is abundantly clear from every chapter in this book that the rights
of children cannot be discussed in any constructive way without
giving some indication, however brief, of the theoretical framework
within which such discussion necessarily occurs. Many attacks on
the Scottish system are the results of confusion on issues of theory,
at the most general level on competing conceptions of what it is to
have a right, and more specifically on the nature of children's
rights. With regard to the first, it is not possible to do more here
than offer brief quotations to indicate the position taken on the
nature of rights. The case for this position is argued elsewhere.[1] Here
it will only be stated that it seems clear that 'To have a right is to have
a claim against someone, whose recognition as valid is called for by

some set of governing rules or moral principles',[2] and that 'a right is ... a legally (or quasi-legally) protected or furthered interest.'[3]

Rights are thus viewed here as having a common normative element and as securing goods or interests within a normative order. What of the rights of children?

The view of rights presented above is consistent with the adoption of any one of the three prevailing theories of children's rights which were all mentioned in chapter 1 under slightly different names. These three orthodoxies can be categorized as 'parentalist', 'child-libertarian' and 'protectionist' (or 'paternalist'). Each approach is the outcome of a particular perspective on the status of childhood. All three are consistent with a common view of adults as rational, self-determining, autonomous agents, but they disagree fundamentally in their perceptions of children and of the status of childhood.

Parentalists hold that parents are and should be the final judges of their children's interests. They acknowledge that children have rights to care, protection and education in their own interests, but provided there is no violation of what are usually called 'human rights' – such as the right not to be tortured, enslaved or degraded, which do not depend in any way on merit, are unforfeitable and non-conflicting, and where recognized are seen as belonging to human beings as such and hence to children too – provided there is no violation of these rights, parentalists hold that it is parents who can and should identify the relevant interests of children.

Child-libertarians, on the other hand, argue that children have no special rights arising from their perceived helplessness and dependency. On the contrary, children have or should have exactly the same rights as adults. No distinction should be made between the two groups. Both views are discussed in chapter 1, and both are seen here as problematic. The first assumes that a child's interests are knowable and in addition largely ignores the fact that from a very early age the child has a distinct character and viewpoint of his or her own which cannot be simply ignored whenever it conflicts with parental desires and opinions. The second view rejects as irrelevant the fact that a child's capacities are not yet fully developed and fails to recognize that the right to develop these capacities may conflict irreconcilably with the rights it advocates, such as the right to choose whether or not to receive formal education. The confusions in both views raise several theoretical and empirical issues.

Protectionists, like parentalists, focus on the relative dependency of children and insist that children may sometimes have to be protected against their own actions by intervention on the part of adults (not necessarily parents) 'for their own good'. The following discussion will attempt to highlight some of the problems, arguing that a modified protectionism offers the possibility of reconciling the positive aspects of each position and that, at its best, the Scottish system does precisely that.

It has been noted that all three theories share similar views of the adult as a rational, self-determining, autonomous agent. It is hard to see how a child could ever become such a person on the first view. Where a child is regarded more or less as an extension of his or her parents, how is the transition from dependent to independent individual ever to be achieved? This is a conceptual as well as a practical problem. At the practical level it is very unclear how anyone who has what is sometimes termed a 'life plan' drawn up on his/her behalf and has never made decisions concerning him/herself could ever learn to do so. Conceptually it remains perplexing that one should argue from the facts of biological reproduction and unquestioned helplessness to an existence as an extension of one's natural parents and a right of total control (within the limits set by the human rights outlined above). It suggests a picture of the child as some kind of robot – it can act on its own but only when programmed to do so. The central question which parentalists and indeed protectionists such as J. S. Mill avoid is: 'What rights (freedom, for Mill), if any, belong to a *developing* individual?' Child-libertarians like Richard Farson and John Holt, mentioned elsewhere in this book, seem to regard this problem as almost irrelevant. According to Farson, 'The incapacity of the child in infancy should only mean that extra steps must be taken to guarantee the protection of his rights.'[4] According to child-libertarians, the child has the same rights as an adult and because of his/her limitations may need to have them protected *in the same way* as an adult who has fallen ill or is in some way temporarily incapacitated. In other words, they do not regard children's limited abilities as in any way relevant in determining their rights.

It is interesting to note, particularly in the context of this book, that the relevance or otherwise of the developmental nature of childhood is a key factor in the controversy between the advocates of the 'welfare model' (who support a treatment ideology), whose views are enshrined in the Scottish hearings system, and the champions of the right to punishment or 'justice model' in the sphere of juvenile justice, who are the main critics of the Scottish system. The former regard the 'immaturity' of juveniles as the key factor in determining how to deal with them; the opposition claims that this is of no relevance at all and that measures taken should be based on the principle of 'equality before the law', which should be applicable to all offenders irrespective of age. The supporters of 'treatment' regard children's rights as definable in terms of specific objective needs and interests, while the advocates of punishment claim that basing decisions on such dubious criteria is a violation of generally acknowledged moral rights which are being systematically denied to children. To recapitulate, the protectionists rest their case on the undisputed dependency of the very young and view this as the most important factor in dealing with children for most of their formative years. The child-libertarians, while in no way denying the initial dependency of infants, regard this state as an argument for providing extra safeguards to achieve equal rights. Protectionists and parentalists too would argue that at least some rights – to liberty, for example – are ascribed only to self-determining autonomous individuals and are therefore inappropriate to the status of childhood, but that the young have special rights to care and protection which are not accorded to independent adults.

Reflections on day-to-day dealings with children seem to lend considerable support to the protectionist argument, but the central dilemma remains: if different rights are accorded to the dependent and the independent, and if childhood is seen as a journey from dependency to independence, how can one decide which rights are to be ascribed to children? The child-libertarian view avoids this question altogether, but it should be clear that, by doing so, it also avoids the reality of childhood. Nevertheless, it must be acknowledged that 'dependency' not only is a vague term, but is often used to support differential treatment in a manner that begs the whole question at issue. There is therefore a need to articulate what might be called a 'modified protectionism'. Here it is not possible to do more than indicate the direction in which a more constructive approach to children's rights must move. It would seem that recent attempts[5] to isolate specific capacities as morally relevant in denying certain rights to children (and possibly ascribing other rights to them) are unhelpful except in the case of the very young, for, as observed in chapter 1, many children do indeed have the capacities of many adults. The key difference would appear to lie not in any capacity, but rather in the different *perspectives* of children and adults – perspectives of what is important, of what is worthwhile, of time. There is no suggestion here that adults are always right, but they do have experience in their favour. A theory of juvenile justice must ultimately accommodate the concept of *development* and some kind of description of *maturity* as that towards which development is directed. It is surely these concepts which embrace the differences between adults and children that constitute the grounds for ascribing varying rights to them.

Having presented this very cursory outline of theories of children's rights as a means of placing an account of the Scottish scene into an appropriate context, it is now possible to turn first to a description of the system of juvenile justice and the rights it guarantees, and then to a discussion of other provisions for Scottish children and young people. It will immediately become apparent that the actual legal rights of children can sometimes be understood and defended from a parentalist viewpoint,[6] sometimes from a child-libertarian stance and at other times from a protectionist standpoint, and even a combination of any of the three, but none of them necessarily guarantees the best possible outcome for the children involved. This might be a reflection of the fact that the developmental nature of childhood makes it an inappropriate subject for a single coherent theory of rights. There may be a need for a system of juvenile justice to be sufficiently flexible to accommodate conflicting theories in order to achieve justice for children, instead of denying the conflicts of childhood in order to achieve a coherent philosophy. It may also be that the Scottish system has the potential to achieve the necessary flexibility.

Juvenile justice in Scotland

The Scottish children's hearings system came into operation in 1971 with the implementation of Part III of the Social Work (Scotland) Act (1968) and the statutory instruments known as the Children's Hearings (Scotland) Rules No. 492. The jurisdiction of the system is limited to those children under sixteen years of age whose environment is thought to be damaging for a number of reasons including neglect and abuse, or who fail to attend school, or who commit offences. In some instances those who have already come within the remit of the system may be referred up to the age of eighteen, but this is not the norm, and first referrals are only until sixteen. All children enter the system via the Reporter's office. There are approximately 100 Reporters, deputies and assistants in Scotland. The Reporter plays a key role in the whole structure, serving as decision-maker, administrator and legal adviser. Children may be referred to the Reporter by anyone concerned with their welfare. In practice, most referrals come from the police and from the departments of education and social work, and approximately 70 per cent of the referrals are on offence grounds. It is also worth noting that very roughly 50 per cent of the referrals to the Reporter are sent to a hearing.

When a child is brought to the notice of the Reporter, it is necessary to establish whether there is evidence of at least one of the statutory 'grounds of referral' (there are ten in all, including 'lack of parental care', commission of an offence, failure to attend school and, most recently, 'solvent abuse'), and whether the child appears to be in need of compulsory measures of care. The Reporter may request information from any people or agencies to whom the child is known, including the child's school, the social work department, the police and medical services. After this there are three possible alternative courses of action. The Reporter may decide to discharge the matter, or to request assistance from the social work department on a voluntary basis, or to bring the child before a children's hearing. In the case of the third outcome, the Reporter has to make all the arrangements for the hearing and is responsible for ensuring that all parties have been cited to attend, as well as for recording any decisions taken and for making sure that they are implemented.

In the context of the hearing itself, it is members of the children's panel and not the Reporter who are the decision-makers. The Reporter's role within the hearing is only that of legal adviser and recorder. Children's panel members are all lay volunteers appointed by the Secretary of State from the general public, on a regional basis, to participate in hearings. There are well over 1500 members in Scotland. Three panel appointees, one of whom must take the chair, constitute the hearing members in every individual case. They meet together with the child and parents in the manner described below, to determine whether or not the child is in need of compulsory measures of care, and make their decision accordingly. The hearing has no power to determine questions of innocence or guilt. Where a child or either parent denies the grounds of referral put to them at the start of the hearing, the case must be either dismissed or sent to the Sheriff court for proof. Where the grounds are established in court, the case returns to the hearing for consideration and disposal.

A hearing usually involves three panel members (at least one man and one woman), the Reporter to the children's panel, a social worker, the child and at least one parent. Depending on the nature of the case, various other people may be present too: teachers, children's home staff, members of intermediate treatment groups, and so on. Occasionally a hearing may proceed in the absence of a child. This usually happens when the child is very young, or in particularly distressing neglect and abuse cases. Hearings also sometimes proceed without any parent present, for, although parents are required to attend and have a right to be present throughout the proceedings, there are no prohibitions against making decisions in their absence. In practice this only happens where a parent refuses to attend, but there is a general reluctance to proceed in such cases and the parents may be charged. A hearing cannot proceed without three panel members, a Reporter and a social worker. The whole procedure is conducted in front of all the participants and the decision is reached in public. Hearing members retire to another room only in very exceptional circumstances. In normal circumstances the proceedings are entirely open.

Once the grounds of referral have been established, the hearings proceed in a relatively informal manner in which it is hoped that all those present are involved. Before reaching a decision, the hearing considers a number of reports which always include one from the social work department and, where appropriate, a school report, as well as written documentation from other agencies such as children's homes, psychiatric units, and so on. Hearings can adjourn to obtain further assessments, and in all instances the hearing is required to decide on the course of action that is deemed to be in the best interests of the child. Both the child and the parents have the right of appeal to the Sheriff against the decision of the hearing. Except in such cases and where the grounds of referral are disputed, the courts and the hearings remain quite independent of one another. (The Sheriff may occasionally request advice from hearings but is under no obligation to act on it.) It should be noted that it is required that

> The chairman shall inform the child and his parents of the substance of any reports, documents and information . . . if it appears to him that this is material to the manner in which the case of the child should be disposed of and that its disclosure would not be detrimental to the interests of the child.[7]

At the end of the hearing, except in cases of adjournment, the member in the chair is required to inform the child and parents of the decision taken, of the reasons for the decision, and of the rights of the family to request the stated reasons in writing and to appeal against the decision to the Sheriff within twenty-one days. Once these formalities are over and usually after the family has left, the person chairing, either alone or together with the other two members, proceeds to write down the reasons for the decision. The written reasons are kept on file, irrespective of whether or not the family requests a copy of them, and regardless of whether or not an appeal is lodged.

There are limited disposals available to a hearing, and there may be a situations in which none of the available options seems to offer the key to a solution. The possible alternatives include: first, discharging the case; second, placement on supervision to a social worker while remaining at home; and, third, a residential supervision order removing the child from home and placing him/her with a family or in a children's home or in a List D school: the Scottish equivalent of the English Community Homes with Education (see p. 74). All supervision orders may be reviewed at any time, subject to certain rules and regulations, and must be reviewed within a year or they automatically lapse. A hearing may also adjourn to obtain further information or to see whether a child can 'get back to school' or 'stay out of trouble' pending an actual decision. The remit of the panel is to act 'in the best interests of the child'.

The underlying philosophy of the system can perhaps be most accurately exemplified by the dictum 'Help for tomorrow not punishment for yesterday'. This is the rhetoric of the system, and it seems self-evident that in the light of this rhetoric the decisions taken will be justifiable (if at all) primarily on forward-looking grounds. This stands in marked contrast to legal intervention in the lives of adults, where consequentialist considerations at most form only one element in the reasons for a decision. According to the rhetoric of the Scottish children's hearings system, the anticipated consequences of the different available disposals are the overriding criterion in all decisions made on behalf of children. The reality can be very different, for often the actual decision is the only one available in the circumstances, or it may (despite the contrasting rhetoric) be taken on grounds involving societal needs or legal requirements. These observations have been substantiated further in parts of the literature cited at the end of the chapter. They are only mentioned in passing here as testimony to some of the shortcomings of the system in practice. One further problem will be mentioned briefly before turning to a discussion of rights within the system.

The inbuilt class bias of the children's hearing system is a frequent focus of discussion which must be mentioned. Where an offence has been committed (as indicated above, in over 70 per cent of the cases dealt with by the Reporter) and compulsory measures of care are felt to be unnecessary, the case is frequently discharged. This occurs more often in the case of children from middle-class families. Both Reporters and panel members are predisposed to look for compensatory provisions for the most deprived members of the community, that is they look for signs of disadvantage in the lives of young people. Hence those from working-class backgrounds (both offenders and non-offenders) will often be treated to more 'welfare' than their middle-class counterparts. It is sometimes suggested that there are insufficient safeguards to ensure that measures taken do not compound existing disadvantages even further. A very stark example of how this may happen is a provision in section 3 of the Rehabilitation of Offenders Act (1974), which lays down that

> the acceptance or establishment of that ground [offence] shall be treated for the purpose of this Act . . . as a conviction, and any disposal of the case thereafter by a children's hearing shall be treated for those purposes as a sentence.

The extension of the Act to the children's hearings system has given rise to a great deal of discussion and various attempts to amend the legislation. The present situation is the result of grafting an English measure on to an area of Scottish law. However, in the meantime the effect of the statute is to restrict the employment opportunities of young people who have been referred to the panel on offence grounds. They are obliged to inform potential employers of their 'conviction' for a period of six months after the *discharge* of the referral, for twelve months following a compulsory supervision order or until expiry of the order if that occurs later, and for the rest of their lives in the case of exempted jobs such as nursing and teaching. The use of the word 'sentence' in relation to a disposal of the children's panel is in itself contrary to the spirit and ethos of the whole Scottish hearings system and has quite understandably given rise to cynicism with respect to the claim that the system operates in the best interests of the child.

The preceding paragraphs offered a brief account of the structure brought into existence by the 1968 Act, together with some serious blemishes. As a result of this legislation, a large majority of children in trouble and deemed to be 'in need of compulsory measures of care' were removed from the jurisdiction of the courts. However, a minority of young offenders over the age of criminal responsibility (eight years) are still directed to the Sheriff court and dealt with under the terms of the Children and Young Persons (Scotland) Act (1937) and the Criminal Procedure (Scotland) Act (1975). The Lord Advocate retains the power to prosecute all children above the age of eight years in the criminal courts. In practice, only certain types of cases involving children are automatically referred both to the Procurator Fiscal and to the Report to the children's panel. Broadly speaking, the key considerations and categories of offence are: the gravity of the offence (cases of murder, rape and armed robbery, for example, have to go for trial under criminal procedure), some offences under the Road Traffic Act by those over fourteen years which on conviction can lead to a disqualification from driving, offences which on conviction permit forfeiture of an article (these are usually firearms offences) and any offences committed by a child acting along with an adult, as well as all offences by children over the age of sixteen who are not already on supervision under the terms of the Social Work (Scotland) Act. It was noted above that the Sheriff is at liberty to ask the children's panel for advice about the disposal of almost all such cases, but remains free to ignore any advice given. Moreover, the courts retain jurisdiction over children in matters of custody, financial provision, some aspects of education and several other areas. Hence the Scottish system of juvenile justice comprises both the courts and the children's hearings system.

Children's rights within the system of juvenile justice

The actual legal rights of children within the Scottish system of juvenile justice vary from one part of the system to another and, as indicated in the first section of the chapter, they can be understood and defended sometimes from one theoretical perspective and sometimes from another. The discussion will first take a brief look at the rights of children in court and then will critically examine children's rights within the Hearings System.

The courts

Offenders The interesting point to note here is that children appearing before the court have a distinct set of legal rights that are not granted to those within the remit of the hearings system. They have the rights of adults on trial including (except in rare cases of extreme violence) the right to a determinate sentence on conviction. In addition, there is separate provision under section 23 of the 1975 Act for the remand and committal of those under twenty-one. In brief, this section of the legislation is designed to keep young offenders apart from adult detainees, either in separate institutions or in self-contained units of adult institutions. With the exception of the provision of separate facilities and the imposition of restrictions on reporting, the law here seems to be much more in accord with child-libertarian principles than with the tenets of protectionism. At least in this area children and adults do appear to have the same legal rights. What are the consequences for the child:

A case study published in 1978 compared a number of boys committed to such care by the courts and by the children's hearings system, and produced results that can only be regarded as deeply disturbing by anyone who professes a concern for the rights of children. The study centred on those sent to List D schools and found among other things that for those included in the sample:

1   There were no significant differences in the home background or in the offence histories of the two sets of boys.
2   A higher proportion of 'court boys' was held in custody both prior to the hearing and during the continuation of their case and, where no List D place was immediately available after disposal, they waited longer than 'panel boys' for a vacancy and moreover had to remain in custody more frequently while doing so.
3   'There was some indication that boys who have been processed by the courts may stay rather longer in the schools and may be somewhat more likely to be transferred to a Borstal, or receive a subsequent Borstal sentence.'
4   'Though asserting that the two sets of boys were no different, it was clear that half the staff interviewed felt that some, at least, of the court boys were subjected to subtle measures of control over and above those imposed on panel boys.'[8]

The findings of the study raise many questions well beyond the scope of this discussion. The most important point to notice here is that granting legal rights in itself guarantees very little. The overwhelming fact is that, in the present system, the 'court boys' from the sample, whose *legal* rights were more like those of adults and were thus more clearly defined, suffered longer terms of confinement before and after trial and more stigmatization than those who were referred to the panel for *similar offences*. It could be argued that this is the result of inherent inconsistencies in a system that allows control and treatment principles to operate side by side. Irrespective of whether this is indeed the case, the point remains that, in the present context, granting certain adult legal rights to certain children seems to make them considerably worse off than similar children denied such rights. The issues are far more complex than either the child-libertarians or the protectionists are prepared to concede. Perhaps this can be illustrated even more forcefully by a brief look at one of the 'protectionist' provisions in the criminal law.

It was stated above that section 23 of the 1975 Act demands separate remand facilities for young offenders. In practice, the results of this requirement are also often very detrimental to the individuals in question. In Edinburgh, for example, the remand facilities frequently used are a self-contained unit of Saughton prison. As a result of the legislation, young offenders are debarred from using nearly all the prison's very impressive recreational and educational facilities, as well as the open workshops. Consequently this category of detainees spends a far greater proportion of the day locked up in cells than do all the other inmates. Once again, the legal rights divorced from an institutional context do little to guarantee action in the child's best interests. One could argue that isolation from adult prisoners is in the child's best interests, regardless of any consequences, but this is not only dubious, it has almost certainly never been discussed. It would seem that in the field of law, just as in the realm of theory, there is an urgent need for articulating more fully what is constitutive of 'a child's best interests'. The area of the law which more than any other seems to take this standpoint is that relating to questions of parental custody and access in matrimonial disputes.

Custody and access in matrimonial disputes   In cases of separation, nullity and divorce, decisions frequently have to be made by the courts concerning the custody of any children involved and access to them by the parent to whom custody has been denied. David Walker writes as follows on the Scottish system: 'The paramount consideration is the welfare of the child or children and the court will consider the child's wishes, and a child in minority is entitled to be heard on the matter.'[9]

In recent years questions of guilt and issues of custody have been separated in matrimonial disputes. The 'welfare of the child' has been redefined to allow considerable weight to be placed on the child's own preferences, although these are not the only views taken into account. A recent decision illustrates clearly that the 'child's best interests' can remain unknown and that, in the absence of any other relevant criterion for resolving the dispute, the child's view can become the deciding factor. In *Fowler v. Fowler* there was general agreement that both parents were in a position to provide their ten-year-old daughter with a home, although in the past neither had put the child's interests first. The mother's former cohabitee had been found guilty of violence towards the girl, and the father had repeatedly given her into the care of others. Lord Stott stated:

> I am fully conscious of the fact that while in questions of custody the interest of the child is of paramount consideration, it cannot by any means be assumed that a child's interests necessarily coincide with her wishes. All the witnesses however agreed that Denise was a highly intelligent girl with a mind of her own and that was fully confirmed by my own impressions of her. I was quite satisfied that she had not been pressurized or brainwashed by either parent and since her views were rea-

sonable and there was no compelling reason to disregard them I have I confess allowed Denise in effect to decide the issue for herself.[10]

In the theoretical discussion it was suggested that neither the child-libertarians nor the protectionists could provide a comprehensive theory of children's rights. It is worth noting that the decision in *Fowler* v. *Fowler* can be fully defended on both child-libertarian and protectionist principles. It is also worth stressing that the decision was made within the frame of reference believed here to be the appropriate one in making decisions about the lives of children, namely a prior statement of what constitutes the child's interests and a prior notion of what might be considered 'reasonable'. The child's right to be heard in such cases is clearly unconditional; the right to determine the issue is more complex and in a very great measure dependent on the actual views expressed, whether they do indeed accord with or at least are not in direct conflict with what is acknowledged as reasonable and in the child's best interests. In all such cases there is general agreement that, except in instances of extreme abuse, it is better for the children to spend time with both parents. Requests to prevent access are viewed with caution. The legal rights of the child in this area are protectionist in that they rest on a view of the child as a dependant, but they are also sufficiently flexible to accommodate the concept of development. They do allow the child to be self-determining within a prescribed limit – the case of *Fowler* v. *Fowler* is clear testimony to this fact. How does this compare with the legal rights of children in the hearings system?

The hearings system

Rights within the hearings system clearly fall primarily, although not entirely, within a protectionist framework. Children appear before panel members where it is thought that they may be in need of *compulsory* measures of care and the remit of the hearing is to act *in the interests of the child*. Within the context of the hearing, children are entitled to be heard (in the same manner as in the custody cases described above), and they have the right to deny the grounds of referral, the right to representation, the right of appeal, the right to request a review after a set period of time, the right to be informed of the substance of any reports which have a bearing on the disposal of the case, provided the information is not considered detrimental to them, and the right to written reasons for any decisions taken.[11]

Sympathetic critics[12] of the system have recently pointed out that there is a certain laxity in some hearings with regard to ensuring that these rights are indeed fully upheld, and there has been increasing recognition within the system of the need to enforce and apply all the procedural regulations which can serve to secure these rights. But this criticism stands in marked contrast to that of the child-libertarians, who deny the realities of childhood for the sake of consistent theory by seeing the rhetoric of the court as embodying a more appropriate attitude to the rights of children and criticize the hearings system accordingly. What they fail to take properly into account is that this is like criticizing a bagpipe for not being a violin! The court, at least in theory, views those found guilty primarily as lawbreakers; the panel sees them in need of help. The language of the one is punitive, of the other supportive. Ignoring for the present the degree to which rhetoric in fact matches reality, it should be apparent that any legal rights enshrined in the two systems *must* be quite different. Where an offence is the sole reason for intervening in a child's life, it is essential, as in the case of an adult, to establish that the offence was indeed committed, and notions of just punishment demand a determinate sentence that is proportionate to the crime. However, in a system that regards a need for care as the criterion for intervention, these rights are as irrelevant as they are to questions of compulsory education and custody and access. The criteria for a just disposal in the first case are well defined and fairly uncontroversial, whereas in the latter they remain hazy at best and the scope for error is enormous. The concern of a court in criminal cases is the pursuit of justice according to law, of what is sometimes called 'legal justice'. In cases where welfare is the issue as in matrimonial disputes, it is the pursuit of some of the ideals of 'social justice', of the best possible outcome for a given individual in given circumstances within the range of options permitted in law. There is no place for 'proportionality' and 'determinacy' here any more than in the present hearings system. The objectives of such a system may indeed be partially misguided, particularly where extended to certain offenders, but it is absurd to criticize it for denying children those rights which are alien to its very existence.

Criticism can be levelled at the hearings system for a different but related reason, namely that in reality not only some of the dispositions but some of the statutory grounds of referral to the system have no place within a welfare ideology but belong rather to the realm of law enforcement, that is to the very area in which considerations of due process are of paramount concern. It can be argued that, in order to be immune from the legalistic criticisms currently being levelled against it by the justice for children movement in the name of children's rights, the children's panel must either openly accept a dual role that includes both care and law enforcement and guarantees the rights of children accordingly, or must refer any cases requiring punitive measures (and it must remain an open question whether there are such cases) back to the courts and concern itself only with those children who are genuinely 'in need of compulsory measures of care'. Here, and not in any move towards child-libertarian principles, lies the path to securing the rights of children within the Scottish system of juvenile justice.

A brief guide to some services for young people in Scotland and rights within them

This section will first present a summary of the age limits which govern the rights of young people in Scotland, and will then take a brief look at the major services provided for young people in relation to health, education, employment, housing and care facilities.

Minors in Scotland are girls between the ages of twelve and eighteen and boys between the ages of fourteen and eighteen. Before reaching minority, children in Scotland are known as 'pupils'. This difference in law is attributable to the differences in attaining sexual maturity in girls and boys. The status difference of minors affords particular rights to young people along with certain responsibilities. The age-related rights of young people in Scotland have been listed in the following way:[13]

Age 5:   You must go to school.
         You may be given alcohol in private (at home).

Age 7:   You can take money out of the Post Office or Trustee Savings Bank.
         You can go to a film at the cinema (as long as the manager doesn't object).

Age 8:   You are considered capable of committing a criminal offence.

Age 12: You can buy a pet.
         GIRLS — become Minors and can therefore:
                — consent to medical treatment (but it's unlikely they'll be treated without their parents' consent).
                — apply for legal aid.
                — open bank accounts/get credit (H.P.) but again they'll probably need their parents' approval.
                — make a will/act as a witness in court.

Age 13:   You can get a job on Saturdays, and for not more than 2 hours on schooldays (not before 7 a.m. or after 7 p.m.) but you'll need the permission of the Education Authority who can make their own rules about the employment of young people.

Age 14:   You can own, or be lent, an air rifle.
You can go into a hotel or restaurant where drink is being served, but only into a bar if the owner doesn't object.
BOYS — become Minors and can therefore do the things which are listed for girls at age 12.

Age 15:   You can use a shotgun if you're supervised by someone over 21.
You can go to see a (15) registered film.

Age 16:   You can leave school.
You can leave home.
You can get married.
You can buy or be given drink (not spirits) with a meal.
You can buy fireworks.
You can buy cigarettes/tobacco.
You can consent to sexual intercourse (girls).
You can get a full time job.
You can join a trade union.
You can claim supplementary benefit.
You can get a licence to drive a moped, tractor, mowing machine, invalid carriage or pedestrian controlled vehicle.
You can get a glider pilot's licence.
You can be sold a lottery ticket.
You can buy premium bonds/open a giro account.
You will be dealt with in the Sheriff Court if you are charged with committing a crime.
You can change your name – but you'll need to get your parents to record the change.
You can carry a donor card (kidneys etc.) but your parents' consent would be needed before your organs could be used.
You can consent to all medical treatment, change your doctor etc.

You can apply for a passport (with your parents' permission).
Boys can join the forces.
You can be elected onto the Community Council (some areas)

Age 17:   You can get a licence to drive a car, motorbike, motor trike or road roller.
Girls can join the forces.
You can apply for a firearms' certificate.
You can hold a pilot's licence.

Age 18:   YOU REACH ADULTHOOD
You can donate blood.
You can vote in an election.
You can be elected onto the Community Council (all areas).
You can take court action.
You can be tattooed.
You can place a bet.
You can drink alcohol in a pub.
You can work in a pub.
You can apply for a mortgage etc.
You can be called to serve on a jury.
You can see any film.
You can drive a lorry up to 7½ tonnes.
Enter into legal contracts for HP etc. or anything else an adult can do except . . .

Age 21:   You can drive any vehicle (lorries over 7½ tonnes/buses carrying over 9 people).
You can obtain a licence to sell liquor.
You can run a gaming shop.
You can consent to a homosexual relationship (in private).
You can stand for election as an MP or Councillor.

Many of these age limits are upheld and enforced throughout the United Kingdom. However, it is worth noting the significance of the age of minority in Scotland, as well as the fact that young people aged sixteen can leave home and get married without parental permission. This is not the case south of the border.

Health

The health service, through general practitioners, community health service, hospitals, clinics and advisory services, offers a reasonably comprehensive range of provision for all members of the community. Specific services of concern to young people often relate to sex and sexuality. Parents have a legal obligation to support their children to a standard relative to their social and financial position. But in the case of health matters, the issue of confidentiality between the medical practitioner and the patient is important even in the case of minors. The Gillick case in England until the decision was overturned on 18 October 1985, raised doubts about the legality of young girls seeking contraceptive advice and treatment from a doctor without parental permission. In Scotland, however, the confidentiality of the patient was upheld throughout the period of the different legal decisions which have come to be known as the Gillick case. Some doctors will, in fact, not give contraceptive advice to girls under sixteen, but they should recommend another colleague who will. Young people under sixteen can legally consent to or refuse medical treatment as long as it is felt that they understand the implications. From sixteen onwards, young people can consent to any treatment, although many hospitals still require parental permission for sixteen- to eighteen-year-olds before an operation can be performed.

Education

The 1980 Education (Scotland) Act places the obligation to provide education on education auithorities and the obligation to attend school for children under sixteen on parents. This means that the rights of children with regard to the choice of school, for example, are nil – it is parents who have the right within certain limits to choose the schools to which their children will go at different stages between the ages of five and sixteen; it is parents who have the right to choose the religious instruction which children will receive there.

The phrase 'compulsory education' sums up the type of service which is on offer. Young people of the appropriate ages have to undergo schooling, whether this is provided by the state, privately or by parents themselves. Pupils (in the non-legal sense of the word) are expected to attend regularly and, if they do not, to offer good reasons – for example, a lack of what the school deems 'appropriate clothing', sickness, or the absence of a school within the prescribed distance for either walking or busing. The school is afforded certain parental powers and in accordance with those powers can exercise reasonable discipline. It has been argued that giving parents the right to choose the school their children go to in Scotland through the so-called Parents' Charter has, in effect, given schools the authority to operate their own systems of rules and regulations. There are questions under the law regarding the rights of children to disregard school rules on issues such as uniform and homework. These have not yet been adequately tested in the courts, but usually schools use 'disruptive behaviour' to substantiate the suspension or exclusion of individual pupils.

Where young people are excluded from school, the education authorities are required to provide some other form of schooling. Sometimes this alternative is hardly adequate, being only of limited duration, or following a wholly inappropriate curriculum, but only the parents can complain on the child's behalf. The young person under sixteen thus has few rights in law with respect to education. Similarly it is parents who may be prosecuted for the non-attendance of their child. Only when a question of non-attendance comes to a children's hearing are the child's own concerns given prime consideration in the process of making a suitable disposal. To a very real extent, the education authorities have their own alternative structure to the children's hearings. This process operates where children are found to be too disruptive or difficult to deal with in the system of mainstream education. At this point there is likely to be an involvement of the education support services, through psychologists, psychiatrists and welfare staff. They can instigate attendance at special schools without taking a particular case to the children's hearing.

For young people over sixteen, section 49 of the Education (Scotland) Act 1980 gives 'the provision to assist pupils to take advantage of education facilities'. This means that in some instances the Sheriff's court will insist that parents continue to support children in education. It would appear from this that the right to education for young people over the age of sixteen is recognized even where there is no longer a legal obligation to participate. Participation by young people over sixteen can be either compulsory or voluntary, depending on the exact nature of the course being followed. What changes is that the duty to attend is placed on the young people themselves and no longer on their parents.

Employment

When young people leave school there is now a fairly well-established right for them to engage in one of the government's Youth Training Schemes. Whether or not this will be made compulsory in the future is the subject of bitter controversy, not least in Scotland, where the 'Say No to YTS Conscription' banners have been flying high. This and the right to sign on for either supplementary benefit or unemployment benefit are common to both Scotland and England and Wales. It is one of the anachronisms of the system that local decisions can make different interpretations of policy. The Department of Health and Social Security uses its 'S' manual to adjudicate on claims. For the Manpower Services Commission there are local area boards which tend to establish differing guidelines for both the establishment and the running of employment schemes.

At the age of thirteen young people can take up part-time employment, with very severe restrictions, some of which will depend upon the policy of the local education authority. At sixteen young people can take a job of up to forty-eight hours per week but may not work nights. They also have the right to belong to a trade union.

Housing

In Scotland young people have the right to leave home at the age of sixteen with or without parental permission. However, this right does not automatically lead to their being able to find suitable accommodation. The responsibility of housing and social work departments for providing housing for those who want to move away from the parental home and for those who find themselves homeless are quite complex. All that the legislation (the Housing (Homeless Persons) Act (1977)) guarantees for young homeless people is 'the right to advice and assistance' from the council. They are not obliged to offer young people accommodation unless they can prove that they are 'in priority need', which in terms of the Act means that they have dependent children, or are pregnant, or are physically or mentally disabled, or are vulnerable for some other reason. They must also be able to prove that they have not made themselves 'intentionally homeless'.

The Shelter report *Homeless Young People in Glasgow* (1984) documents how the local authority used the Housing Act to help young people with their housing needs. In August 1984 this led to the council's ratifying the right of sixteen- and seventeen-year-olds to hold council tenancies. This move has been followed by other Scottish district councils who have begun to accept applications from young people of this age on to their waiting lists for accommodation.

The board and lodging rules, introduced by the Social Services, Secretary Norman Fowler on 29 April 1985, but suspended by the ruling of Mr Justice Mann in the High Court on 31 July 1985, caused severe problems for young people faced with housing difficulties. The regulations limited the rights of young people to move away from their home areas and seemed likely to force the closure of some hostel accommodation for vulnerable people, including the single young homeless. The limitation of benefit levels to within local limits could take some privately rented accommodation off the market and restrict the availability of board and lodgings. On 13 December 1985 Lord Justice Glidewell in the Appeal Court confirmed that Mr Fowler's original regulations were illegal and refused an appeal to the House of Lords.

In care

Young people who are taken into residential care may arrive there for a variety of reasons. It may be as a result of decisions by either a children's hearing or a court or because the police, parents or the young person themselves did not think that adequate care was available in the home. The rights of children in care vary somewhat, depending upon whether the admittance to care is voluntary or compulsory. Residential staff will in most cases take decisions about young people in their care in much the same way as their parents would normally be expected to do. This includes decisions on schooling, pocket money, clothing, etc.

Young people in care have the right to be told about all meetings and decisions which effect their future. They also have the right to request a 'review' of their case. In addition, some areas of Scotland are attempting to draw up codes of rights for young people in the care of the local authority. In Strathclyde Region, the report *Home or Away* outlines the rights the local authority would wish to give to young people in its care. These rights might be regarded as a manifesto, or as a statement of the direction in which policy is and should be moving. Given that Strathclyde is the largest region in Scotland, serving half the country's population, this document is extremely important. The proposals are aimed to secure the rights of children in care to:

develop their physical, emotional and intellectual potential;
family life, preferably in their own family, but if this is not possible, within a substitute family;
individual respect;
be actively involved in all decisions about their care;
know the contents of all reports which might affect decisions made about them, however painful;
know the full details of the personal and family circumstances and to have help to accept the implications of this information;

have help in putting forward their own point of view in all
forums making decisions about their future;

have a written contract outlining the plans for their future and
the expectations and duties on themselves and all workers
involved in their care.

The rights for young people over twelve who are in the care of the
authority and which are enforced are:

the right to privacy;

the right to space;

the right to individual property;

the right to an independent income and control over it;

the right to a say in the purchase of personal items like clothing
and food;

the right to a say in the running of the establishment in which
they live.

Interestingly, this list of rights for young people in care far exceeded
the rights of young people living at home with their families.

The way forward

It was stated at the beginning of the chapter that 'modified
protectionism' seems to offer the most appropriate framework for
securing the rights of children. Such a framework was said to require
a prior statement of children's interests and a prior notion of what
might be considered 'reasonable alternatives'. From this perspective,
the right of children to be *involved* in any decision-making process
affecting their lives is unconditional, but the right to determine
outcomes is partially dependent on whether or not the actual views
expressed are in conflict with what is acknowledged as reasonable
and in the interests of children. It should be clear that, at its best, the
Scottish system of juvenile justice is sufficiently flexible and open to
accommodate these principles; however, there is a strong case for
further safeguards (for example, the giving of written reasons for all
decisions, the availability of all reports to families, possibly the
provision of child-representatives, etc.) to ensure that the system
remains needs-based rather than deeds-based and to guarantee that
the right of children to be heard is understood as an absolute right
and not a matter of discretion. It is also apparent from the preceding
paragraphs that there is an enormous divergence in the rights secured

for children and young people both in law and in practice (including unacceptable regional variations) with respect to services. These will be examined in turn.

The position in Scots law regarding children and health care is exactly that viewed as appropriate in the first section of this chapter. The law here can accommodate the concepts of development and maturity, giving doctors discretion in the case of minor children in deciding whether to dispense with parental consent. However, as already indicated, doctors in Scotland are reluctant to take an independent stand in this area, and practice is usually in accordance with the law south of the border – that is, parental consent is sought in almost all cases involving those under sixteen. Hence, although the Gillick ruling was not strictly applicable in Scotland, had the decision not been reversed in October 1985 it would have had far-reaching effects throughout the United Kigndom and constituted a step backwards in the light of the principles advocated here. Scotland is in a unique position to take an independent stand on children's rights in this area, and it is to be hoped that the opportunity will be grasped by the medical profession in the future.

The position with respect to education is almost the reverse of the situation existing in matters of health. Here children under sixteen have no rights in law beyond the general right to be given education. The Education (Scotland) Act explicitly views children as entirely dependent and nowhere recognizes that they may have their own point of view. This is clearly not the case within individual schools, which may range from those with a compulsory curriculum to those with individual timetabling; from those which regularly consult with parents to those which barely keep parents informed of their children's progress. However, the fact remains that the legal status of children with regard to their own education remains far from ideal and, although the law does no more than provide a framework within which the education system can operate, it would seem desirable for children to be given some legal standing in this area in the future.

In the areas of employment and housing, the position was until recently moving in the direction advocated here; however, any compulsory Youth Training Schemes would be regarded as a regressive measure. The rights of children in care in Scotland have also been developing in the direction advocated in this chapter, and it is to be hoped that the rights outlined in the Strathclyde code will soon be fully implemented in practice and enshrined in the law. There is no cause for complacency, and a great deal remains to be done. However, it should be clear from the preceding account that in the area of child care, as in several other areas, imaginative attempts have been made over the past decades to secure the rights of children in Scotland.

Notes

1 See R. Adler, *Taking Juvenile Justice Seriously* (Scottish Academic Press, 1985). The first three sections of this chapter are based on material contained in chapters 2 and 3 of that book.
2 J. Feinberg, 'The nature and value of rights', in *Rights, Justice and the Bounds of Liberty* (Princeton University Press, 1980), p. 155.
3 T. D. Campbell, *The Left and Rights* (Routledge and Kegan Paul, 1983), p. 27.
4 R. Farson, *Birthrights* (Penguin, 1978), p. 73.
5 See, for example, L. Houlgate, *The Child and the State* (Johns Hopkins University Press, 1980).
6 The clearest example of parentalism enshrined in the law is probably in the field of education, where children have the right to education but parents and parents alone the right to request placement in certain schools, exclusion from religious education, and to refuse corporal punishment.
7 Children's Hearings (Scotland) Rules (Statutory Instruments, 1971, No. 492 (S. 60)), 17, 3.
8 M. Rushforth, *Committal to Residential Care*, Scottish Office Central Research Unit (HMSO, 1978), esp. pp. 24, 26, 67.
9 D. M. Walker, *Principles of Scottish Private Law* (Clarendon Press, 1982), vol. I, p. 282. Minor children in Scotland are girls between the ages of twelve and eighteen, boys between fourteen and eighteen years of age.
10 *Fowler* v. *Fowler* (1981), SLT (Notes), 9.
11 It is worth noting that the Social Work (Scotland) Act and the Children's Hearings (Scotland) Rules (Statutory Instruments, 1971, No. 492 (S. 60)) give all these rights to parents as well as to children. In addition, parents, unlike children, have a statutory right to be present at all stages of the hearing (S. 41(1)).
12 See particularly F. M. Martin, S. J. Fox and K. Murray, *Children out of Court (Scottish Academic Press, 1981)*, and J. P. Grant, '*Protecting the rights of the child*', in *Children's Hearings*, ed. F. M. Martin and K. Murray (Scottish Academic Press, 1976).
13 Bob Stead, *Basic Rights: information for young people in Scotland* (Citizens Rights Office, 1984).

Further reading

M. Clark and A. Dearling, *Leaving Home* (Scots Group and IT Resource Centre, 1985).
F. M. Martin and K. Murray (eds), *The Scottish Juvenile Justice System* (Scottish Academic Press, 1982).

F. M. Martin, S. J. Fox and K. Murray, *Children out of Court (Scottish Academic press, 1981).*

SCOLAG, monthly bulletin of the Scottish Legal Action Group with a regular Child Law Brief and a considerable number of articles on the law relating to children in Scotland, published by Scottish Legal Action Group, 40 Perth Road, Dundee.

The Scottish Child, a journal of policy and practice affecting children in Scotland, published quarterly by Scottish Child Publications, c/o 56 Albany Street, Edinburgh.

Shelter (Scotland), *Homeless Young People in Glasgow* (Shelter, 1984).

Notes on Contributors

Robert Adams teaches social work at Humberside College of Higher Education. He was formerly a Borstal deputy governor and director of a community social work project for delinquents.

Ruth Adler is research fellow on a child law project at the University of Edinburgh.

Alan Dearling is publications and training officer at the Scottish IT Resource Centre.

Bob Franklin is a research fellow at the University of Leeds.

Patricia Hewitt, formerly of the NCCL, works for the Labour Party as press secretary in the Office of the Leader of the Opposition. She co-authored *First Rights*, one of the earliest guides to rights for young people.

Richard Ives works for the National Children's Bureau. His current project is concerned with responses to solvent abuse. Formerly he was a youth worker and teacher.

Tony Jeffs teaches social policy in the School of Government at Newcastle upon Tyne Polytechnic. He has also taught in schools.

Gerry Lavery has been a local authority social worker and was until recently an action research worker in a community social work project. He now teaches on a part-time basis in the School of Social Studies, Leeds Polytechnic.

Sue Lees teaches sociology at North London Polytechnic.

Emma MacLennan is a research officer for the Low Pay Unit in London. She is currently on secondment to the Labour Party.

Jenny Mellor teaches sociology at North London Polytechnic.

Keith Popple teaches in the Department of Social Work, Health and Community Studies, Plymouth Polytechnic.

Shahin Popple teaches education at the College of St Mark and St John, Plymouth.

Index

234   INDEX